WHEN MEN LOST FAITH
IN REASON

WHEN MEN LOST FAITH IN REASON

Reflections on War and Society in the Twentieth Century

H. P. Willmott

Studies in Military History and International Affairs
Jeremy Black, Series Editor

Westport, Connecticut
London

303.66
W73w

Library of Congress Cataloging-in-Publication Data

Willmott, H. P.

    When men lost faith in reason : reflections on war and society in the twentieth century /
H. P. Willmott

      p. cm. — (Studies in military history and international affairs, ISSN 1537-4432)
    Includes index.

    ISBN 0-275-97665-3 (alk. paper)

    1. War and society. 2. War—Psychological aspects. 3. World War, 1914–1918—Social
aspects. 4. World War, 1939–1945—Social aspects. 5. Military history, Modern—20th
century. 6. Militarism—History—20th century. I. Title. II. Series.

UA10.W478   2002

303.6′6′0904—dc21   2002019627

British Library Cataloguing in Publication Data is available.

Library of Congress Catalog Card Number: 2002019627
ISBN: 0-275-97665-3
ISSN: 1537-4432

First published in 2002

Praeger Publishers, 88 Post Road West, Westport, CT 06881
An imprint of Greenwood Publishing Group, Inc.
www.praeger.com

Printed in the United States of America

The paper used in this book complies with the
Permanent Paper Standard issued by the National
Information Standards Organization (Z39.48-1984).

10 9 8 7 6 5 4 3 2 1

Dedicated to FY1645
and
in Praise of
Dissent, Uncertainty, and Tolerance

Contents

Acknowledgments

In the preparation of this book acknowledgement must be made to those who, over many years whether in the form of conferences, lectures, exchange of letters or general conversation, provided me with the basis of knowledge and critical facility that made this work possible. To attempt to list these people is impossible, but they have the satisfaction of knowing that without them this book could never have been written and also that they are not responsible for the various errors that may be within its pages.

Nonetheless there are two individuals whose critical facility and unwavering personal support and loyalty command acknowledgement. These were Michael Coles and Steven Weingartner, and invidious though it might be to name names within this category I do so with the simple statement that the book could not have been attempted, still less completed, without their quiet contribution and benefaction. I trust only that this acknowledgement of the debt I owe them provides no cause for embarrassment.

Second, I would acknowledge my debt to those without whose patience, tact, and ability this book would probably have gone the way of the many of the formations cited in these pages; specifically one would cite one's debts to Heather Staines and Penny Sippel of Praeger and also Klara King of Communication Crafts, and trust that they will accept this acknowledgement of their support, good judgement, and efforts on my behalf: I trust they will not try to amend this poor acknowledgement of their endeavors.

Third, a special acknowledgement has to be made to those professional colleagues and friends who provided me with support at a time of professional disasters, and without whose support times that were truly difficult would have been near-impossible. Among those I would acknowledge are Tim Bean, Patrick Burke, Tony Clayton, Martine and Nigel de Lee, Christopher Duffy, and Paul Harris, and Spenser Johnson and Jack Sweetman, Cliff Krieger, George Raach, and Gerald Roncolato, and John Votaw (and Cantigny First Division Foundation and the Cantigny conference, 2/3 March 1994) and John Andreas Olsen and Tomatsu Haruo. I would not wish to thank one more than another, and those who helped me the most know who they are without my elaboration: to these especially, but to all who so aided me, I owe a special debt, which I will discharge in due course.

I would also make reference to one person who, alas, is no longer with us. After this manuscript was completed and accepted, a colleague and very good and loyal friend, Raymond Sibbald, joined the majority. Inevitably this meant that his name was moved from one list, only to be noted separately, sadly, and for all the wrong reasons, in a class of its own. Very simply, he was an honourable and above all, a gentle man, and one who has been and will continue to be missed. Sailor, rest your oar.

H.P. Willmott
Englefield Green
Egham, Surrey
19 June 2002
being the 58th anniversary
of the Battle of the Philippine Sea

There remains one group that always appear in my acknowledgement section and for one reason: they have always been the means of ensuring sanity. I would acknowledge my debts to and my love for my dogs, Everton, Sherry, Kondor, Jamie and Suki: I trust they are at peace. I would acknowledge my present debt to and love for Lancaster, Mishka, and Cassie, and for Junior and Yanya: I trust that much time will pass before they join their predecessors and chase together across the celestial fields.

WHEN MEN LOST FAITH IN REASON

1

New Perspectives: Twentieth-Century History, War, and Wars

The years 1989–95 were years of unprecedented plenty for historians, or at least alleged historians who defected to the entertainment industry. The anniversaries of campaigns and battles of 50 years ago may well have been commemorated by the many, but one must admit to a certain distaste for some of the outpourings, not least because they would seem to have fallen into one of three categories: the catch-pennies of no great worth; the shameless exploiters of national prejudice; and those produced by individuals who toiled under illusions of competence in the sure belief that they had explained events that they had merely described.

In terms of historical perspective, one of the least attractive features of the 1994 commemorations marking the Normandy invasion was the manner in which presentation demonstrated refusal to move beyond self-satisfied predictability. So Normandy was the decisive campaign, the climactic campaign, of the Second World War—or so we were told. It is difficult, if not impossible, to resist the conclusion that the issue of victory and defeat in the European war was resolved in 1943, if not before. If that was so, how can any campaign conducted after the decision of the war had been reached been decisive? How can any single campaign in a war of six years' duration be climactic unless it is the one with which the war ended? The Normandy campaign was critically important, most crucially in the shaping of the postwar world, but with reference to the outcome of the Second World War one suspects that its impact was probably minimal. It is difficult to see, if Operation Overlord had miscarried, how the outcome of the war and the timing of its end would have been affected. The Soviet advances of 1944–45 would not

have been significantly slowed, still less prevented, as a result of an
Anglo–American defeat in the west. Few German formations in the
western theater could have been released after summer 1944 in any fit
state for service on the Eastern Front, and such forces did not represent
the difference between Germany's defeat and victory in the east. And, in
terms of victory and defeat, wherein lies the significance of the operations of the 3rd U.S. Army and its breakout from Normandy? The
conventional explanation is that it was the means of victory, but it is hard
to resist the conclusion that the breakout was the product of and completed a victory that had been won over the previous two months.

Given the manner in which popular history has pandered to national
mythologies and the fact that Anglo–American historiography remains
crippled by the Carlyle legacy, whereby the story of events must be
explained in terms of the deeds of great men, it is hardly surprising that
we consider Normandy in the wrong context, failing to see it for what, in
effect, it was: the third battle of the Somme. If one compares the first
battle of the Somme in 1916 with the campaign in Normandy in 1944,
one cannot but be struck by the similarity in the way they were fought,
their relative length and losses, and the physical condition of the battlefields. One tends to forget that Normandy in 1944 was scarred by
trenches, that the battle was characterized by massive artillery strikes—
albeit often from the air—and swarming, costly infantry attacks. In terms
of length and casualties, the symmetry is not exact but striking nonetheless. In 1916 the battle of the Somme lasted for 142 days and resulted in
some 1,197,024 casualties, whereas the Normandy campaign lasted for
two months and resulted in about 510,000 casualties. With approximately 8,500 daily casualties in both battles, the real difference lay in the
fact that whereas in 1916 losses were more or less evenly balanced, in
1944 losses were about 2:1 in favor of the offensive and that at the
campaign's end an intact and mechanized army was available to the
attacker for further offensive operations.[1]

Moreover, we fail to recognize in Montgomery's conduct of the Normandy campaign the essence of American generalship in the 1991 Gulf
campaign—force-packaging, reliance upon *matériel*, the concern to minimize casualties, the ability to read "deep battle"—though perhaps this
failure to recognize what binds Montgomery and Schwarzkopf is understandable: the thought of Montgomery as Schwarzkopf's mentor does
seem somewhat incongruous. But so many British and American historians remain trapped in personal and national arguments that serve only
to convince the skeptical that there are some who apparently cannot put
pen to paper without detracting from the sum of understanding. If the
British performance in Normandy was as poor as some writers would
have us believe, how was it that the British managed to secure Caen
before the Americans secured St. Lô, and did so when faced by three-

quarters of the German armor in Normandy? Which of the Allied armies inflicted greater casualties on the German armies in Normandy and suffered fewer casualties in the process? And if the British were so good, why did the breakout on their front prove so elusive? The arguments that one associates with the Normandy campaign and which have been paraded endlessly do not lead anywhere. Yet we are still afflicted by interpretations that remain narrowly focused in terms of national perspective and lacking real understanding of these events and their context.

With respect to the events of the Second World War and the role that the British and Americans assign themselves, there is no escaping the fact that the Anglo–American experience of this conflict is deceptive. In one very obvious sense, Britain and the United States were marginal to the conflict. Neither was subjected to a campaign on home soil or to occupation, and, as one eminent American observer has noted: "As experience . . . the suffering was wasted. . . . America has not yet understood what the Second World War was like and thus has been unable to use such understanding to re-interpret and re-define the national reality and to arrive at something like public maturity."[2]

Undoubtedly this was one of the reasons why Vietnam was so traumatic. For Britain and the United States, the Second World War was one of shortages: for vast sections of Europe and Asia it was one of sacrifice. This is not to denigrate Britain and the United States: they could take upon themselves no more than that part of the war which lay within their respective areas of competence and responsibility. But both were primarily naval powers, and the protection afforded by salt water and distance that in peace gave a measure of choice to appease or to oppose that was denied continental powers ensured in war that neither Britain nor the United States was obliged to bear the burden of continental warfare. One hears and reads much about how terrible were the British and American losses: the shock to public opinion caused by the Tarawa casualties, the awfulness of one company suffering 96% losses on the Normandy beaches. Of every 100 Soviet males of the draft of 1941, three remained alive on 12 May 1945. We are not talking about 4,000 casualties in the taking of an atoll in the central Pacific, the 13,000 casualties incurred by the British in 12 days at second Alamein, the 10,000 Allied casualties on 6 June 1944. We are talking about continental warfare, about the annihilation of a generation, about murdered civilizations that reached from the Volga to the Channel to the Aegean and extended across the whole of Japanese-occupied China.

Britain lost some 380,000 dead in the Second World War, the United States just under a quarter of a million. In the course of any week of its Great Patriotic War, the Soviet Union suffered more deaths than the United States incurred in the whole of the Pacific war. Even excluding the killed and missing, the battle of Stalingrad between November 1942 and February 1943 was as costly for the Soviet Union in the numbers of soldiers who died of their wounds as was the whole of the war for Britain. More Soviet soldiers were killed in forcing the Dnepr in autumn 1943 than the United States lost in the entire war, and, other than a specialist historian, who in the west has ever heard of Mga, a small town outside Leningrad, where in 1941 the Soviets lost three times as many men as the British lost in the whole of the Battle of the Atlantic? This was the reality of the Second World War, and it presents the obvious questions: How do we understand this war? How could industrialized states in the first half of the twentieth century have waged this kind of war? How could such states as the Soviet Union and Germany have kept going despite such losses? To the latter question there is an obvious answer, at least for countries such as the Soviet Union and China: they were denied the right to collapse by the nature of the enemy they faced. The same applied to Germany—the Allied demand for unconditional surrender ensured that it was obliged to fight to the bitter end. There is a second, equally obvious, answer, at least with respect to Germany and the Soviet Union. Both were totalitarian states, and their coercive power, and willingness to use it, were formidable. But such matters describe as much as explain, explain everything and explain nothing, and one needs to look beyond the immediately obvious in order to grasp the meaning of this war and to understand both this war and its place in history.

Inevitably, in seeking to address such questions, we face an insoluble problem: both as individuals and as societies we lack the imagination to understand basic terms about the Second World War. We have read the history books and, depending on source, we have read that the Soviet Union's death toll during the Second World War was between 20,000,000 and 32,900,000.[3] A Russian general staff paper issued in 1992 estimated Soviet losses as 27,000,000, and this was the figure used by President William J. Clinton in May 1995 at the ceremonies to mark the fiftieth anniversary of the end of the European war. But whatever the figure, in an obvious sense it means nothing because we cannot imagine a mound of 27,000,000 dead or 27,000,000 individual killings as part of a single process. Even for societies, such numbers make little sense. If one has to identify a defining moment in the British national existence in the twentieth century, the point in time when things were never the same thereafter, one thinks instinctively of the first day of the Battle of the Somme. Perhaps third Ypres, perhaps the First World War as a whole, should be identified in its place. Alternatively, it is possible to see 15 May 1940, the day that the French army was defeated on the Meuse, as the moment when Britain's world changed. If one looks outside the two world wars for such a moment or occasion, the Suez humiliation may be seen to possess singular significance. But to wander around English country churchyards, to look at memorials such as those in one's own little town, with its 305 names, leaves the indelible impression that the First World War scarred Britain, changed it for ever. If only for the sake of this argument, one would select 1 July 1916 as the day Britain's world was forever changed. On that day, north of the Somme, in one attack, the British Third and Fourth Armies sustained almost 60,000 casualties, of whom about 19,000 were killed. The Soviet dead of the Second World War amounted to 19,014 a day every day between 22 June 1941 and 11 May 1945. How could a society sustain itself when it incurred the first day of the Somme every day for six weeks short of four years, for 1,420 days? One dead every 4.5 seconds. If the Soviet dead were laid along the road between Moscow and Berlin, each corpse would be allowed 2.82 inches, less than a headstone. One does not demean British or U.S. losses: for those thus reduced to statistics and for their people, the loss could not have been greater. But the first day of the Somme every day for four years? We hear from our parents' generation about rationing and, if British, how hard life was during the Second World War because of the shortages. But we do not know what it means to die of shortages, to have a period in the history of our second city known as the Time of the Cannibals, as was the fate of Leningrad in the winter of 1941–42. The same sort of comparisons can be made for China and Poland. How can one understand such events, be they the wars or battles of these wars? One has stood on the top of Fort Douaumont and looked to the north and east over the ground crossed by German infantry on that day in February 1916, and one has turned to look across to Vaux and Souville. For all that one has heard and read and seen, Verdun makes no sense at all, and the Menin Gate at sunset, with its panels bearing 40,000 names of British soldiers who died at Ypres and who have no known graves, provides no clues. We—or perhaps it is merely a writer who is the product of a rationalist, dissenting upbringing—cannot grasp the reality of the two world wars because it is beyond our experience and our understanding.

But for all the attention paid in the last decade to its various battles and campaigns, the real matter that we should consider is the context of the Second World War per se. There is no doubting the accuracy of John Lukacs' observation that the two world wars dominate the landscape of the twentieth century, but one would add a rider. If the two world wars are the mountain ranges of the twentieth century, they were separated by low-lying ground. The Great Depression of the 1930s was in many ways as important in the unfolding of the twentieth century as the two world wars—most particularly its impact upon the colonial empires and the economic system that had been developed by the European states. But that being noted, the basic point remains, and misleadingly so. We as societies look to the two world wars as the yardsticks against which other conflicts are measured. In a sense this is natural and inevitable, but it is exactly the wrong way to consider these conflicts. The more relevant way of looking at the twentieth century and the two world wars is to start from the premise that these wars were so very different in so many ways from wars that came before and since that they should be regarded as exceptions and discounted from consideration as a basis of comparison except with and against each other. With such an argument, historical investigation is free to pose three questions that are seldom addressed: what is the context of the Second World War within the twentieth century, and, much more important, what was the twentieth century, and what was the place of war in its unfolding?

* * *

The second question is, of course, mendacious, but we instinctively look to decades or centuries with a view to attach labels that define their character. But no single definition or interpretation of a period can provide more than a partial explanation of events. What would be relevant in a European context would not necessarily be appropriate to North America, still less to the Third World. How can one bind into a single explanation matters so diverse as the two world wars, the Cold War, the Green Revolution, decolonialization, the proliferation of technological change, and the changing patterns of production and trade, any one of which could be used as the starting line for an examination of the twentieth century? But, of course, this question begs the real one: why should we look at history in terms of decades or centuries? The problem is that to Westerners a decade is an Era, a century an Age. It is difficult to resist the idea that Westerners, in dividing history on the basis of moving noughts, look down the wrong end of the telescope. But accepting Western terms of reference, even if these are of dubious worth, it is hard to resist the notion that the history of the twentieth century is best understood in terms of war. Certainly there is no serious doubting the correctness of the Lukacs thesis that the two world wars dominate the historical landscape of the twentieth century. It is only in the last few years, since the Soviet Union passed from the scene, that the world has moved beyond the legacy of the Second World War; it is only in this period that one can see the unfolding of events that were not the product of the Second World War and its immediate aftermath.

* * *

We consider the Second World War in very narrow terms and with precise dates: 1939 and 1945. But Japanese official histories date the Second World War from September 1931 and the conquest of Manchuria. Even if one is inclined to regard July 1937 as a more reasonable starting line, one would not deny that the China Incident was nurtured in Manchuria: the link between the two Japanese military efforts on the Asian mainland in the period between 1931 and 1941 and between these efforts and the outbreak of the Pacific war can neither be dissolved nor contradicted. No less important is the question of when the war ended. Officially, it ended in 1955 with the various declarations that proclaimed the end of hostilities notwithstanding the failure to conclude peace treaties between once-warring powers.[4]

But in the history of the twentieth century, it may be that the only way to consider this war is in terms of its forming but one part—the most destructive single part—of a series of struggles that were decades in their unfolding. Some thirty or so years ago it was fashionable to consider the two world wars as one, a European civil war separated by a twenty-year truce. This view commanded more attention than its speciousness warranted. The *sine qua non* of a civil war is a common shared identity of the combatants, which most certainly did not exist in the form of an awareness of a kindred European identity in the first half of the twentieth century. The real point, however, is the place that the Second World War occupies in the emergence in a world system that lost its nineteenth-century Eurocentric hue, which very largely survived the First World War. When this order passed, and the many factors that were involved in the process, is difficult to determine, but 1975 commends itself as the year when the events set in train in eastern Asia by the Manchurian Incident can be said to have resolved themselves with the fall of Saigon. It was a year that also saw the end of the Portuguese empire in Africa: for the first time in history virtually every part of the earth was under the jurisdiction of some form of indigenous sovereign authority. The diffusion of power has been perhaps one of the twentieth century's most significant developments. It may be, therefore, that, rather than considering this conflict in terms of its 1939–45 conventional time frame, we should look at events as a series of wars of transition waged between 1931 and 1975 that formed the link between very different international orders.

More usefully still, perhaps, the period could be extended to sometime between 1989 and 1994—the period of the collapse of the Soviet system between the unification of the Germanies and the withdrawal of the last Russian troops from the new Germany and the Baltic states. Perversely, however, it is possible to see very different patterns to events. The idea that the First World War was the first war of the twentieth century is not new. The Victorian era is often portrayed as having ended with the outbreak of war in Europe in 1914. But in an obvious sense any century concerns itself with redressing the sins of omission and commission of its predecessor: by such reasoning, it is possible to see the Second World

War as the last war of the nineteenth century. How does one understand the Second World War other than in terms of the warring powers drawing upon a 100 years of slowly defined hatreds? The nineteenth century witnessed the cultivation of hatred, the twentieth century the reaping. The Second World War, by drawing upon ideas that belonged to the second half of the nineteenth century, was the last war of the Victorian era, the final curtain on that century: Queen Victoria, quite contrary to popular belief, died on 15 August 1945—the date when, in historical terms, the twentieth century dawned.

Alternatively, one could impose upon events an interpretation that saw the end of the Second World War, in 1945, as the starting point of a golden age, a period when real hatreds were suspended, to return only when the Cold War ended with the collapse of the Soviet system. But whatever pattern one sees to events and irrespective of the date or event chosen as the basis of interpretation, one is obliged to ask oneself what pattern to events might future generations discern that we cannot. Just as the name, the *Hundred Years' War*, was bestowed upon a series of wars and the parties to these conflicts had no awareness of such a concept, so it may be that with respect to the wars of the twentieth century, those who follow us will see a period of struggle, with dates and elements of continuity and change that will cast several decades together, and with a suitable historical shorthand to define in a single phrase the moment of time of which the present is unaware.

* * *

The reputations of too many historians have foundered as a result of their owners' predilection for prediction to be anything but aware of the one and only rule of reading a chart at sea: keep off the green bits. In the business of historical interpretation, one never knows one's present position, for a very good and obvious reason: one cannot understand the present with regard to the recent past, still less with reference to the future. One example will suffice to illustrate the problem: the context of the 1991 campaign. More than a decade has elapsed since this campaign, yet it remains very difficult to understand what it foreshadowed with respect to the nature and conduct of war. What was fought in 1991 was not a war, but a campaign, and Western problems in dealing with Iraq since February 1991 have stemmed from the fact that those members of the Western political and military leadership with the power of decision in 1991 never understood the distinction. The Gulf War, which began on 2 August 1990 with the Iraqi invasion of Kuwait, ended on 9 September 1996, when, with the Iraqi reconquest of the northern provinces, the United States found itself in a position similar to that of France in summer 1925 after its two-year occupation of the Ruhr—no longer able to confirm an earlier victory with every passing year. For the American-led coalition, the campaign of 1991 was won, but the war of 1990-1996 was lost.

* * *

In seeking to interpret the 1991 campaign, one could suggest certain conclusions, provisional and tentative though they may be. This conflict was the first in which space—in the form of comprehensive satellite communications and navigation and surveillance systems—provided a hitherto unrealized dimension to war. This campaign witnessed the arrival of the 24-hour battle in which night was not an obstacle to operations but deliberately used as cover and without loss of any real offensive capability: one could add that this campaign heralded a capacity to conduct major offensive operations irrespective of season and weather, though certain reservations have to be entered against this particular claim. This was a campaign that demonstrated an unprecedented reach inland of naval units in terms of direct fire, since never before have naval units at sea been able to engage a target more than 330 miles inland. The 1943–45 central Pacific campaign notwithstanding, it is hard to resist the idea that the 1991 campaign was the first in history when ground elements operated in support of air and naval power. One would suggest that the 1991 campaign was the first in which air power, rather than being one part of an overall offensive effort directed against enemy forces, was the primary agency of destruction in the sense that the outcome of the battle had been decided before ground forces closed with the enemy.

In addition, one could argue that the 1991 campaign was illustrative of a trend to use air power either primarily or alone in the conduct of war: the Israeli strike against the Osirak nuclear plant in Iraq on 7 June 1981, Operation Peace for Galilee in southern Lebanon in June 1982, the U.S. attack on Libya in April 1986, and Operation Deliberate Force, the use of air power by the North Atlantic Treaty Organization in Bosnia in 1995, providing supporting evidence of this trend. But even if this is not accepted, there can be no serious disputing the fact that this was the first campaign in history when a state of reasonable size and depth—only five states in Europe are larger than Iraq—was subjected to attack across its entire area in an initial offensive operation, and it is certainly possible to represent this campaign as unique in two respects. It could be claimed that this campaign witnessed the comprehensive defeat of a nation that was quite separate from the defeat of its armed forces, and indeed it may be argued that Iraq could have been defeated without its armed forces having been subjected to attack. It could also be asserted, less contentiously, that this campaign witnessed the conclusive defeat of a state without the necessity of having to complete the wholesale destruction of its industrial infrastructure, society, and armed forces.

These latter points form the basis of legitimate dispute, yet lurking on the sidelines are two questions that are profoundly important in terms of the future conduct of war and the structure of military establishments throughout the world. It could be argued, for example, that the 1991 campaign was the first occasion when it was not necessary to fight for air supremacy: air supremacy was commanded, and the advantages it conferred enjoyed, by the use of an air power that, by virtue of its size, diversity, and sophistication, rendered formal battle for air supremacy superfluous, irrelevant. This, of course, begs one obvious point—the nature of victory in air warfare. Victory in the air, and at sea, is never definitive and never decided in time or place with a set result, as is the case with the land battle as a result of possession of the battlefield, but it has to be maintained by repeated offensive operations as the maintenance and the exercise of supremacy become one and the same. But if the main argument begs a point, it does address one that the obvious counterargument so often heard—that in 1991 the Iraqis did not contest coalition air supremacy—misses entirely: the scale, diversity, and technological superiority of coalition forces meant that the Iraqis could not contest coalition air supremacy.

More significantly, it can be argued that this campaign marked the point in time when the power of decision of war was restored. Though seldom acknowledged, the indecisiveness of military force has been one of the most obvious characteristics of warfare in the last 100 years. But, arguably, by 1991 the unprecedented accuracy and destructiveness of certain weapons systems, plus the overwhelming advantage conferred by state-of-the-art information technology, produced a double consequence that was barely perceived even in 1991. The new technology employed in this conflict could permit a recourse to war below the nuclear threshold, with every possibility of the realization of aim by conventional firepower alone. This, combined with the possibility that Warden's "Five Circles" and Deptula's "Inside-Out Warfare" were, if not proven in 1991, then harbingers of what will be reality within the next decade, may well provide the future terms of reference of war—perhaps.

The restoration of the power of decision of war and the realization of aim by firepower alone may not represent an accurate reading of the signs. But the new technology may well herald a new instability in the sense that precision munitions will weaken restraints upon the employment of force by making war both practical and winnable. One of the most distinguished of British commentators has noted that the coalition effort in the 1991 campaign represented "a striking exemplification of the inutility of the Western way of warfare,"[5] and so it may be, but equally the 1991 campaign may point in exactly the opposite direction and herald a period of unprecedented effectiveness in the conduct of the Western way of warfare, either in the prosecution of total war or, because of the power and effectiveness of modern weaponry, by virtue of an ever-closer definition of the political at the expense of the military. In fact, the new technology may serve to render the distinction between total and limited war meaningless by making it possible for an advanced, sophisticated state to conduct total war without having to wage war totally.

Herein is a point of significance that is too easy to miss: a country reckoned at the time to be the fifth-ranked power in the world in terms of size of military establishment was comprehensively defeated in 43 days at a coalition cost of six dead and one aircraft per day. The wonder of the 1991 campaign was not the scale of the coalition effort but the extent of the victory and the speed and economy with which that victory was recorded, and a contrast between 1991 and the Second World War is not without interest. The latter conflict lasted 2,193 days, in the course of which Britain and the United States lost 40,379 aircraft operationally, or 18 aircraft a day every day for six years: once it entered the conflict, the United States took 44 months to achieve the defeat of a Japan that was then the fifth-ranked power in the world. The contrast with the events of 1991 needs no further elaboration.

The future significance of the 1991 conflict may well lie in a return to the element of decisiveness in the conduct of war and a lessening of restraints upon the future employment of force. The example of 1991 may well encourage, on the part of middle-ranking and even small states, a search for the means of precision that hold out a promise of victory over less favored neighbors that would yield more plentiful dividends more quickly than anything that could be achieved by any other means. The 1991 campaign may well mark the point in time when the genie escaped from the bottle, though in setting down this and other possible conclusions that may be drawn from this one campaign, three cautionary notes need to be sounded. It is always dangerous to draw conclusions about war from the experience of one war, and whatever the 1991 campaign might herald in terms of change, it will be noted only in one aspect of warfare and under certain specific conditions. Other forms of warfare, such as insurgency, are unlikely to be overly affected by any redefinition of the terms of reference of combat in this one particular field. Certain very specific conditions that pertained in the 1991 campaign in terms of terrain, Iraqi morale, and passivity in the face of attack, and the question of the relative value of timings and different forms of air attack, must be considered in the weighing of the conclusions to be drawn from this conflict. A certain wariness has to be exercised in the consideration of any air force claims. The movement of the horizon is perhaps one of the most profound changes to have taken place in the conduct of war, but time has shown that postaction analysis invariably results in the claims of air force personnel to be able to make the earth move being revised downward. Be that as it may, perhaps there is a point about the 1991 campaign that represents the most profound and fundamental of changes in that the conduct of the campaign represented the point where immaculate performance represented obsolescence, that this was an effort directed against a state and that such efforts will be ever less relevant because conflict in future will be between peoples or groups within a state or group of states or directed by political, ethnic or religious groupings against individual or groups of states.

* * *

But whatever significance one reads into the events of 1991 one matter cannot be disputed: this was a campaign fought at long-range and, indeed, at least in part, beyond the line of sight: more than half of all Iraqi aircraft destroyed in air-to-air combat were destroyed by airmen who never saw their victim. Herein one touches upon perhaps the most important change in the conduct of war to have occurred in the last hundred years, and by seeking to define the terms of reference of war one assigns oneself the thankless and impossible task of defining warfare since the cooling of the crust, or only slightly later: warfare, given the fact that the dividing line between love and hate is called marriage, began with God's creation of woman. Other than the Ant, Man is the only species that practices organized mass violence to the death against its own kind, and one can date and identify the character of warfare with some accuracy. If Man and Warfare are synonymous, we may infer the form and character of the dominant form of warfare that has been practiced for the greater part of Man's existence. Aboriginal tribes discovered this and last century have been found to conduct what is immediately recognizable as guerrilla warfare. It may be assumed that throughout previous existence such people have practiced the same for want of the sophistication to practice anything else. By about 8000 BC, however, Man and Warfare in one part of the world at least had developed beyond guerrilla warfare's terms of reference. In the Middle East pasture and the domestication of animals gave rise to settlements. Jericho was the first city, and its walls reveal that with it being settled, Man, at least in this part of the world, had organized himself sufficiently to build and defend walls or to destroy them. We know, moreover, the form of warfare that was practiced. The Book of Joshua tells us what happened when Jericho was taken by the Israelites: "The people went up into the city, every man straight before him, and they took the city. And they utterly destroyed all that was in the city, both man and woman, young and old, and ox, and sheep, and ass, with the edge of the sword."[6] The Old Testament is in large part the tale of war for possession of territory and the right to survive. Wars were wars of racial extermination with captivity and enslavement the only lesser alternative. Genocide has passed over Europe, Asia, the Americas, the Caribbean and Australasia: the Final Solution of the Second World War and, most recently, Bosnia-Herzegovina, have a long, and not very distinguished, pedigree.

For all but the last 100 years or so war, or more accurately combat, did not change overmuch. Throughout the greater part of Man's existence combat, whether on land or at sea, was fought at or only marginally beyond the length of an arm. Battle, its definitive terms of reference provided by the horizon, was fought in an area that could be scanned from a single vantage point and seldom lasted longer than the hours of daylight of a single day. Battlefields widened and many battles, such as Kandurcha in 1391 or Leipzig in 1813, lasted longer than a day as, of course, did sieges, but these basic rules of thumb in defining battle and combat stand scrutiny. Before the second half of the nineteenth century battle and warfare had altered but little since the age of antiquity. A commander of the classical era would have recognized, with due allowance for changes of weaponry, the basic form of warfare as exhibited in the Napoleonic or Crimean Wars: Alexander, Hannibal, and Caesar would have understood Waterloo. The movement away from close-quarter battle was a characteristic of twentieth-century warfare, and while one must be careful to recognize that much combat still takes place at very short range, the movement of the horizon does indeed represent the most important change to have taken place in the business of war. Drake or Nelson would have understood at a glance the battle of Manila Bay in May 1898: Manila Bay and Santiago, in terms of the conduct of battle, together formed the last actions in the Age of Sail. But they would have been at a loss to understand the battle of Leyte Gulf in October 1944 in which the battle area covered some 110,000 square miles and the area of deployment was almost three times greater.[7] Such was the impact of air power on the conduct of naval operations in terms of the extension of the battle area even as the period of engagement shortened.

The movement of the horizon is inevitably associated with the aircraft, but in fact began in the nineteenth century with the development of the railroad: the initial movement of the horizon was not in depth but lateral. By the end of the Russo–Japanese war of 1904–05—during which powered flight by a heavier-than-air machine celebrated its first birthday—battle had been extended over 40 miles and three weeks. By 1918, frontages extended over many hundreds of miles and battles could last for months, while the distinction between a war and its constituent campaigns had become blurred almost to the point of having been rendered meaningless. The latter was not the product of the aircraft's impact on war, but in terms of impact, and irrespective of cause, the movement of the horizon does indeed represent a fundamental change in the conduct of war, in military affairs. From Bailey's and many others' one, via the Tofflers' three, to Krepinevich's ten, historians, real and alleged, have been constantly identifying revolutions in military affairs at various stages in history—gunpowder, the long bow, fifteenth-century France, the Swedish system of the late sixteenth century via the changes of 1916–18, to contemporary developments. One wonders if the very term *revolution in military affairs* is not much abused.[8] Most of these revolutions have been associated with technological change, but no single development in itself changes the terms of reference of war or the conduct of operations: the introduction of a single weapon or system cannot be anything other than limited and local in terms of its impact and effect. Moreover, the introduction of a new weapon to the battlefield is always evolutionary, involving as it must the recognition of the need for this weapon, its production, and the development of organization and doctrine that govern its employment: to borrow an observation: technology alone does not a revolution make.[9] And nothing in war is wholly new: the Old Man in the Mountain and his assassins in Alamut in the twelfth and thirteenth centuries would recognize Inside-Out Warfare for what it is, as would any disciple of Sun Tzu with respect to his instruction to use double agents and disinformation to paralyze the decision-making processes of an enemy.

* * *

The statement that the movement of the horizon represents the most important, indeed perhaps the only, fundamental change to have taken place in the business of war was in the form of a proposition rather than an assertion, and realistically it must be conditioned by a statement of the obvious. The conduct of war cannot be separated from its context, specifically the nature of war, most obviously in terms of the ability of states to wage war. Herein lies a change that took place in the course of the twentieth century and was certainly no less, perhaps even more, important to the nature of war than the changing terms of reference of battle. The conduct of total war in the first half of the twentieth century was synonymous with the rise of the state, and the process by which the two emerged together was mutually supporting: the emergence of the mass state inevitably meant that the greater and more powerful the motives of the war, by so much closer would that war approach its absolute form. War between great powers in the first half of the twentieth century could only be prosecuted by a process that could not but result in the cultivation of more powerful motives.

* * *

The relationship between the organization of society in order to wage war and its willingness to do so is subtle and often missed: it explains the indecisiveness of the Western Front in the First World War. But more pertinently, there would seem to be strands woven together that are critical to any understanding of twentieth-century history. The history of the twentieth century can be related around the theme of warfare, yet equally it can be related around the theme of the state, and the two are indissolubly linked because in the first half of the twentieth century total war gave rise to the mass state and the emergence of the mass state necessitated total war.

Yet the history of the second half of the twentieth century provides a triple paradox, which is all the more striking because of the success of the state in previous years in the generation of power. The Helsinki treaty of August 1975, with its provision for guaranteed human rights and international supervision, marked the demise of the Westphalian state system and the essential characteristics of the state and the concept of sovereignty as these had evolved after 1648.[10] The second half of the twentieth century has played host to a proliferation of states, to the point where perhaps as many as three-quarters of the states that presently exist must have question marks placed against their viability in terms of identity and financial base. But in the last three decades of the twentieth century governments in the advanced Western countries, despite the evidence of the first seven decades of the century, set about the prescription of state activity and proclaimed their own inability to act, except in matters that are electorally advantageous: governments seemed to have divested themselves of a shared view of society that had emerged in the first 60 years of the twentieth century. The state, as that concept came to be understood in the course of the greater part of the twentieth century, has in the last 20 years come under an attack that was without precedence. In part this attack has developed under the double impact of new technology: the Information Revolution has drained power from the state while the proliferation of newspapers and television channels has undermined the basic elements of social cohesion as the latter had developed by and in the second quarter of the twentieth century. But the attack has developed for another reason—the reassertion of the Right— and in this there is an irony in the sense that, at least in Britain and the United States, those who have conducted this assault on the concept of the state are those very same people who have sought to claim credit for military success that was only rendered possible because of the existence of the very state structure that they repudiated and were determined to dismantle.

But to suggest that the assault upon the concept of the state has been the monopoly of the Right is clearly simplistic. The profound disillusionment with government, the emergence of what Ulrich Beck has referred to as changes happening in the area of "subpolitics,"[11] and the lack of youth involvement in the representative process have affected virtually all the advanced democracies in the latter part of the 1980s and throughout the 1990s. Persistent and high levels of unemployment, seemingly intractable industrial, financial, and economic problems in many of the established democracies, and the emergence of organizations and forces—such as disease, a 24-hour money market and enormous multinational trading companies with budgets greater than most states—are illustrative of problems that have emerged in the period of financial deregulation and with which even the most powerful national governments cannot cope. All these matters together point to the fact that the changes that have taken place in terms of social cohesion, perspectives of society and the state, and the institutions of governance cannot be attributed simply to the rise and rhetoric of the Right, though the latter has probably been the most obvious single factor in this development.

* * *

The history of the twentieth century can be told in terms of warfare, and it can be related in terms of the role of the state; the growth of state power was directly related to the demands of total war to the extent that the state of 1914 had more in common with the state of 1815 than with the state of 1918. The First World War brought about a transformation of the state in terms of the strengthening of its bureaucratic institutions and its intrusion into the lives and welfare of its citizens; the Second World War repeated the process. The role of the state in the Second World War followed the pattern established in the previous conflict, with two results that are easily missed. For all the many imperfections of their systems, Britain and the United States proved much more efficient in the mobilization of resources than Germany, Italy, and Japan: indeed, the latter was so incoherent in the formulation of strategic policy and priorities that it did something that was seemingly impossible, which was to have made the Confederacy seem a model of rationality and organization in comparison.

Moreover, and in sharp contrast to enemies that were committed to the waging of war to the exclusion of everything else, by 1942 Britain and the United States had begun to turn their attention to the form of postwar society and were acting upon the evidence of their war efforts in terms of political programs that reflected the success of the command economy and the forging of a new social consensus during the war. In Britain the war served as a leveler, specifically of income but, unusually, a leveling upward in terms of postwar expectations. There was both in Britain and the United States during the war years an increasingly widespread belief that what could be achieved under state direction in wartime in terms of the public good could equally be achieved in peacetime. For Britain this process is identified with one name, Beveridge, and the commitment of government to address what he had defined in December 1942 as the scourges of the prewar period: want, disease, ignorance, squalor, and idleness. For Britain in the Second World War the Beveridge Report was no less important than Alamein. The experience of the war produced in the two western democracies a commitment to reduce social injustice through deliberate state policy and by economic expansion. Both in the United States and throughout Europe after 1945 it was the Left that reaped the benefit of this change to the extent that, whether in office or not, it held the intellectual initiative and dictated the political agenda for more than a generation.

* * *

If the Second World War can be seen as the last war of the nineteenth century, the final struggle between Rationalism and Romanticism as the twin products of that century, then the immediate post-1945 period and the triumph of the Left in this time can be portrayed as the swan song of a Rationalism that reached back to the eighteenth century and had as its basis concepts of human betterment, the common good, and social advance through deliberate state policy. The line that links the ideas of eighteenth-century Enlightenment and the political and social reforms of the post-1945 period is direct, and the achievement of the Left after 1945 is considerable. After 1949 the growth of Western economies, in large measure the product of American benevolence toward Europe in the form of Marshall Aid but also the result of the emergence of the social market and the arrangements crafted at Bretton Woods, allowed the realization of much of the Left's program in Europe. In education, health, welfare, and employment the postwar period was one of massive social change achieved on the basis of a general understanding of what society was and should be. The movement of parties of the Right into the center provided the basis of social consensus as the state embraced a collectivist culture, thereby provoking the obvious questions: when did this consensus unravel, and, with it, when did the Rationalist tide ebb?

* * *

It is difficult to resist the notion that 1968 marked the end of the primacy of the Left, that by that time the Right was beginning to emerge from the shadow cast by Hitler, Mussolini, and the Second World War while the Left, having apparently slain so many dragons, had spent itself. Certainly one can see in the events of 1968 proof of the exhaustion of the Left's credibility and ideas. The crushing of the Prague Spring was evidence, as if the erection of the Berlin Wall had not provided evidence enough, of the moral bankruptcy of Soviet creed, that the Soviet system had nothing to offer, while the evident failures of Johnson's Great Society and the profound conservatism of the ramshackle Wilson administration were tokens of radical exhaustion. Alternatively, 1973 may really mark the end of the immediate postwar period: the combination of the onset of unprecedented inflationary pressures in the Western world, the collapse of the Bretton Woods system of fixed exchanges and the devaluation of the dollar, and the first oil crisis destroyed the industrial and financial order and stability that had been set in place after 1949.

Whether one sees either of these two years, 1968 or 1973, or indeed any other specific year, as the point in time when the Left's intellectual primacy passed, one faces the obvious problem of interpretation; in setting out any *fin de siècle* argument there are obvious problems in identifying both periods and the circumstances of change. For example, it is possible to identify change, an end of one phase of history, in terms of the invention of the DRAM chip invented in 1970, the microprocessor in 1971, or the introduction of the Intel 8086 microprocessor in 1978, developments that together brought the cost of computers within range of the private individual. Conversely, 1979 was massively significant in terms of industrialized society as it had developed over some two centuries: it was the year when the world's production of plastics exceeded that of steel. But—specifically addressing the proposition that the decline of the Left marked the end of the postwar era and with it a much more important phase of history—1968 presents problems in the sense that the process most certainly was not complete by this time, and whether the crises of that year were specific or a reflection of deeper trends is difficult to determine.

The 1960s as a whole witnessed a fragmentation of the Left, and certainly there were groupings on the Left that had embraced violence before the events in Paris in May 1968 that many hold to have been the watershed in radical fortunes. The phenomenon of the New Left is very often identified with the 1970s and the politics set in train by the events of 1968, but in fact the New Left was a term applied from the beginning of the 1960s and that decade as a whole was one of alternative rebellion and one that sapped the corpus of the democratic Left. *International Times* first appeared in October 1966, the British *OZ* in January 1967. Both reflected and were born of the decade when youth was, or seemed to be, in the ascendancy. The Roundhouse seminar took place in July 1967, and it was the image of a decade of alienation and rebellion, with much of the force of this alienation and rebellion gathered in opposition to the war in southeast Asia. The 1960s was the decade of sex, drugs, and rock 'n' roll, and the images that come down to us through the years, blurred through an acid haze, are those of the one-dimensional man Herbert Marcuse; the pre-Newport Bob Dylan; Timothy Leary in his own Spiritual League; the innocently conspiring Angela Davis; Black Power and Mexico; Guy Debord making an antisocial spectacle of his situation; the indescribable Grateful Dead; Guevara, the poster not the man because the poster was the more useful; New York's answer to culture, Andy Warhol; the Faithfull Mars Bar; Stokeley Carmichael taking liberties with dialectics; a howling Allan Ginsberg; Michael Harowitz, Abby Hoffman, Janis Joplin. The background tune, inevitably on account of its association, is "Lucy in the Sky with Diamonds" of 1967.[12] The 1960s was the decade of the lithograph and the Underground, and in the fervor, excitement, and passion of these years, at a time when love was a social panacea, there was a violence against the values and system that had created a generation that was unique in that it did not know real poverty and privation.

It is possible to dismiss the whole of the Alternative Society as cosmetic and dilettante, a self-indulgence on the part of individuals who enjoyed the liberty bestowed by full employment and who proved conformists when confronted with the realities of choice. Perhaps the real Alternative Society had begun to emerge among those whose protest was directed against the powerless of the intellectual Left, the basic message of which had been "accommodated" within a political, social and economic system at the expense of genuinely radical and democratic change. There may, however, be another explanation: the protest movement of the Left, despite its collectivist origins and rationale, was essentially individualist, and the radical Right that emerged in the 1970s clearly had its immediate origins in the protest movement of the previous decade. Be that as it may, it is difficult to resist the notion that the drug culture, hedonism, and insistent self-expression of the decade spelled the end of a civic culture that the Left had embraced and which had provided the basis of what success it had commanded. Certainly the new values represented a massive assault on collectivism and in its emphasis upon individualism and nonconformity paved the way for the Age of Self; it is no less difficult to resist the notion that in this decade the Left and popular music reflected one another. The simplicity, honesty, sincerity of their individual parts were lost in a welter of self-indulgence, confusion, and self-destructiveness. The term "heavy metal" was coined at the end of this decade about the alleged music of Jimi Hendrix: the world had come a long way, in less than a generation, from the innocence of the Big Rock Candy Mountain. A mere five years separated the Magic Dragon and the crisis of 1968.

The intellectual primacy of the Left was the victim of the 1960s, yet in representing 1968 as the year that marked the destruction of that primacy, three codicils must be noted. The rebelliousness of the decade and the year was not primarily directed against the Left, which was undone more by exhaustion and disillusionment—and its failure to provide a genuinely radical alternative in the 1960s—than by direct assault or fragmentation. The most spectacular casualties of the upheavals of 1968 were from the Right. In France de Gaulle survived the challenge on the streets in May 1968, only to be forced from office in April 1969. Five months later the Christian Democrats went into opposition for the first time since the establishment of the West German state. Even fascist Spain seemed to waver when pushed by the Basques, but another seven years were to pass before Franco, deservedly, descended piecemeal and painfully into Hell. Moreover, the Left's defeats that followed were desperately narrow and not seen at the time as irreversible: indeed, at the time the slenderness of the Republican victory in November 1968, the narrow and unexpected Conservative Party's success in Britain in June 1970, and the desperately close victory of Giscard d'Estaing in the second round of the presidential election in May 1974 were anything but proof that the Left was in irreversible decline. The election in 1972 of the first Labour government in Australia since 1946, the overthrow of the dictatorship in Portugal in April 1974, the recovery of the Democrats in 1976 and of parties of the Left in Europe in the 1970s, and the French socialist victory in May 1981 would seem to provide evidence that after 1968 the radical agenda was not dead. If one wants to date the end of the Left's primacy, the end of the immediate postwar world, then one faces an embarrassment of choice and an impossible problem: no single date can explain the process of fragmentation. But the parties of the Left had no effective program to deal with the problems of the 1970s and 1980s, and it is difficult to resist the notion that the Left, if it did not die in the 1960s, emerged from it mortally wounded. Perhaps the more appropriate metaphor would be that it entered the 1970s a condemned man on appeal. But if for no other reason than convenience and to draw this section of the introductory chapter to a close, one can select 1968 as the point in time when the postwar primacy of the Left passed into history. The Tet offensive in February, the currency crises and introduction of a two-tier price for gold in March, the Paris uprising in May, the assassinations of Martin Luther King in April and of Robert Kennedy in June, and, disastrously, the Democratic Party's convention in Chicago in August together represent the moment in time when the Left's domination of the political and intellectual agenda in Western society died, when the rationalism that reached back to the Age of Reason faltered, *when men lost faith in reason.* How else can one explain Richard Nixon? And the slimy *Triturus*, from both sides of the pond, that were to follow him through the gutters?

* * *

So Queen Victoria died in 1945 and Voltaire expired in 1968? But of course: the twentieth century only lasted 23 years. Such an argument cannot be sustained, its various weaknesses argue for themselves, yet at the same time the new millennium presents reason enough to reconsider the events of the last century in order to try to understand the present time and what beckons in the future, to look for explanation that lies outside predictable terms of reference. No doubt in time an orthodoxy will emerge that historically dates the end of the twentieth century with the destruction of the Berlin Wall or the demise of the Soviet Union, though one would admit one other possibility. Given the fact that the term "postmodern" is often used of the present time and that the change between the modern and medieval world was Man's replacement of God at the center of Creation, if someone can date the point in time when the human being's place was usurped by the television, one would have the key to an understanding of the present. But in the aftermath of the collapse of the Soviet system and the end of the Cold War, both opportunity and necessity to reconsider the history of the twentieth century come together, and without terms of reference supplied by the demands of Cold War rhetoric. It would be easy enough to see in the demise of the Soviet Union a drawing of the line beneath the Second World War, and in one sense that is correct: we live in a Europe that bears a very odd resemblance to the map of Europe as it existed between March and November 1918, that brief period between a German victory in eastern Europe and a German defeat in the west. For the moment the rivalries in eastern Europe remain, and one is reminded, as one considers Yugoslavia in 1999, that in the Jasenovac death camp, where prisoners prayed for "a golden death" by bullet, the Croat guards often wagered who could kill the most prisoners. The supreme achievement was registered by a guard who in one night slit 1,378 Serbian throats. The past is still very much with us, the ending of the Cold War has brought with it a loosening of its disciplines, and only a fool would deny that the force of nationalism throughout Europe, not just in the Balkans, is stronger today than at any time since 1945.

* * *

Herein lies much of the rationale for a collection of chapters that have not been written in the form of a history or a comprehensive analysis of either the twentieth century or war in the twentieth century. Moreover, the individual chapters have not been standardized in order that each and every one considers the same basic aspects of different wars. The various chapters have different form and substance. Some have as their subject an examination of the nature of war and others the conduct of certain wars. Most obviously, those chapters primarily concerned with the two world wars of the twentieth century have examined specific campaigns and episodes, and concern has primarily been with how these campaigns and episodes have been represented: the final chapter deals primarily with doctrine and the 1991 campaign in the Middle East. There are, obviously, overlapping terms of reference in each chapter, since these deal with subjects that do not lend themselves to ready, ordered compartmentalization, but each chapter is distinctive and separate from the others.

These chapters began life, more than a decade ago, in the form of a number of essays, each devoted to some aspect of the Second World

War. One basic consideration lay behind the idea and its various parts. Attendance at various conferences and listening to various papers on the subject of the Second World War prompted concern because so many papers seemed to be microanalyses to the point of loss of context and perspective and the reality that this war, while certain of the commemorative events on television were either staid presentation or blatant sensationalism, or noted for their proclamations of new material and interpretation where neither existed. But it was when the draft of *Queen Victoria's Last War* was completed that the realization came that the effort that had been expended represented effort wasted: far more serious than any concern about the way in which the history of the Second World War was being written were two matters—namely, a fear for the way in which the history of the twentieth century was being written and presented, and a concern for standardization of view, specifically with respect to representation of the events of 1991 in the Middle East.

This second episode, the 1991 campaign, emerged initially as a result of my time in Washington, at war college. There was, in my second year there, a group of service personnel, mostly drawn from the U.S. Army, who, with their hold on Maneuver Warfare doctrine, possessed a certainty of knowledge and insisted on enforcing their own narrow and ill- or uninformed views on their colleagues: the mark of their professionalism was the request that I inform them of the name of the author of, or provide them with, a suitable Clausewitz crib. These individuals always wanted the answer in six lines, failing to realize that distillation over six lines of necessity means work over many pages—not to mention years and even decades—and, of course, to ask for a Jominian guide to Clausewitz encompassed an irony, and a comment upon themselves, that these individuals simply could not appreciate.

It took three years for the various parts of *When Men Lost Faith in Reason* to be slotted into place, the final chapter, the only one primarily concerned with the events of 1990–91 in the Middle East, being one of two basic problems that beset the recasting of the terms of reference. The other concerned Maneuver Warfare per se, and here a series of doubts and reservations came to the fore during the writing of these chapters. I did not understand why maneuver had been represented as the counterpoint to attrition, since, clearly, they are not opposites. I was at a loss to identify a war in which both sides had abjured maneuver, and I simply could not understand how such a concept could have any place in matters dealing with war at sea and in the air. Moreover, so much of what had been written about Maneuver Warfare doctrine seemed to represent firepower and maneuver as opposites rather than as complementary. During the writing of various chapters, but specifically those dealing with the Second World War and the 1991 campaign, my major reservation about the whole Maneuver Warfare concept took shape with the realization that what the new doctrine was about, and what it could have been better named, was *Decisive Warfare*—that what had emerged in the aftermath of the Vietnam War was a concept of war that aimed to restore the element of decision to war.

The problem that this definition of what was being sought was the Maneuver Warfare school's repudiation of so much of warfare in the industrial age. There most definitely seemed a most willful and mendacious treatment of warfare, specifically in the First and Second World Wars, a deliberate *ex post facto* classification of battles, campaigns, and wars that seemed to have as its only basis the desire to arrange matters to a predetermined end. Yet I considered, as I thought of the examples provided by history, wars that had been decisive. I thought in terms of defeats that could be permanent, and herein the example of history seemed to point in the direction of decisiveness only where states or societies were destroyed, where entire populations were systematically massacred. The obvious implications of such a thought would seem to argue for themselves, but in seeking to examine history dispassionately, I found myself coming back, so often, to the example of the Eastern Empire. Here seemed to be an example of a society and a state that provided evidence of everything that those who were in the ascendancy in the last decade of the second millennium repudiated. Here was a state that was a direct contradiction of the fundamental principle drawn from Clausewitz's writings. To the Eastern Empire war was not an instrument of state policy: the state existed to wage war and was organized to wage war on a permanent, not an occasional, basis. Faced by enemies whichever way it turned, the Eastern Empire faced the obligation of perpetual war, and it was organized as a command economy geared to raise money and manpower to meet its military commitments. The command state existed from the seventh to the eleventh centuries, from Heraclius to Basil II Bulgaroctonus, and herein, with these two individuals—the first to bear the title of basileus and the second, arguably, the greatest of the emperors—was evidence of the indecisiveness of war. The survival by the Eastern Empire in the face of the great crisis of August 626, the culmination of deepening problems over the previous two decades, was then followed by the defeat of the Persian Empire. This defeat saw Roman armies reach Isfahan, and it saw victories that were unprecedented in Roman history. It saw the restoration of provinces that had been lost over the previous 20 years, and, most important of all, these victories resulted in the return of the True Cross to Jerusalem in 629. The victory that was won by the Eastern Empire was remarkable: from the battles fought on land and at sea in 626 to final overwhelming victory, in effect it destroyed the Avar empire and left the Persian Empire dependent on its western neighbor. And within 10 years all that had been reconquered had been lost, and within another 20 years one-third of the Eastern Empire would have been lost and the Persian Empire disappeared into history. From a position of very considerable security in 629, the Eastern Empire was handed a defensive commitment that lasted for two centuries. In the first 100 years its very existence was on the line, and when finally it emerged from the shadow of defeat, it was given a series of rulers who provided the Empire with a measure of security unknown throughout that time. It was finally afforded an Emperor who reestablished the Empire on the Danube for the first time in more than 400 years, registered massive gains in the east and south, and genuinely brought to the Empire a security against invasion that predated Justinian the Great in the sixth century.

But in the long history of the Eastern Empire, no individual front better illustrated the indecisiveness of war and its capacity to change rather than to solve problems than the one presented by the Bulgar state. For some 200 years the Empire waged war against the Bulgar state, which doubled its size in the process, and when finally under Basil II the Empire destroyed the Bulgar state and established itself on the Danube for the first time in four centuries, it inherited insoluble problems. The Bulgar population, though conquered, was never reconciled to Imperial rule; the Empire faced on the Danube new enemies that presented a graver threat than had the Bulgarians; such peoples as the Serbs and Croats, who previously had made common cause with the Empire against the Bulgars, were no longer under such obligation. Even in success, therefore, were the seeds of future defeat, because war in itself could not be, and intrinsically cannot be, decisive.

One looks not just at Bulgaria and the Haemus in this respect; searching through history, it is difficult to identify a battle with a result so wholly different from its context, so vast in its repercussions, as the unlikely Imperial victory outside Antioch in 995. Yet for this success, and despite the creation of eight new military administrative areas (themes) during the period of Basil II's rule, within less than 50 years of his death the Empire had been expelled from Italy and sustained a defeat at Manzikert that in effect condemned it to a long, lingering death. Certainly with the loss of the Anatolian heartland in the wake of the 1071 debacle there was never anything more than a partial retrieval of losses.

The point, of course, is the impermanence of victory—that even in this period of unprecedented Imperial victories there were the seeds and ingredients of defeat. This does not begin to examine the fact that on Basil II's death the command state was dismantled by rulers and nobility that sought only personal enrichment and indulgence while the army, in effect, was destroyed from within. If one reads through accounts of these campaigns and battles, one is struck by two thoughts—of the permanence of influence of geography and the transient nature of victory. The passes through which armies marched in 626–628, and again when Basil II annexed territories in the east, were the same as those through which Alexander the Great had led his army. Men, weapons, and tactics may change, but, within certain limits, geography and strategy do not, and no victory possesses any element of permanence. To acknowledge what was written hundreds if not thousands of years ago: *O quam cito transit gloria mundi.*

* * *

Such, then, were the more important of the arguments and considerations that at various times moved to center stage as I sought to shape chapters—individual essays—anew. This first chapter sought to place before the reader perspectives unlikely to have intruded much upon his or her attention, most obviously the propositions that what we understand to be the Second World War was really no more than one part—the most destructive single part—in a series of wars between 1931 and 1975 that reshaped the international order, and that what we understand to be the Cold War was the time when real hatreds were suspended, to be resumed when the Soviet Union and its system were no more. As the product of postwar society—born in 1945 and having graduated from university in 1967—and so conservative as to be incorrigibly Old Labour, the author has long wondered where it all went wrong, how society could possibly inflict the Shrew of Suburbia upon itself. This first chapter was, in some ways, an exercise in self-indulgence, but nonetheless it was seriously intended, to pose the question of what, in historical terms, the twentieth century was and to define certain lesser times within its terms of reference.

The second chapter concerns itself with two matters: the First World War and the interwar period. In terms of its examination of First World War matters, its concerns are twofold. The chapter aims to set out the reasons for tactical stalemate, the battlefield impasse, whereby it was impossible for any single state, or group of states, to win a decisive victory in either a single battle or a campaign. The reason why this subject commands much attention in this chapter is the belief that in setting out the standard reasons for deadlock, various historians and commentators have merely described the battlefield and not explained why it was impossible to secure victory on it. The problem with this analysis is that there are different levels of explanation, and, moreover, there are individual campaigns and battles in which specific matters need careful explanation, since they would be missed in any general examination of this subject. Thus the German offensive of spring 1918 is considered in general terms but also specifically, in terms of being conducted on too narrow a frontage and against too little of the Allied forces on the Western Front to be able to register strategic paralysis, which was essential, the *sine qua non* to the success of this endeavor. Perhaps more importantly, however, the second chapter examines the nature of war in terms of its relationship to the state, specifically the changes that affected the state in its waging of total war. In terms of the mobilization of opinion, combined with the legacy of nineteenth-century hatreds, there is the basis for an understanding of the emergence of Nazism and its place in German success in the 1939–42 period and in German failure in the 1943–45 period. What binds these various parts together is the iden-tification not of material factors as decisive in the conduct of war, but of moral and political considerations as crucial, if not in terms of the outcome of specific wars, then in terms of the nature of war.

The third chapter is very different from all the other chapters because it primarily concerns itself with how historical evidence has been pre-sented. It represents an attack on both "standard" presentations from both sides of the North Atlantic, American and British, specifically with respect to Normandy and, more generally, the Mediterranean theater of operations. The main casualties in this examination are popular sub-scribed myths such as the "British way of warfare" and the increasingly popular thesis in the United States that an invasion of northwest Europe could have been accomplished in 1943. Both of these arguments are considered against the background provided by historical evidence: the "British way of warfare" against evidence provided over hundreds of years in which Britain invariably made its main military effort in any war in which it found itself in the Low Countries, northern France and western Germany—that is, in the strategic heartland of western Eu-rope—while the 1943 thesis is considered against such matters as the Battle of the Atlantic, available shipping and convoy cycles, German force levels, and the practical experience that was registered by Allied armies in the Mediterranean theater of operations.

The last part of this section of the third chapter concerns itself with air power and the Normandy endeavor, and this leads naturally to an examination of the strategic use of air power in both the German and Japanese context, to a question of the value and morality of bombing efforts directed against civilian and industrial targets in 1945. This also allows a questioning of one of the more curious historical arguments used to justify the use of atomic weapons against Hiroshima and Naga-saki—namely, how it was that American calculations indicated that more casualties would be sustained in an invasion of the Japanese home islands than were incurred in Normandy, when the quality of most Japanese divisions was low, most obviously in terms of armor, transport, and communications, and certainly much lower than overall German levels in Normandy.

In its middle section this chapter reaches into the German concept of offensive operations, generally known as *"Blitzkrieg"* but more properly as the "*Schlacht ohne Morgen*" [the battle with no tomorrow] and this then passes into an examination of the Nazi–Soviet conflict and the wider question of the Soviet military performance in the Second World War. The author is of the view that in the waging of total war every little helps, and just as in alliance warfare victory and defeat are not the preserves of individual states though the input of one may be the most important single contribution to this process, so one must consider the Second World War properly, without the constraints and restraints imposed by Cold War rhetoric and shorn of claims of national exclusiveness.

The fourth chapter has more in common with the second chapter than with the third: it is an analysis of the dynamics of deterrence and, very separately, warmaking in the first 30 years of the Cold War. Critical to the analysis are three absurdities: the creation of permanent, standing alliances with strategic forces permanently at readiness with the task of ensuring against war, the separation between deterrence and defense, and that in fighting for values in the conduct of "Limited War," the only war that can be fought is one that, in the final analysis, the protagonist must be prepared to lose. This latter point was simply never appreciated until it became reality in the course of the Vietnam War. In the analysis of this particular war are two conclusions that are unlikely to recommend themselves to many: that the cause of American failure lay in an inability to understand the enemy and in the inversion of one of Clausewitz's basic definitions—that if war is an instrument of policy, then so is peace, and if war and peace are both instruments of policy, then they are one and the same or, perhaps more accurately, the two sides of a coin called "struggle," in which what cannot be won on the battlefield must be won on the international political stage and in terms of domestic opinion. Critical here is a thorough examination of the concept of revolutionary guerrilla warfare, specifically the teachings of Mao Tse-tung, and the identification of the critical components of revolutionary struggle—not the three phases of preparation, guerrilla warfare, and conventional offensive action, but, based on the idea that war is above all a political phenomenon, the critical trinity of abstracts—time and space and will. Against such criteria there is an examination of various campaigns: specifically, the British in Malaya and the French in Indochina and what made for their very different endings.

Thereafter, the chapter divides attention between two areas of interest, the first being the disastrous Algerian campaign, or perhaps more accurately the emergence, as a result of the Indochina debacle, of a counterinsurgency doctrine—*La Guerre Révolutionnaire*—that was applied with such disastrous results in Algeria. Herein, of course, was the element of contradiction: *La Guerre Révolutionnaire* was a disaster not because it provided the French army with a blueprint for failure, but because it was so successful—indeed, so much so that it had to be destroyed by the

French state: it was more important for the French state to lose a war than for the French army to win a campaign. The second area of interest is a counterpoint to Algeria and *La Guerre Révolutionnaire*: the Cuban revolution and, more importantly, its legacy in the 1960s in terms of the emergence of a new concept of revolutionary warfare, the concept of "revolution within the revolution," which failed throughout the length of South America. The underlying factors at work in these various campaigns—both in Cuba and in the revolutionary defeats of the 1960s—are examined alongside the growing crisis within Western society that came to a head in 1968. In an obvious sense, therefore, this chapter reaches back to this first chapter in terms of events and fact, though not of interpretation and presentation, and thence to a new concept of revolutionary struggle—urban guerrilla warfare.

The latter emerged in the late 1960s, and for the most part the challenge that it presented to established Western society was defeated in the next decade. The 1970s, however, saw the crumbling of many of the standard features of Western society as they had come to exist after 1945, and it was also the decade, the encapsulation of obsolescence at the peak of achievement, when the Soviet Union attained parity with the United States in terms of superpower status and capability. It was a time that was traumatic for the United States as it struggled to come to terms with defeat and the aftermath of the war in southeast Asia and a time that saw five developments, singly or more relevantly together, holding massive consequences for the future. The Vietnam War—and for that matter the U.S. commitment to European NATO—were basically of Second World War vintage: not so much in the air but certainly on land and at sea this was the case; by the mid-1970s the weapons systems of the Second World War and their derivatives of the immediate postwar period had come to the end of their allotted time. In their place were weapons of unprecedented accuracy and destructiveness. Alongside were massive changes in society, most obviously in terms of production and the onset of the Information Revolution to which this chapter has referred. All these together spelled change, as did the founding of Training and Doctrine Command (TRADOC) and what amounted, under the Carter Doctrine, to American acceptance of a forward commitment in the Middle East.

These various developments, or at least most of them, really came together in the 1991 campaign in the Middle East, an examination of which forms the second part of the fifth chapter. The first part of this chapter brings together the various developments cited in the previous chapter and traces the emergence of the Maneuver Warfare school of doctrine and the process that was to lead, via various intermediate stages, to the concept of AirLand battle. The coincidence of timing with events in the Middle East in 1981 is noted in the form of the analysis of the Israeli offensive into southern Lebanon, which went under the name "Peace for Galilee." The greater part of this chapter is devoted, however, to a detailed analysis of the 1991 campaign, while the final part of the chapter represents an examination of this campaign in terms of how far it accorded with current doctrine or whether it represented something that was new and that promised to bring with it new definitions that would result in fresh terms of reference as these would affect the nature and conduct of war.

* * *

What these chapters would claim to be was reflective and analytical rather than disciplined and narrowly scholarly or academic. Together, they constitute a series of examinations of war in the course of the twentieth century not with an prescriptive intent and not for purposes of prediction. Rather, they represent an attempt to trace the journey that has just been made, the basic strength of which lies in not seeking to impose a set order upon individual wars and in not forcing each and every conflict to conform to a Jominian checklist. Its various conclusions are offered on the proper basis, for what they are worth, if anything, and as the starting point for the reader's individual consideration of conflict in the twentieth century and not as the conclusion. The author would stand by his final comment that in war everything is uncertain, and wars invariably assume courses and outcomes very different from that intended by their authors. The whole notion of being able to control warfare, whether it be definition of "end-state" or offensive operations of surgical precision, runs directly counter to the fundamental Clausewitzian element in war, chance. War is not the preserve of the intellect and is not intrinsically rational or scientific. Man made War in his own image, complete with all the elements of human failure, misjudgment, and incompetence therein, and, hopefully, thus it will remain. Current doctrine and predictions for the future of war that are now on the table would seem to assume otherwise, that somehow the certainties provided by technology will provide certainties in the conduct of war that will in themselves transform the nature of war, and would seem to represent the end of the primacy of Man in terms of the nature and conduct of war.

Such is the reasoning behind this work, and here I would make just one final point. My concern is that the power of image, in fixing in the public consciousness a set view, presents a most dangerous development in that it will deny the level of objectivity and learning that will lead to new perspectives, in part because we are now so far from the major events that have shaped the history of the twentieth century. At the present time we are further in time from the Munich agreement of September 1938 than a person in 1938 was from the Congress of Berlin and the end of Reconstruction—and in part because the written word seems to command so little power of redress. But if popular perception has changed but little, history, as Peter Geyl taught us, is an argument without end, and I would be disappointed to find acceptance of the views expressed here in this first chapter, and indeed in the book overall, that were written in the hope of providing a starting point of a reconsideration of history and warfare in the twentieth century, and not an end in itself.

NOTES

1. By the same token the 1991 campaign can be defined as the fourth battle of the Somme. If one identifies as the basis of calculations not personnel but formations and assumes the destruction of a one-third under-strength division a day for the duration of the campaign, the daily losses in 1991 correspond to those of 1916 and 1944, while the balance of losses between the defensive and offensive confirms the trend identified in the 1944 returns.

2. Paul Fussell, *Wartime: Understanding and Behaviour in the Second World War* (London: Oxford University Press, 1989), p. 268.

3. David M. Glantz and Jonathan House, *When Titans Clashed: How the Red Army Stopped Hitler* (Lawrence, KS: University of Kansas Press, 1995), pp. 298–299.

4. The arrangements that formally led to the end of the European war were the treaty of 31 August 1990 between the two German states that were to be unified and the "Four plus Two" treaty—Britain, France, the Soviet Union, and the United States, plus the German states—of 12 September 1990; unification of the Germanies took place on 3 October 1990. A treaty between Japan and Russia (successor state to the Soviet Union) remains elusive.

5. John Keegan, *A History of Warfare* (New York: Knopf, 1994), p. xi.

6. The Book of Joshua, VI, 20–21.

7. Giuseppe Fioravanzo, *A History of Naval Tactical Thought*, transl. Arthur W. Holst (Annapolis, MD: Naval Institute Press, 1979), p. 203.

8. For example, Alvin and Heidi Tofflers, *War and Anti-War: Survival at the Dawn of the 21st Century* (New York: AOL Time Warner Book Group, 1995), and Andrew F. Krepinevich, "Cavalry to Computer: The Pattern of Military Revolutions," *The National Interest*, No. 37 (Fall, 1994). Amid a mass of publications on the subject, one would note just a number of perhaps the more important works: Jonathan Bailey, "The First World War and the Birth of Modern Warfare," in Macgregor Knox and Williamson Murray (Eds.), *The Dynamics of Military Revolution 1300–2050* (Cambridge: Cambridge University Press, 2001), pp. 132–153; Michael Duffy, *The Military Revolution and the State, 1500–1800* (Exeter, U.K.: University of Exeter, 1980); Geoffrey Parker, *The Military Revolution: Military Innovation and the Rise of the West, 1500–1800* (Cambridge: Cambridge University Press, 1988); Clifford Roger (ed.), *The Military Revolution Debate: Readings on the Military Transformation of Early Modern Europe* (London: Routledge, 1999).

9. Thomas A. Keaney and Eliot A. Cohen, *Gulf War: Air Power Survey: Summary Report* (Washington, DC: Department of the Air Force, 1993), p. 238.

10. The Stockholm treaty of September 1986, with its provision for international inspection as part of the confidence- and security-building process in

Europe, represented the administration of the last rites, but, of course, the erosion of the concept of state sovereignty predates Helsinki and Stockholm. In the European context the establishment of the Organization of European Economic Co-operation (1948), the Court of Human Rights, and the European Coal and Steel Community (1952) represented massive inroads on the idea of noninterference in the domestic affairs of states. In the case of the latter, there is an irony seldom noted by historians. The principle of noninterference was adopted in the Treaty of Westphalia as a means of trying to avoid another Thirty Years' War; the concept of state sovereignty was crafted as part of the attempt to avoid total war. After the Second World War, the European Coal and Steel Community emerged as a means of integrating the economies of western Europe in large measure in order to ensure against their nations going to war with one another—the concept of state sovereignty was eroded as part of the attempt to avoid total war.

11. Ulrich Beck, *Risk Society. Towards a New Modernity,* transl. Mark Ritter (London: Sage, 1992).

12. The abiding image of the decade, however, is the film of Vietnam, the B-52s dropping their bombs and the background supplied by Joan Baez singing "There but for Fortune"; but that image dates from television and the 1970s and either documentaries on the Indochina war or flash-back years. The alternative songs of the 1960s, perhaps, are "The Times They Are A-changing," "Blowin' in the Wind," and Procol Harum's "A Whiter Shade of Pale"—though my own preference remains "Mr. Tambourine Man."

2

The First World War:
Deadlock and Hatred

For some four centuries, and for the only time in human existence, it was easier to move around continents than across them. It was this fact, made possible by the discovery of how to sail against the wind, that was to transform the smallest and poorest of the continents into the greatest, that was to ensure that the mark that was placed upon the world was that of Europe. Inevitably, Europe's reaching beyond its shores was not a peaceful process, and in this sense this author is always struck by the incongruous title: the *First World War*. If it was a world war—and it can be argued that it was a European war that tipped but briefly, in small measure, into certain other areas—then it most certainly was not the first. It was the first only in terms of the twentieth century. Yet, in another sense, the name the First World War is thoroughly appropriate, because it was the first war in Europe for some five centuries in which there was a non-European dimension that manifested itself in terms of Europe's fate. Europeans had fought one another outside Europe in these centuries, and non-European territories changed hands as a result of the outcome of European wars, but it was not until the First World War that the outcome of events within Europe was to be influenced substantially, even decided, by non-European factors. Other than the Australian troops who were present at the burning of Washington and who fought at Waterloo and the Canadian soldiers who served in the Crimean War, the Franco–Prussian War of 1870–71 had seen the arrival on European battlefields of the first non-Europeans since the thirteenth century, but in too small numbers to have any impact upon events. By contrast, the First World War saw divisions from the French and British empires, labor from the Far East, U.S. Army and naval forces, and Japanese warships make their way to Europe, and it was the Allies' ability to draw upon the resources of a world beyond Europe that decided the conflict in their favor.

* * *

The question, "Why was there war in Europe in 1914?" would seem to provide overwhelming evidence of the truth of the dictum that history is argument without end. The cycle of evaluation and reevaluation, interpretation and reinterpretation, is the essence of history and is, of course, the basis of the statement that anyone who wants to change history should become a historian. But the question is one that has generated much controversy, mostly unenlightening. Contending national perspectives and political persuasions have jostled with one another as their champions labored in pursuit of that most elusive of historical substances—incontrovertible fact. Against such a background, it is small wonder that this is a question that has perplexed generations of students, though in part the question's elusiveness lies in its deceptive simplicity: the form of the answer is dependent upon where in the question emphasis is placed.

The question invites consideration of two very separate but related matters. The question of why in 1914 Europe was plunged into war cannot be divorced from the wider context of how Europe was led into a war that began in 1914, but it is a question that cannot be answered until that context is examined. Yet it is this context that has invited the most mendacious of interpretations by historians. History is not the product of single causes; rather, events unfold as a result of an interplay of factors. In the decades that preceded the First World War, one can identify certain factors that conspired together to produce war in 1914. Different schools of thought have blamed secret diplomacy or the capitalist system for the outbreak of war, but because secret diplomacy could be considered to have preserved the general peace of Europe for a century, and because every state in Europe was capitalist such interpretations provide little in the way of explanation. Likewise, the argument that prewar alliances and arms races, even imperial rivalries, led to war provides a less-than-adequate interpretation of events. The war that began in July 1914 was not the product of extra-European rivalries: the European powers were never prepared to countenance a war within Europe on account of imperial rivalries beyond its shores, and if alliances and arms races did indeed have their own logic and did impart a certain pace to proceedings, they remained the manifestation rather than the cause of deeper divisions and rivalries.

Undoubtedly the succession of crises in the decade before 1914 had the effect of weakening restraint, and most certainly there was a militancy and belligerence within Europe in 1914 that made the outbreak of war welcome to a continent unfamiliar with its realities. Equally certainly, this dissonance reflected an increasingly strident nationalism and a heightened sense of insecurity on the part of all the major powers. The developments of the previous decade had left the Entente powers fearful of German intent. Conversely Germany, despite its increasing primacy within Europe, was, in the years immediately before the outbreak of war, very conscious of the long-term implications for its security presented by the lengthening of both Russia's railroads and the French periods of service with the colors.

Within Europe there were two rival alliances, and within both alliances there was fear on the part of all states that their major ally would cease to regard their partner as *bundnisfähig*. Just as there was an awareness in both France and Russia that their alliance could not survive continued refusal to provide one another with support, so Germany recognized that it could not always refuse to stand by its only ally, Austria–Hungary. In 1914 there was a certain brittleness to the cause of peace that flowed from tension within alliances. But if the factors that produced war in 1914 were long in the making, the fact remained that war broke out as the result of calculations, and miscalculations, made in various capitals, primarily in Berlin: the drafting of the German ultimatum to Belgium by the Chief of the Greater German General Staff before Russian mobilization was ordered provides incontrovertible evidence that the war that began in 1914 was primarily a German war.

* * *

The war that was fought between 1914 and 1918 was siege warfare conducted on the scale of alliances and continents. The Central Powers—Austria–Hungary, Germany, Turkey, and Bulgaria—found themselves engaged in a war with powers that could call upon the resources of the rest of the world. This was a war noted for trenches, and futile stalemate, but outside the Western and Italian theaters fronts often moved over scores of miles in the course of single offensive operations. Strategic mobility was not quite as dead in the First World War as rumor suggests, and in the initial weeks of the war there was considerable movement, most obviously in the west. Here Germany sought to defeat France in six weeks by moving through Luxembourg and Belgium around the French left flank, and thence into eastern France, where its armies would fight and win a battle of encirclement and annihilation before the bulk of these forces were moved to the east. Politically, the German plan of campaign was flawed, but the violation of neutral states, with the resultant loss of goodwill on behalf of other neutrals, was set aside by the dictates of "military necessity." Militarily, however, the plan set German forces the impossible goal of an advance of some 800 miles and fighting a series of encounter battles and then the main engagement, all inside six weeks. The two leading German armies were able to advance to the Marne by the first week of September, in no small measure only because after crossing the Belgian–French border, ammunition demands were relatively light. But as the French armies recovered from the fearful mauling they took in Lorraine, so they and the British were able to counterattack at the Marne in the second week of September and drive the Germans back to the Aisne. Thereafter both sides sought to turn the open flank, their failures resulting in a series of actions known as the "Race to the Sea," which this process was not, and which culminated with the indecisive battle of Ypres in November. In the east the Russians experienced mixed fortunes. Two Russian armies in August moved against East Prussia, and one suffered a disastrous defeat around Tannenberg, but at the same time, in a series of closely fought battles, Russian forces ultimately routed Austro–Hungarian armies around Lemberg in Galicia. Their ally's defeat brought German reinforcements to the east, but in two major offensives these were fought to a standstill. In February 1915, however, the Russians suffered emphatic defeat around the Masurian Lakes, at the very time when their forces again inflicted a heavy defeat on Austro–Hungarian armies in Galicia.

With the winter of 1914–15, the question of how the war was to be continued presented itself in urgent form for both sides. None of the powers had anticipated a war lasting longer than a matter of weeks, and none possessed the means to prosecute a protracted war. But the elusiveness of victory in 1914 forced all the powers to begin a double process of widening the war in which they found themselves. This involved the long-term mobilization of their societies and the geographical spread of the war. With Germany having successfully brought Turkey into the conflict in October 1914, throughout the winter of 1914–15 both sides tried to play the Italian card. The Entente powers sought its support, the Central Powers its neutrality, but most Italian ambitions could only be met at the expense of Austria–Hungary, and the only concessions that it could make were ones that would not meet Italian demands. The Entente thus secured Italy's entry into the war in May 1915, but it was the Turkish dimension that was the most important single factor in determining the course of events in 1915. Turkey's entry into the war produced another front for Russia, but it also provided Britain and France in 1915 with the option of moving against Turkey and its non-Turkish possessions. The year 1915 saw the start of the campaigns in Mesopotamia and the Sinai and Palestine, but more importantly of the Gallipoli venture. The rationale behind this Anglo–French enterprise was the need to help Russia, to open Russia's Black Sea ports to supplies of war material, and, by driving Turkey from the war, to conjure into existence a Balkan alliance that would present Germany and Austria–Hungary with yet another commitment in southeast Europe. These various calculations were nonsense. Britain and France had neither shipping nor war material to send to Russia, and the fact of the matter was that none of the great powers had anything to gain by the adherence of minor states that were liabilities to be supported rather than additions to strength. The fate of Europe was never going to be decided in southeast Europe by the adherence to one side or the other of countries such as Romania.

If sea power and the Turkish dimension provided the British and the French with the option of extending the war, it also presented the dilemma of choice, but the failure of the Gallipoli operation ended strategic arguments for the western allies, because thereafter the primacy of the Western Front was never disputed. But Germany was also presented with the dilemma of choice, and 1915 saw its initial effort made in the west, at second Ypres in April, before its main effort unfolded in the east. In May and June the Central Powers cleared Galicia and in the next two months Russian Poland; thereafter their attention was directed against Serbia, which was overrun between October 1915 and January 1916. It was a campaign that saw Bulgaria join the Central Power and Britain and France send forces to Salonika in a vain attempt to support Serbia. The Allies remained in Germany's "largest internment camp" until September 1918, when Allied forces were able to drive Bulgaria from the war and clear most of the Balkans. In so doing they achieved one notable first. The breaking of Bulgarian formations in the Kosturino Pass by air attack in September 1918 was perhaps the first occasion when aircraft played the decisive role in the registering of a tactical victory; certainly this was the first time when intact ground forces were broken by air attack. The caveat that must be noted, however, is that Bulgarian morale was crumbling, and the air attack arguably was merely the *coup de grâce*.

The year 1915 was known as *l'année sterile* to the Allies, the various British and French offensives on the Western Front in the course of that year being singularly notable for their costly futility. But the year saw the determination of both sides to continue the war harden, and 1915 ended with both sides increasingly confident of better fortune in 1916. By 1916 Britain and France could call the resources of their empires to the battlefield, and Russia, for the first time since September 1914, could meet the German and Austro–Hungarian armies on a basis of equality in numbers of divisions at the front. Between December 1915 and February 1916, to make maximum use of their positional advantage, the Allies arranged to synchronize their efforts. British and Russian weaknesses meant that these efforts were to be made in June and July, but Germany, in choosing to make its main effort in 1916 in the west, forestalled this intention. Thus in February began the battle of Verdun, which was to last until December. It began as a German attempt not to secure Verdun but to force the French to fight in its defense and thereby be bled to death; it rapidly became a battle in which the process of hemorrhaging applied to both sides. It was a battle that saw the French, in spring 1916, be the first to systematically fight for air superiority over the battlefield, but more immediately important was the fact that this battle forced a reduction of the French commitment to the summer offensive astride the Somme: the latter battle, between July and November, attained a notoriety that matched that of Verdun.

If not before, then certainly by the end of 1916 the European powers should, by any rational standard, have sought an end to the war. There were, indeed, individuals who foresaw the prospect that faced Europe if it continued with the war—the ruination of all the powers and the unleashing of revolutionary forces that would sweep away the existing order. But there was no basis for ending the war. The sacrifices that all the powers demanded of their peoples could only be justified by victory. For the British and French, unable to consider peace with the Germans occupying most of Belgium and northern France, 1916 ended with the belief that a major effort in 1917 could break a Germany that must have been weakened severely in 1916. More to the point, in the course of their last counterattacks in front of Verdun in October and December 1916, the French had outfought the Germans as a result of tactical innovation: thus was bred the certain conviction that success could be repeated on a scale that would unlock the front in 1917. From this success was to emerge the debacle of the Chemin des Dames Offensive of April 1917, which reduced the greater part of the French army to mutiny—in most cases a refusal to undertake offensive operations in the summer. This development was to lead the British army into the offensive at Ypres between July and November that is forever associated with the squalor of the First World War. The Passchendaele Offensive was proof, if ever proof was needed, that for the military the difference between genius and stupidity is that genius has its limits.

The mutinies of the French army in spring 1917 and the extent of the disaster that overwhelmed Italian armies at Caporetto in October–November were symptomatic of a growing war-weariness in Europe, but, of course, it was in Russia, with the February and October Revolutions, that antiwar sentiment manifested itself to greatest effect. As Russia slowly sank into a revolutionary morass, its loss was more serious to the British and French than the promise presented by the entry of the United States into the war in April. The latter had been provoked by Germany's decision, taken in response to a hardening suspicion that its armies could not achieve victory, to wage an unrestricted campaign against Allied shipping in the belief that Britain could be forced from the war before the United States could intervene effectively. The German decision was made after its battle force had been worsted in the only fleet action of the war at Jutland (31 May–1 June 1916) and in response to the growing effectiveness of the Allied blockade. It was a decision based on results that the Imperial Navy assumed it had obtained in restricted campaigns, but German calculations made no allowances for British countermeasures, and in April 1917, with shipping losses at their peak, the British belatedly introduced oceanic convoy. This measure, combined with Allied shipbuilding resources and pressure on the neutrals to keep trading with Britain, ensured that shipping losses fell to manageable proportions. As a result, British and French salvation was assured, though, of course, they first had to survive the German spring offensive of 1918.

This offensive was intended to break the British armies in France before the Americans arrived in strength. But the Michael offensive against the British on the Somme in March–April failed, and thereafter the follow-up German offensives conformed, strategically, to the law of diminishing returns, until the point of balance was reached with the Marne–Rheims offensive in July in the Champagne. There, for the first time, a German effort was halted by major counterattack by the French. Thereafter, the tide of war turned, and with an American army in the line, the Allies were able to launch a series of separate offensives that may have lacked strategic coherence but nevertheless inflicted a series of major reverses on the German army and broke its belief in victory. With Germany's allies going down to defeat and numbed despair at the prospect of trying to survive another winter of blockade, German national will to resist was broken in autumn 1918 as a result of the failure of the army to win the victory that had been promised. In order to avoid total, comprehensive defeat, the German military insisted upon an armistice, but Germany's enemies exacted terms that ensured that it could not resume hostilities after 11 November 1918.

* * *

In the previous chapter it was noted that "The relationship between the organization of society in order to wage war and its willingness to do so is subtle and often missed: if nothing else, it explains the indecisiveness of the Western Front in the First World War." If one asks why there was deadlock on the Western Front, specifically between November 1914 and March 1918, one immediately encounters problems of interpretation and context. The problem of interpretation is obvious: several generations of historians and military commentators have provided the answer, and, unfortunately, it is the wrong answer. There is no single answer, because "trenchlock" was not the product of any one cause but the result of the coming together of a number of factors. Two, whether singly or in combination, always form the first line of alleged explanation: the superiority of defensive firepower over offensive firepower and the superiority of strategic mobility over tactical movement. Clearly, both were important: there is no disputing that offensive firepower could not neutralize a defense, and any breach in the front could always be sealed by a defense that was able to move formations by rail to the threatened sector more quickly than an attacker could move by foot and hoof across the battlefield in the attempt to maintain any breach that was opened. One more matter is often cited as complementary to these two: the lack of the systems that in the Second World War were to unlock fronts. These individual systems are usually identified as the tank and the aircraft, the point being that during the First World War their very limited capabilities precluded their use as the means of breakthrough. The problem with the identification of these two systems as providing the means of breakthrough is that a measure of motorization of at least part of the mass of armies was necessary to achieve the rupture of an enemy front. The critical development, however, was not tanks, aircraft, or motor transport, but the miniaturization of the radio, which made possible effective command and control at the point of contact.

The second line of argument usually paraded as an explanation of trenchlock is that terrain worked against the attack, that surprise was difficult to achieve, and that the past means of ensuring mobility, the use of an open flank, was not available. To these can be added another factor. Given the rapid degradation of formations committed to offensive operations, any attack invariably reached its culminating point very quickly—witness the returns registered in the British offensive at Amiens in August 1918. On the first day, with 456 tanks, the offensive recorded gains of seven miles; on the second day, with 145 tanks, gains of three miles; and on the third day, with 67 tanks, gains of one mile, at which point the offensive was abandoned. All these facts of life, and others, were at work and contributed to the tactical impasse of the First World War. It was very difficult to register surprise, and no enemy position could be outflanked. The Germans had the pick of the ground after November 1914, and therefore Allied armies, committed to the offensive because the war was being fought on their soil, were faced with a major difficulty, and one that worsened over time because of the defense added to its power in terms of depth and firepower with every year. A rudimentary trench system in 1914 evolved by 1917 into a defensive system with three main lines of resistance, sited on reverse slopes wherever possible and with the forward positions held lightly. The German defensive systems on the Western Front between 1914 and 1917 successively involved a tier a year and evolved one step ahead of the attack, at least until November 1917. In so doing the defense acquired a depth that ensured that it could not be broken in a single offensive. To put the matter in reverse, successive Allied offensives were conducted a year behind requirement. With each successive year there were tactical innovations: the hurricane bombardment in March 1915 at Neuve Chapelle, the creeping barrage in 1916 at Verdun, fire without registration in 1917 at Cambrai. In addition, there was the first use of fire and mobility tactics on the part of the infantry in 1916, and at various times new weapons (such as the tank) provided some element of surprise. But, in effect, what was attempted in 1915 was what would have been needed in 1914 to have overcome a defensive position, and this phenomenon repeated itself with every passing year, at least until March 1918—and therein was irony. The German offensive in 1918 was again a year behind requirement because of the strategic reality Germany had created by bringing the United States into the war against itself in April 1917.

Here one begins to get to the real reasons for trenchlock on the Western Front: the identification of a mental rather than a material problem at the heart of indecision. The offensive, burdened as it was by problems that did not encumber the defense, could not match the latter in terms of rate of learning. The inauguration of new infantry and artillery techniques under the terms of the *Der Angriff im Stellungskrieg* 1918 field manual provided German armies with a means of unlocking the Allied front but did not address the problem of strategic mobility, and for all its tactical success it proved ruinously expensive: between 21 March and the end of July the German armies incurred some 963,000 casualties, the British about 448,000, and the French 490,000. But leaving aside the detail of the German spring offensive, even the basic point—the faster rate of learning of the German defense compared to the Allied offense—begs one obvious question of how to overcome a defense that was too big to be defeated. At the heart of the indecisiveness of the Western Front in the First World War are two realities. Armies had become so large and possessed such powers of recuperation that they could not be defeated in the course of a single battle or campaign. The fact was that military deadlock in the First World War was the result of a decisive victory being beyond any power because all armies were too strong to be overwhelmed in a single attack. And herein lies the complementary reason for the deadlock of the Western Front in terms of mental attitude and the problems inherent in the conduct of operations: for the most part high commands were committed to the idea of a battle of annihilation, which was incapable of realization.

In one very obvious sense, the inability to break the deadlock of the Western Front between November 1914 and March 1918 stemmed from a basic failure of understanding of the nature of war and the nature of a campaign—specifically the latter with respect to the confusion of a campaign with a single battle. Investment of belief in the "decisive battle" served to obscure the reality that only a campaign that embraced simultaneous and separate efforts offered any chance of victory. If there was to have been a way in which the deadlock of the Western Front was to be broken, then it was to be by a series of related limited offensives. This was precisely what the French military envisaged in the interwar period. Its concept of the Methodical Battlefield sought victory through a series of set-piece battles fought on the basis of overwhelming local superiority of material, the individual efforts being short in duration and synchronized with one another, and, critically, conducted across the width of the enemy front. Here is a point that is often overlooked in examinations of the German and Allied offensives of 1918. The German Army's failure in the *Kaiserschlacht* was in part the result of its attacks being conducted across little more than one-third of the immediate theater of operations and against one-sixth of the total number of Allied divisions on the Western Front. With no fewer than 61 of the 175 Allied divisions available in March 1918 held in reserve, the element of shock and paralysis that the Germans needed to induce across the Allied entirety in order to have any chance of registering strategic success could never be secured. The German attack was too narrowly concentrated to affect the mass of Allied forces, with the result that enemy reserves could be redeployed to effect. The success that attended the Allied offensives in and after July 1918 was in no small part the result of their being staged across virtually the whole of the active part of the Western Front. The Allied offensives did not register tactical success on the scale of the *Kaiserschlacht*, but their strategic significance lay in their relationship to one another in terms of timing and their being conducted across the theater of operations.[1]

The *Kaiserschlacht* anticipated the concept of the Methodical Battlefield but for two very significant differences: scope and the balance of forces. In effect the German offensive of spring 1918 sought strategic victory as a result of a series of successive tactical successes in the course of a single campaign, but if the first attack was not successful, there was little chance of the second or third attack achieving strategically significant results— and this offensive was conducted when there was a rough balance of forces on the Western Front, and one that tipped against the Germans in the course of their offensive because of the appearance of increasing numbers of U.S. divisions on the battlefield. The Allied conduct of operations in the second half of 1918 conformed to the Methodical Battlefield idea, but their success at that stage probably had less to do with this concept of operations than with a series of other considerations, specifically German exhaustion. If the majority of military historians and commentators identify such factors as the imbalance of firepower and mobility, the problems of ground, lack of surprise, and the absence of an open flank as the cause of tactical deadlock on the Western Front during the First World War, these other factors seldom command much attention. The changing nature of the defense, specifically the increased depth of defense in these years, is often acknowledged, but the capacity of states to wage war by generating resources on an unprecedented scale is very seldom defined in such terms. Refuge is taken in the notion that wars between great industrialized powers are necessarily protracted and attritional and hence cannot produce decisive campaigns or battles. But the problem with all of these explanations of deadlock on the Western Front is that they are not explanations. Whether singly or together, they describe the battlefield rather than explain the indecisiveness of battle.

* * *

If one wishes to understand deadlock on the Western Front after November 1914, one needs to look beyond conventional wisdom; perhaps the best explanation is provided in an often-quoted passage from *Tender Is the Night* by F. Scott Fitzgerald, in a conversation between American tourists looking over the Somme battlefield in the 1920s:

"This land here cost twenty lives a foot that summer.... See that little stream—we could walk to it in two minutes. It took the British a month to walk to it—a whole empire walking very slowly, dying in front and pushing forward behind. And another empire walked very slowly backward a few inches a day, leaving the dead like a million bloody rugs. No Europeans will ever do that again in this generation.... This western-front business couldn't be done again, not for a long time. The young men think they could do it but they couldn't. They could fight the first Marne again but not this. This took religion and years of plenty and tremendous sureties and the exact relationship that existed between the classes. The Russians and Italians weren't any good on this front. You had to have a whole-souled sentimental equipment going back farther than you could remember. You had to remember Christmas, and post cards of the Crown Prince and his fiancée, and little cafés in Valence and beer gardens in Unter den Linden, and weddings at the *mairie*, and going to the Derby, and your grandfather's whiskers."

"General Grant invented this kind of battle at Petersburg in 65."

"No, he didn't—he just invented massed butchery. This kind of battle was invented by Lewis Carroll and Jules Verne and whoever wrote *Undine*, and country deacons bowling and *marraines* in Marseilles and girls seduced in the back lanes of Württemberg and Westphalia. Why, this was a love-battle—there was a century of middle-class love spent here. This was the last great love battle."

"You want to hand over this battle to D. H. Lawrence ..."

"All my beautiful lovely safe world blew itself up here with a great gust of high-explosive love."[2]

In less than one page Fitzgerald noted one matter missed in most histories of the First World War. Deadlock in the First World War was not the result of imbalances of firepower and movement, size of armies, conditions of ground, or technical factors affecting the conduct of operations. It had nothing to do with either the capacity of the powers to wage total war or even possession of the means to do so; it was their willing-ness to wage total war, their willingness to continue to prosecute war despite the indecisiveness of battle, their hardening determination to fight to a finish in justification of the losses that had been incurred that explains the phenomenon of trenchlock. It was the willingness of socie-ties to fight on, despite and because of the elusiveness of success on the battlefield—a social cohesion and a failure, perhaps an inability, of soci-eties to collapse under the strain of total war that by rights should have destroyed them—that explains deadlock on the Western Front during the First World War. Trench deadlock was a military phenomenon, but primarily it was a military reflection of a political and mental phenom-enon.

* * *

The tendency to explain the deadlock of the Western Front in terms of material—a military determinism—is unusual in Anglo–American his-toriography, yet somewhat strangely it has a parallel in one aspect of the Second World War. German success in the opening years of the latter conflict is usually attributed to *Blitzkrieg*, and there is no doubting that no small part of German success was the result of the Germans' better understanding than that of their various enemies of the existing balance between offense and defense. But German success was also the result of an ability to fight not a war but a series of campaigns separated in time and distance from one another and each conducted against enemies weaker in terms of population, industrial resources, and mili-tary power. Certainly in a number of campaigns Germany began with advantages of position and geography that rendered the defeat of its enemies a formality, and, critically, in every campaign Germany was opposed by enemies with no idea of what kind of war awaited them and without any relevant experience on which to draw. The latter point is not to be underestimated. The fighting on the Eastern Front witnessed *Blitzkrieg* conform to a law of diminishing returns as the Soviets ac-quired, at hideous cost, the technique needed to counter it. One of the most important reasons why the Americans in the Ardennes in 1944 escaped the fate that befell the French in 1940 was the fact that the Americans had paid their insurance premiums in terms of two years' experience and technique, whereas the French had no such reserve on which to draw. But German success in the opening years of the war stemmed more from moral factors than from technique or operational factors. Say it sotto voce: what provided the *Wehrmacht* with its cutting edge was not *Blitzkrieg* or any material or technical advantage, but Nazism, specifically belief in the *Führer*, racism, and a sense of assured destiny. Arguably, and by the same token, the most important single factor in Germany's defeat was Nazism: there was nothing in Nazism that enabled Germany to consolidate its victories because all that it could offer subjected peoples was slavery and death.

* * *

It is not hard to see why the moral factor should have been afforded little real attention in considering either deadlock in the First World War or German success between 1939 and 1942. The need to exonerate military leadership from blame for the situation that prevailed on the Western Front by stressing that the imbalance between the attack and defense was insoluble was quite clearly the major factor at work, and blame could hardly be switched to governments that demonized the enemy and societies that refused to accept anything less than total victory. The post-1945 need to separate the German people from Nazism and the determination of German generals to gather for themselves credit for victories may well be the reasons why Western interpretation should have adopted a materialist hue in seeking to explain the period of German success in the Second World War. But if interpretation has provided difficulties enough, the real puzzlement is why the conventional wisdom should have persisted for so long, and why the context of deadlock on the Western Front during the First World War should have been so misunderstood. To turn the argument around, the Second World War is synonymous with movement, at least in terms of public perception, yet the codicil is obvious: the First World War saw much movement, and the European war between 1939 and 1945 was witness to prolonged periods of static warfare. Perhaps only two campaigns during the Second World War in Europe—those in 1940 in the west and in 1941 in the east—were mobile campaigns as opposed to campaigns noted for movement. On the Eastern Front positions barely shifted in 1942 and 1943 between the Baltic and Voronezh. The Minsk salient and Lvov–Sandomiercz sector, from which the Soviet offensives of June and July 1944 began, had remained quiet since the previous November, and after August 1944 the starting lines from which the Soviet army was to begin the Vistula–Oder offensive in January 1945 remained largely undisturbed. In Italy the front line was static between October 1943 and May 1944 and between October 1944 and April 1945. To borrow and slightly amend a comment by reversing the order of presentation, the Second World War was "a bloody slogging match in which mobility was only occasionally of real significance. . . . It was not a war of movement, except on those rare occasions when the enemy was in retreat."[3] The last part of this observation does bear careful consideration: movement occurred when armies, having been broken at the forward point of contact, were in retreat, not when armies were advancing. Overall, this line of argument can be developed with reference to other wars, but, very oddly, we continue to see the First World War as unique in terms of the nature of the battlefield. What was undoubtedly unique at the time has retained a remarkable tenacity of hold on public perception, despite the evidence of other wars and ample proof of the indecisiveness of battle through much of the twentieth century, not just during the First World War.

* * *

In terms of public perception and understanding, the First World War has been and continues to be overshadowed by its successor, for two reasons. The Second World War was a much larger and longer conflict than the First World War, and the fact that the 1939–45 conflict followed so quickly after its predecessor inevitably meant that the First World War was relegated to the status of starter relative to the main course. One suspects, moreover, that the fact that the Second World War was a cinema war was also at work in this development. Film had come of age, and footage of the Second World War is recognizably modern, whereas film of the First World War, indeed even into the early years of the Third Reich, has that jerkiness and inflexibility of movements that dates it immediately, marking it out as belonging to another time.

But in terms of an understanding of war, the state, and the twentieth century, the First World War clearly provokes a number of questions. Perhaps the most obvious is the sense of wonderment caused by the fact that the nature of war was so little appreciated before 1914. Inevitably historians have seized upon the fact that there were a number of individuals who had appreciated that firepower kills or who predicted that war would be attritional and protracted. Ivan Bloch's *The Future War in Its Technical, Economic and Political Aspects*, published in 1898, could not exonerate an entire generation, but reading some accounts prompts the thought that this individual in his five-volume analysis has come damnably close to doing so. Bloch, however, was not alone; among the many observations that could be cited in defense of the argument that the forthcoming crisis of war was foreseen by more people than is generally recognized, one comment, written in 1887, bears examination, in terms both of its apocalyptic anticipation of future war and the basis of its correctness:

This would be a universal war of unprecedented scope, unprecedented force. From eight to ten million soldiers will destroy one another, and in the course of doing so will strip Europe clean in a way that a swarm of locusts could never have done. The devastation caused by the Thirty Years' War telescoped into three to four years and spread over the entire continent . . . hunger, epidemics, the universal engagement of both troops and masses, brought about by acute need and hopeless jumbling of . . . trade, industrial and credit mechanisms . . . all this ending in general bankruptcy . . . the collapse of old states and their vaunted wisdom . . . the utter impossibility of foreseeing how this will end and who will emerge victorious from this struggle. Only one result is absolutely beyond doubt—universal exhaustion.[4]

The observation, made by Friedrich Engels, owes its percipience to the fact that rather than being a Marxist analysis of war, it is a Clausewitzian interpretation of the state and society as they would affect the nature of war. Its understanding of the changing nature of war stems from Engels having understood the forces of change within society as these were to affect the conduct of war. What this analysis does not represent is a Jominian interpretation of past wars in order to predict the nature of future conflicts, wherein was the basis of the contemporary military's general misunderstanding of the significance of developments before 1914 when the considered wisdom in most countries was that the recent Russo–Japanese war, which lasted 16 months, was a long war. In some measure, the deadlock of the First World War had followed from this fundamental misappreciation of the nature of warfare and the impact of industrialization upon the conduct of war. As it was, the ability of the warring states—and specifically Germany—to embrace command economies more or less at the outset of war had the effect, seldom properly appreciated, of ensuring that the war did not end in 1914. Without the war ministry assuming powers of direction with respect to raw materials, Germany probably could not have sustained itself into 1915.

* * *

Certain honorable exceptions apart, there is, however, no serious disputing the assertion that the impact of new weapons on the conduct of war and the changing nature of war as a result of societal change were but little and very imperfectly appreciated before 1914. One must note, however, that general staffs of the major armies, which made very careful studies of conflicts such as the Russo–Japanese war, were very aware that artillery developments would make the conduct of the attack more difficult than in the past: likewise, the requirement for dispersal and the need to fight defensively at a tactical level within the context of the strategic offensive were recognized. The latter, however, had been appreciated by the Elder Moltke before 1870 and does not represent much in terms of mitigation. The lack of any war in Europe between great powers for over 40 years was certainly a factor in a general failure to appreciate what awaited on the battlefield, and the Balkan Wars of 1912–13 most certainly did not provide any clues. These were conflicts that failed to conform to the trend: they produced results and did so quickly. In the Balkan wars first Turkey and then Bulgaria were rapidly defeated and for a very simple reason: overcommitted on several fronts, both were overwhelmed by enemies that held the initiative and decisive advantages of concentration and position.

Recent European wars thus served as a poor guide to the general staffs in their preparations for the war that was break out in summer 1914, but there was one little-known exception to the basic failure to understand the basic problems that war and the conduct of operations would present. The exception was Russian and derived from the experience of the war of 1904–05. In the scale and duration of the battles that were fought and lost in Manchuria, the Russian army was provided with a decade's forewarning of the First World War, and if that time was but little or ineffectively used, there were nevertheless three developments that formed a very interesting counterpoint relative to the lack of anticipation both in other armies and within the mass of the Russian army itself. In the aftermath of this war, Russian staffs very hesitantly began to feel their way toward a concept of operations at a level between armies and divisions, at what we would understand today to be the operational level of war. Inevitably this concept was only very imperfectly understood and failed to command official endorsement, and it seems that the term "operational art" was not coined until the 1923–24 period by Svechin. At the same time, in this period between the Russo–Japanese and the First World Wars, the problems presented by continuous fronts, defended in depth, was addressed, specifically in the form of proposals that the break-in battle should be conducted across a general sector with concentrated efforts made on a number of preselected narrow frontages, the anticipation being that simultaneous efforts would result in a measure of success that would elude the single "decisive-battle" effort. The Brusilov offensive (1916) and Soviet concepts of break-in operations have a longer pedigree than is sometimes realized. Even more contentiously, the experience of the war in Manchuria convinced at least one Russian officer, Neznamov, that the demands of war could only be met by a militarization of society. Such a line of argument curiously anticipated the arguments within the Soviet political and military leadership in the 1920s and again, under the prodding of Ogarkov, in the 1970s. The parallel between Neznamov and Ogarkov is close in that both the states that these two served, and which rejected their views, were to pass from the scene within a generation of their decisions.

This exception notwithstanding, there is no doubting that the understanding of war and battle of European states and armies in the period before the outbreak of the First World War left something to be desired, and in the process of misreading the nature of battle and warfare before the First World War, the French army is always afforded special consideration, to a predictable conclusion: it managed to get things wrong in 1870 and 1940, and therefore 1914 was merely par for the course. That, of course, is grossly unfair to the French army: for all its mistakes and failures, its record in two world wars of played two, won one is infinitely superior to that of the armies of Germany. Moreover, in such matters as the question of the violation of Belgian neutrality and relations with the United States, the French high command never made errors that littered German deliberations to the point that the German high command snatched defeat from the jaws of victory. Indeed the French high command never displayed logic of the kind that cast interesting light upon the German military psyche. In developing the Schlieffen Plan, the German military staff worked out where the French would have to send an armistice delegation: to the rail station at Provins in Seine-et-Marne. In presenting its case for the start of an unrestricted submarine campaign against shipping, the German naval staff, with mathematical precision, had worked out the month if not the day when Britain would be forced to sue for terms on the basis of calculations such as the price of cheese, the calorie content of the average British breakfast, and the yardage of imported wool in women's skirts.[5] But with the likes of de Grandmaison, d'Alenson, Nivelle, and Foch among the most fervent of the advocates of the offensive within its ranks, one must admit that before 1914 the French army did labor under exceptional difficulties.

The French army's love affair with the offensive before 1914 has become notorious, but few accounts of this period examine what factors were at work in shaping an offensive doctrine that brought France perilously close to defeat in 1914. French failings have been afforded prominence at the expense of an obvious consideration: before 1914 it would have made no sense whatsoever for the French army to have adopted anything other than an offensive doctrine.

For the best part of two centuries France was the most populous state in Europe, Russia and perhaps the Ottoman Empire excepted. In 1870 France found itself opposed by German states that collectively were demographically its equal: in the next four decades it found itself outbred. In 1870 no less than 45% of the German population was under 20 years of age, and by 1914 France was outnumbered 2:1 in terms of males of military age. Herein lay one of the most powerful single factors that was to determine the French commitment to the offensive: faced with such massive inferiority of numbers, the defense held out only the prospect of prolonging, not winning, a war against Germany, with one obvious corollary. The offensive alone offered France some hope of forestalling German plans and perhaps preventing the full weight of superior German resources being brought to bear on the battlefield. Moreover, the needs of the Russian alliance underpinned this basic consideration. Signed in 1892 and given its military clauses in a series of agreements after 1894, the Russian treaty was the basis of French security but imposed obligations and responsibilities. France could not consider waging a defensive war, with Russia left with the burden of offensive operations. Given their individual inferiority to Germany, France and Russia were obliged to undertake offensive operations together or risk separate defeat and destruction.

In one sense, however, this state of affairs does not fully explain the French army's commitment to the offensive: strategic necessity may well have determined that the French army embrace the offensive, but not necessarily to the exclusion of everything else, not least reason. The fact was that the French army's embracing of a doctrine of *l'offense à outrance* was in large measure institutional, the result of the army's turning inward upon itself in the two decades before the outbreak of the First World War generally as a result of its always difficult relationship with the Third Republic and, specifically, of attacks upon it as a result of the Dreyfus Affair (1894–99). In this situation the French army sought a return to soldierly virtues, to what it saw as its own traditions and values, and inevitably it was the offensive that it saw at the core of its history. With the Napoleonic legend so potent at this time, there was really nothing other than the offensive that could be at the heart of the French military tradition. Predictably, the shame of 1870 added to myth: this defeat was seen as the result of the French army's having been false to its tradition of offensive action.

In seeking to understand the French army's obsession with the offensive before 1914, these are the obvious factors that shaped choices; yet underpinning all these was another—a hardening nationalism that saw the offensive in terms of suiting the French national temperament. One need not subscribe to such an idea, but the real point was the fact that such notions as national characteristics, racial qualities, and cultural superiority had emerged as common currency in Europe by the end of the nineteenth century. The French were not alone in picking their way along this particular path, but in terms of an understanding of the twentieth century the development of such ideas was one of the most important legacies of the nineteenth century.

* * *

The rise, and subsequently the decline, of the state and the relationship between war and the state in the course of the twentieth century can only be understood in terms of the context provided by nineteenth-century developments. Perhaps predictably, the physical changes wrought by the industrialization of war have commanded the greater part of historical attention in dealing with the nineteenth century. There is good reason why this should have been so. In the hundred years between the closing of the Napoleonic Wars and the outbreak of the First World War, the basic forms of warfare that had developed over hundreds of years were destroyed by the accelerating pace of technological change. Possibly the most immediately obvious elements of change manifested themselves at sea: the symmetry of centuries disappeared as iron and then steel replaced wood, guns replaced cannon, coal, steam, and electricity replaced wind, ropes, and muscle power. By the turn of the nineteenth century naval warfare had ceased to be one-dimensional, with the development of mines and torpedoes, the invention of the submarine, and a proliferation of new weaponry and ship types: barely a dozen more years were to elapse before navies took to the skies. Probably the most significant element of change that presented itself was in the technology that enabled men to take warfare into the air and beyond the horizon. But the most important and immediate changes of the long period of nineteenth-century peace affected armies, and these changes and their implications can be defined more easily than they can be explained. Industrialization—specifically the spread of railroads and the changes of weaponry brought about by developments in the metallurgical and chemical fields—profoundly altered the balance between mass, firepower, and mobility.

But however important these changes, they were probably less important and relevant than the growth of the size of armies in this period. This growth was the result of several factors, the most obvious, and important, being a demographic increase that saw the population of the seven leading European states rise from 227,000,000 in 1850 to 345,000,000 in 1910 despite the loss of some 22,000,000 emigrants to the United States alone. Scarcely less important, however, was the development of non-European food sources, which, with the introduction of refrigerated ships and the canning of meats and fruit after 1879, resulted in increasing numbers of young males outside the food-production process. The effect of these various developments was an enormous increase in the pool of military manpower in the second half of the nineteenth century. The railroads, which in Europe both doubled in carrying capacity per track and almost tripled in length between 1870 and 1914 from about 65,000 to some 180,000 miles, provided the means whereby these greater numbers could be deployed quickly and effectively. But the latter could not be divorced from the increasing power of the state: indeed, the raising of greater numbers of men under arms could only be achieved by a well-developed and powerful state bureaucracy of the kind that simply did not exist until the latter part of the nineteenth century. In the process, one matter was to be of very great significance. By the period 1871–1914, the pace of technological advance and obsolescence of design were such that armies had to be reequipped every generation, navies every decade. This necessarily meant direct state investment, involvement in the funding of industrial enterprises, and direction of scientific research, but more importantly it also involved enormously heavy financial demands added to those imposed by conscription. Given the advance of the principle of constitutional and representative government throughout Europe after 1848, the justification for military preparations by states in seeking appropriations from their elective legislatures had to be by direct comparison with neighbors. The aspect of self-fulfilling prophecy became obvious over time. As a consequence, immediate comparison with neighbors sharpened differences of a public perception that was increasingly shaped by a popular, tabloid press. The first newspaper chain began life in 1879. The Hearst press in the United States was founded in 1895, one year before the first British tabloid, *The Daily Mail*, appeared.

The emergence of a sensationalist press that pandered to a semiliterate population, an increasing portion of which was enfranchised, was vitally important in the emergence of a xenophobic paranoia throughout Europe that was to contribute significantly to the atmosphere of crisis in the 10 years before 1914 and which made war, when it came, so welcome in all the major capitals of Europe. A vulgar press and its readership, their diet of imperialism, and a steady stream of reports of war beyond Europe that provided a element of brutalization and added to the value of white-supremacy currency were present in this process, but there were deeper currents at work. The war was not the product of the labors of a scurrilous press intent on servings of nationalism and militarism or the result of the scribblings of the likes of Erskine Childers and William Le Queux. Certainly popular sentiment, in the form of nationalistic sensationalism, ran ahead of any serious clash of real interests, and certainly the fervent nationalism throughout Europe that greeted the outbreak of war in 1914 was in part the product of years of demonology in the gutter press. But it was also something more: it was evidence that the idea of the nation and the state commanded general support and genuine endorsement on the part of their populations that was unprecedented and indeed perhaps unthinkable even 30 years earlier. The point was that by 1914 it was the state, not any regional, sectional, or group interest, that commanded popular loyalty and affection, and it was specifically German ideas about the nature of the state that had come to the fore after 1871 as the German example was, to varying degrees, adapted throughout Europe.

Britain, France, and the United States are essentially eighteenth-century states and have remained constant to a very careful delineation between war and peace as these terms came to be defined in the Age of Reason. The nineteenth century, however, saw a new idea of the state emerge and a new concept that blurred the distinction between war and peace. As the state, under German prompting, assumed mystical and God-given characteristics, so the concept of struggle assumed ever greater prominence in European thinking.

It is one of the curiosities of the nineteenth century that the concept of struggle owed much of its intellectual basis to two Britishers who were contemporaries and to two more individuals, German émigrés, whose main work was done in Britain. It cannot be coincidence that Spencer and Darwin (and Wallace and Huxley, for that matter) lived and worked in an aggressive capitalist system at its height and worst. It is difficult to believe that the development of the idea of struggle—Spencer's "survival of the fittest," Darwin's "struggle for existence," and Marx and Engels with their idea of class struggle as the basis of existence—was divorced from the evidence of *laissez-faire* capitalism of Victorian Britain.

But if in these countries capitalist development was largely separated from the state, the same was not true elsewhere, for two reasons. The state "was not established for the benefit of the individual," but, according to Hegel, "is divine will . . . is the reality of the moral idea—the moral spirit as the revealed will apparent to itself, substantial, which thinks and knows itself and accomplishes that which it knows and insofar as it knows it . . . and acts therefore according to purpose." This is a definition with which one would probably disagree, were one able to understand it in the first place; but—and merely for the purposes of the argument—to accept as more easily comprehensible the idea that the state was "the institutionalization of God on earth," the basic nature of the Hegelian state is discernible. It was an entity, indistinguishable from society, with its own rationale, volition, and purpose, "the true embodiment of mind and spirit," and only in and through it could the individual find self-expression and fulfillment.[6]

Hegel in the last decade of his life recognized that a society shaped by market forces was certain to possess within itself an underclass that represented a threat to the state itself. Some 50 years later Bismarck set about "negative integration": the provision of state welfare was an attempt to provide social stability and order as the basis of a successful foreign and imperial policy, and to disarm socialism by the integration of a dispossessed proletariat within the existing economic order without altering the political and social status quo. At the same time, of course, Germany's four armies—there was no German army until after the First World War—sought to mold an impressionable youth delivered annually into their ranks with conservative values. In this effort the military became, and not just in Germany, "The School of the Nation." In this process, however, the French and German experience was to differ considerably, for reasons that reflected their differing concepts of the state and society. In France after 1871 the rights of citizenship were tied to obligation, specifically military service; for much of the period before the outbreak of war the French military called something like 85% of all eligible manpower for the annual draft. In Germany, however, the draft took only some 57% of eligible manpower until the years immediately before the outbreak of war. Demographic factors account for this disparity at least in part: France had to conscript more of its manpower and for a longer period than Germany simply to match its neighbor's numbers. But Germany's refusal to develop its manpower advantage to the full was in large measure the result of a refusal on the part of the state to undertake an effort that had to involve the dilution of an aristocratic or at least propertied officer corps. But to return to the main point: the values that were gaining ground throughout Europe were not simply conservative values but ones underpinned by what can only be described as the certainty of knowledge.

* * *

Jacob Bronowski, in the most compelling *coup de théâtre* this writer has had the privilege of watching, expounded upon his Principle of Tolerance in the eleventh part of his *The Ascent of Man*. The stage on which he chose to do so was Auschwitz, using as he did as the basis of his argument von Heisenberg's Principle of Uncertainty. To Bronowski the basis of democracy was tolerance, and the basis of tolerance was uncertainty: those who would aspire to absolute knowledge that has no test in reality would destroy the basis of democracy. In Germany, however, the basis of democracy failed in 1848, in part because it had failed already. Perhaps the failure stemmed from the Thirty Years' War in terms of the impoverishment of Germany and the stunting of middle-class development as a result of the subsequent concentration of power in the hands of rulers. Certainly it owed something to the teachings of Luther, in particular his concept of piety toward the state, and obviously to both the War of Liberation and its fanning of nationalist ardor and to the reaction against the French Revolution and Napoleon after 1815. The reconstruction of society and the international order after the Napoleonic Wars had to be attempted on the basis of antilibertarian principles—the reestablishment of links with the past and continuity, the creation of the national idea as the bulwark against the Rights of Man, the primacy of society, and the dependence of the individual upon society as a whole. Be that as it may, long before 1848 there was in Germany a concept of obedience to and veneration of the state that was unthinkable in such countries as Britain, France, and the United States. Antidemocratic sentiment—specifically contempt for parliamentary institutions and practices—was widespread in Germany. Liberalism failed there. In a choice between liberty and unification after 1848 the latter, in the form of the Prussian state, prevailed, and in the liberal failure and eclipse of the democratic form was a conservative victory that was able to "accommodate" the emerging bourgeoisie, even the working classes. It was able to do so because of its success in achieving national unification and through the inculcation of an increasingly strident and assertive nationalism tied to, and supported by, racist concepts that appeared to be supported by the latest scientific developments.

One never ceases to be amazed by the prevalence within Europe in 1900 of racist ideas that would never have been countenanced for a moment in 1800. *On the Origin of Species* was not responsible for such a situation: like Clausewitz, Darwin is more often quoted, or misquoted, than read. But what is so notable about his writing and career is the way in which, in spite the furor of 1860 and the Huxley–Wilberforce clash, by the time of his death in 1882 Darwin was an honored citizen. Despite the flawed nature and failure of *The Descent of Man*, in a little more than two decades Darwin's idea of the struggle for existence had provided intellectual and social respectability to Spencer's concept of the survival of the fittest as applied to societies. Logically, while certain of the ideas that emerged in this period, such as those of Darwin and the geologist Lyell, reinforced one another, these various strands of thought were hardly complementary. The Hegelian concept of historical development and Darwin's ideas were most certainly not interdependent, but Darwin's line of argument reinforced the Hegelian concept that history was the clash of vast impersonal forces. It also served to buttress other ideas that were flowing into the mainstream of European intellectual and social consciousness and teetering on the brink of acceptability. There were 29 phrenological societies in Britain in 1832. As late as 1883, one year after the publication of Ratzel's *Anthropogeographie,* their very serious studies were still being duly reported in equally very serious journals. Such activities, coming together with such influential publications as de Gobineau's four-volume *Essai sur l'Inégalité des Races Humaines* (1853–55), were helping to mold a more sharply conscious patriotism that was increasingly identified with race, the notion that what marked different nationalities apart in Europe was not cultural but racial and genetic. There was afoot in Europe—and Darwin was to cast his cloak of struggle as the basis of existence around it—a biological and sociological determinism, which, coming on top of the emerging concept of the state and antidemocratic sentiment, represented a dangerously potent, poisonous mix. The nineteenth century concerned itself with many things, but mostly with the cultivation of hatred.

* * *

Given such views, specifically the view of struggle, the connection between the state, society, and war was self-evident—so much so that Spengler defined war as "the eternal form of higher human existence" and, in a comment that demonstrated the failure of Clausewitz, said that "states exist for the purpose of waging war."[7] It was a comment indicative of the extent to which the concept of struggle moved to center-stage in the nineteenth century. By the time of the outbreak of hostilities in 1914, the sentiment that war was a biological necessity of the first importance as a racial and social cathartic whereby the health of nations is maintained was common, and not just in Germany. The comment that "the nation must . . . prove its right to exist among other nations by a war of all against all in which only the stronger survive" may well be German, and it certainly indicates, at least in part, its Darwinian pedigree, but for all its apocalyptic vision it would have encountered little contradiction in any major country in Europe.

* * *

The victory over France in 1870–71 was to provide Germany with a political, military, and intellectual primacy—to which was added by 1900 the industrial leadership of Europe, which that was to last until 1918. It was to be this primacy that ensured that German ideas gained widespread currency throughout Europe after 1871, though it must be noted that Germany had no patent upon racism. Chamberlain was British, de Gobineau and Sorrell were French, and the Black Hundreds in Russia needed no foreign encouragement. But what is so remarkable about these ideas and the development of sharply defined racist attitudes in the period after 1871 is that the existing political and social system was able to keep them in check. The state system was able to accommodate these extremist ideas, just as it was to blunt the socialist appeal, by partially stealing their clothes. The result was that it was not until after the First World War that many of these ideas, very literally, came onto the streets.

* * *

Perhaps the most interesting question to present itself for consideration is why such notions did not come to the fore during the First World War. It is quite obvious why they emerged after 1918: the fact that they flourished primarily in the defeated states explains much. But one suspects that such ideas never took hold in the course of the First World War, for three reasons: The genuine support in all countries for war made such ideas superfluous. These extreme nationalist ideas held sufficient sway to make their formalization unnecessary. The various European states had problems enough simply in the prosecution of the war itself, and there was no time or opportunity to develop such political consciousness as there was, for example, in Germany after 1933. The latter is important, if only because it is too easy to miss the full significance of the changes that affected the state in the course of the First World War.

* * *

The state in 1919 was in many ways unrecognizable from the state of 1914: the latter had more in common with the state of 1815 than it had with its end-of-war equivalent, most obviously in two critical respects. The 1914 state, despite the development of social legislation and provision, was still predominantly committed to *laissez faire* and was still, despite the process of industrialization, remarkably weak in terms of bureaucratic controls outside the finance and military departments. The First World War forced massive changes upon the state, which had to assume direct control and direction of industry. It could not survive and prosecute the war by any means other than by its own powers of regulation and governance, though herein was ambiguity. The First World War saw the state both gather power to itself but also power drain from it in favor of private organizations and institutions without which it could not organize society and the economy. But in terms of the growth of the power of the state, it was obliged not just to assume direct responsibility for, but actively to promote the welfare of its citizenry—an increasingly impossible task for Russia and the Central Powers as the war lengthened. Industry could not function, and the armies could not be supplied with manpower and material unless the populations were kept supplied with adequate food, heating, and light, and it is particularly notable that the German collapse in 1918 came when failure and defeat in the field came on top of the exhaustion of these three commodities.

In addition, the state had to assume a corporate identity in terms of social mobilization. Despite industrialization, the states of Europe in 1914 had changed but little over the previous 100 years in terms of political and social organization. They were monarchical—there were but two republics in Europe—and aristocratic. The class lines, though softened in the decades before the war in such countries as Germany, nevertheless remained clearly defined, and in many societies constitutionalism was a substitute for properly representative and responsible government. Only one of the great powers, France, was fully democratic in terms of a properly accountable government to an electorate in which all adult males had the vote: in Britain, with a population of some 46,000,000, the franchise was restricted to one in nine. In Germany the largest single party, the Social Democrats, was checked by a weighted system of representation that worked in favor of Prussia within Germany and the aristocracy and monied interest within Prussia. Though as late as May 1918 the Prussian *Landtag* vetoed an attempt to abolish the existing system of (mis)representation, the First World War destroyed any rationale for a restricted franchise in terms of a male population that had served and a female population that had contributed fully to the national war efforts, particularly in industry. The waging of the First World War broke down the old social barriers in favor of a new egalitarianism in which birth and privilege were increasingly at a discount: clearly the shattering of the aristocratic principle was directly linked to the rise of antidemocratic populism. Moreover, one would have to note one more casualty. The losses of the First World War came as a terrible shock to a Europe freed from the realities of protracted war for 100 years, and the greater part of that shock had to be directed against a liberal democratic system that for that period had stressed the primacy of the individual. In the aftermath of the First World War it was very difficult for a system built around the Rights of Man to justify itself in terms of millions of dead and wounded: the new levelers had no such trouble.

The First World War was a collectivist war. It turned out to be a siege war fought on a continental scale; the price that it exacted was the weakening or destruction of the old order and, for all the warring nations, its replacement by an authoritarian but directly responsible state. The latter was particularly important in that it provides the key to an understanding of a seeming paradox—that the advance of democracy was attended by an intensification of war: war became ever less manageable in terms of definition of aims and its conduct. War between peoples was infinitely less controllable than wars between kings, as many people noted at the time. The First World War witnessed the mobilization of some 63,000,000 men, the vast majority of whom were Europeans. That such numbers could be raised was evidence of a massive development of state power, but even more obviously it demonstrated an unprecedented political will, commitment, and solidarity of societies, though it needs be noted that the effort that was made shattered four of the great powers and left all the warring European nations exhausted. Herein lies the significance of the Fitzgerald observation on the Somme battlefield. Perhaps on the Somme, but if not there, then in the course of 1916, prewar liberal Europe died, because during the First World War those elements that had made Europe great—its rationalist skepticism, its spirit of scientific inquiry, its diligence and industriousness—were turned inward upon Europe itself.

For the Europe that had existed before 1914, the war was an inversion of all those values that made for future hope. The very act of going to war broke with that hope, and thereafter the socialization that all states performed in the disciplining of society's members was effective. There was very little popular opposition in any state to the outbreak of war, as patriotism ensured conformity and overwhelmed dissent. The outbreak of war, like the war itself, was a deluge; when it had passed, it had carved new channels through a landscape hitherto dominated by consent, rationalism, and right. In the course of 1915 a new landscape began to take shape, and during 1916 its main features became discernible as the states of Europe dug ever deeper into their reserves of intellectual and moral stamina in their pursuit of victory. In the place of consent came leadership, and will displaced rationalism as the demands of society prevailed over the rights of the individual, and obligation exacted ever greater sacrifice. The year that witnessed Verdun, the Somme, and the Brusilov offensive was a year that saw a hardening of resolve on the part of the warring nations of Europe. Failure strengthened determination as very slowly national leaderships changed with the casting aside of those identified with the old order and their replacement by those committed to the waging of war to the bitter end. It was to be in the following year rather than in 1916 that this process was complete, but with the fall of the Asquith government in Britain, the emergence of Clemenceau to challenge the Briand–Caillaux combination in France, and the progressive erosion of civilian authority in Germany by a military command after September 1916, headed by Hindenburg and Ludendorff, the future course of events had been charted by the end of 1916. In eastern Europe the position was somewhat different, but Austria–Hungary and Russia were dependent upon decisions made elsewhere. By the end of 1916 these two empires were acutely aware of the dangers that confronted them, but if the leaderships of both Austria–Hungary and Russia could recognize the exhaustion of their empires and their need for peace, there was no escaping the fact that neither had the power to break with its allies and that there was no basis for peace with their enemies. To an extent all the great powers were trapped by the same remorseless logic, but for the two empires whose quarrel over the Balkans had set in train these events, the winter of 1916–17 brought home this the reality of their position.[8]

* * *

To this author the consequences and nature of the First World War are more interesting than its military narrative and chronology. Of course, there are aspects of operations that do command interest. The Schlieffen Plan inevitably commands attention for an obvious reason—its many transgressions of common sense and reasonableness. Yet one notes the neat contrast between the achievements of Germany and its western enemies in the course of the war. Each year of the war, at least until 1918, the advances of Germany's enemies would be measured in terms of a handful of miles while Germany conquered whole countries—in 1914 Luxembourg and in effect Belgium, in 1915 Serbia, in 1916 Romania, and in 1917 Russia. The war ended in 1918 with German defeat and the victory of the Western democracies. It was a war that witnessed the greatest victory in British naval history, though no one realized it at the time and it took 30 months for the full enormity of the victory to manifest itself. Never before had there been the surrender of a complete and undamaged battle fleet; the abject internment of 9 battleships, 5 battlecruisers, 7 light cruisers, and 49 destroyers in the Firth of Forth on 21 November 1918 was proof of the extent of British success at Jutland.

The citing of Jutland and British success at sea provokes the obvious comment that here was the first of two victories at sea that were without parallel other than with one another; the second was in September 1943 with the surrender of the Italian battle fleet. But the real interest at sea during the First World War lies in the fact that it marked a profound change in the conduct of war and profoundly affected naval planning in the interwar period.

The war at sea marked a return to total war in a way that, rather oddly, the war on land did not. The reemergence of total war was possible only because of the mobilization of societies, and with it the blurring of the distinction between combatant and noncombatant. Of course the distinction had always been tenuous, as the inhabitant of any town under siege had always fully understood, but the fact is that the distinction had been recognized, if only in its being ignored, since the time of Aquinas. But in the prewar period such ideas as the deliberate bombing of cities or the sinking of unarmed merchantmen on the high seas without warning had been unthinkable to societies confident in material progress that seemed synonymous with an advance of a civilization that precluded such barbarism. But the First World War could only be fought by deliberately taking the war to civilian populations, in the German case by long-range bombardment and by the sinking of merchantmen, and in the Allied case primarily by blockade. Admittedly, the Allies, specifically the British, were the first to turn to strategic bombing if single-aircraft German attacks on Liege and Paris in August 1914 are discounted from consideration. The attacks on the Cologne railway station and the airsheds at Düsseldorf on 8 October 1914 were the first strategic bombing raids and on Christmas Day the Royal Navy conducted its first such raid, against the Zeppelin base at Cuxhaven. For the most part, however, bombing raids on cities were notable for their lack of precision and for the fact that the effort involved in mounting attacks precluded sustained campaigns being waged against civilian targets. The best-known raids were those made on London first by Zeppelins (31 May–1 June 1915 and 19–20 October 1917) and then by heavier-than-air aircraft (26 November 1916 and 19–20 May 1918). The first squadron attack by Zeppelins was made on 13 October 1915 but not repeated until 2–3 September 1916, and only in one week, 24 September to 1–2 October 1917, was London subjected to sustained attack, with six raids, all conducted under cover of dark. The strength of the defense, even at this early stage of proceedings, prompted the Germans to abandon daylight raids. The war was to end with the Royal Air Force one week from mounting an attack on Berlin, but with the Royal Navy having recorded three notable air firsts: the first engagement of a target beyond the horizon at the Dardanelles by the battleship *Queen Elizabeth*, supported by a spotter aircraft; the first sinking by aerial torpedo, again at the Dardanelles, in August 1915, and the first attack beyond the coastline with the destruction of the airship sheds at Tondern on 18 July 1918 by aircraft launched from a carrier. Perhaps even more notable is the fact that the first concept of strategic bombing, and one specifically directed against an enemy civilian population with the aim of undermining and destroying enemy morale, was penned in 1915 by a naval officer. The bailiwick of such individuals as Douhet, Mitchell, and Trenchard, one might have thought that it was one of these, or such individuals as Robida, Conan Doyle, or H. G. Wells, who first put such an idea on paper, but in fact it would seem that the first to do so was a certain Lieutenant Nakajima Chuichi of the Imperial Japanese Navy. Throughout the First World War, however, the primary means by which naval power was directed against civilian populations remained the blockade.

* * *

The consequences of the naval war are somewhat curious. Much of the historical attention of the interwar period concentrated on either the refighting of Jutland or the struggle for primacy between battleship and carrier. These matters were at the forefront of American, British, and Japanese naval debate, yet, very oddly, what perhaps should have been the two main subjects of historical consideration in terms of naval concerns of interwar period have been afforded relatively little attention.

The first, and perhaps the least obvious, was the future of amphibious operations, and the experience of the First World War in this aspect of the operational art was distinctly discouraging. In the First World War the amphibious experience was dominated by the Gallipoli failure. One of the less obvious facts about the war is that certain states with lesser reputations in amphibious operations should have conducted successful enterprises. The First World War provides evidence of successful amphibious landings, though one caveat needs be noted. Geography and the pattern of industrialization in effect ruled out amphibious options in western and central Europe, where armies commanded great numbers in relatively small areas, where the rail and to a lesser extent the road systems were extensive, and where coastal regions were restricted. The element of vulnerability increased, however, away from the core areas of western Europe, and amphibious opportunity existed in those areas where communications were poor and defensive forces few. Such conditions applied to Gallipoli; but there were special conditions surrounding the circumstances of that endeavor that explain failure—not least the fact that in terms of amphibious operations the Dardanelles was not a policy but an operation masquerading as a policy; a substitute for one. Policy was defined in August 1915 with the decision, admittedly by default, that the Dardanelles endeavor had sought to avoid: the concentration of the British army where it really mattered, on the North European Plain.

But there was also something else at work in this substitution of an operation for policy: what was on the line in late 1914, when the navy appeared to be doing little even as the army was bleeding to death, was the question of role. The Dardanelles initiative came after the navy had lost the critical roles-and-mission argument with the army but nevertheless remained committed to a maritime as opposed to a continental strategy and still aspired to a major role in the Mediterranean because of its own institutional requirements. The point of present-day relevance, of course, is that the Dardanelles venture must be seen against a background of a decade of furious argument between the services and a most deliberate manipulation of historical argument and peddling of self-justifying mythology by the navy in its attempt to secure its own perceived *raison d'être*. As it was, perceived *raison d'être* lay behind the successful search by U.S. Marine Corps in the interwar period for the lessons of Gallipoli and the requirements of a campaign in the Pacific, and this search has been contrasted sharply and unfavorably with the British indifference to amphibious operations during this time. Yet the point of perceived *raison d'être* repeated itself. Without a real enemy for most of the interwar period and with the army committed to imperial policing, there was no imperative for the British to pursue the amphibious option. When an enemy did present itself, the amphibious option disappeared, because the army would proceed to France; there was no amphibious option in dealing with Germany.

The second of the main issues that might have commanded more detailed study is the question of reaction of the *Kriegsmarine* to failure and defeat. After the war the German Navy was faced with the very real problem of trying to understand why, after so much investment and attention, it had achieved so little, and just how, why, and in what ways another war might be fought to a different result. To the first question there was, inevitably, a very simple answer. The German navy's failure was the result of the building of a fleet without regard to its hopeless geographical, numerical, and psychological inferiority to its enemy, which left it in a hopeless strategic situation in which its desire to do battle was but the minimum tactical response to its lost strategic cause. But the German navy could not admit that throughout the First World War the fleet had been no more than a coastal defense force and that the waging of a *guerre de course* was no more than an instinctive reaction to its own strategic futility.

Recognition that a victory in the North Sea had no strategic value given Britain's geographical position was acknowledged in 1926 by Wegener, whose main line of argument was that sea warfare was concerned with the struggle to control lines of communication and the defense of trade; a parallel argument held that the German failure during the First World War was not to have occupied Denmark and southern Norway and thereby either broken or pushed back the British blockade and provided Germany with direct access to the North Atlantic. The argument was facetious: a German fleet in southern Norway would be scarcely better placed to defend German oceanic trade than a fleet in home ports. But the disastrous implications inherent in Wegener's line of reasoning went unnoticed within the German navy. In forcing attention upon what was assumed to be the strategic purposes of sea power (the maintenance of lines of communication) by stressing one aspect of Germany's strategic situation (geographical position) and by belittling the importance of battle, Wegener embraced the premise that sea warfare was about lines of communication, whereas it was concerned with command of the sea. Wegener failed to appreciate that war at sea involved control of an enemy's movements as a means of breaking his lines of communication, and the control of an enemy's movements was in large measure dependent upon the outcome of battle. In so constructing his argument, Wegener moved to the notion that command of the sea was something that was divisible and could be localized. In his confusion of the struggle for and exercise of command of the sea, Wegener pointed out a path that led to the idea of sea denial and blockade. On this basis other ideas built, most obviously that the distant blockade imposed by Britain during the recent war was economic in nature and shorn of strategic purpose. This was part of a process that saw the German navy identify naval warfare solely in terms of economic war in which it was not important for a continental power to secure command of the sea for itself. In this way the German navy moved away from challenging an enemy's formal command of the sea and away from battle, which had to be avoided rather than sought, and adopted the position that command of the sea was simply and wholly identifiable with control of maritime lines of communication, that war at sea was an economic struggle shorn of military aspects, that avoidance of battle was desirable, and that sea denial in terms of area or time was as effective as possession of command of the sea.

The irony of these arguments was profound. The German navy's argument in 1916 in favor of a *guerre de course* was that if it could sink 600,000 tons of shipping for six months, neutral shipping would be forced to abandon its British trade, and Britain would be compelled to surrender. The argument was proved to be false, and the consequence—the United States' entry into the war—was disastrous for Germany. Wegener began the process whereby the German navy was forced to confront the reality of its disastrous policy and to address the fundamental question of its strategic role and aim. But by the time the Second World War began, the German navy was equipped with a doctrine that held that if raiders—primarily submarines—could sink 750,000 tons of shipping a month for a year, then Britain would be forced from the lists. Perhaps the only conclusions that can be drawn from this circular trip around naval doctrine are that the only people who argue about sea power are those that do not have it, and that for all the alleged German proficiency in war, the experience of the interwar German navy would seem to furnish ample evidence that the German military have never properly understood the distinction between war and fighting. Lest the point be doubted, the *Kriegsmarine* record in the Second World War illustrates the comprehensiveness of its failure. The ineffectiveness of the campaign against Allied shipping is obvious, but it has obscured the fact that German naval power was unable to prevent successive Allied landings in German-occupied territories, to protect German oceanic trade despite possession of Denmark and Norway, or to prevent the destruction of two-thirds of the German merchant marine and the elimination of German coastal trade in the course of the Second World War. Responsibility for such a state of affairs cannot be laid exclusively at the door of the *Kriegsmarine*, but consideration of its record suggests that the French army would seem a paragon of percipience by comparison.

* * *

The First World War was Europe's most destructive war for three centuries. A European rather than a world war, despite its name and the fact that it was fought on three continents and five oceans, it cost an estimated 9,000,000 lives on the battlefield, and it has been calculated that worldwide three times that number died in the winter of 1918–19, most of them from hunger and malnutrition-related disease that were directly attributable to the effects of the war. But any familiarity with history suggests that the Muse is but casual in her human book-keeping: careers and the course of events are seldom considered in terms of the countless lives sacrificed upon the altar of personal or national ambition.

Nevertheless, the human cost of the war goes to the heart of the observation that for the victors success was bought at a price that was all but indistinguishable from defeat. This may have been true of Britain and France, but it was not the case for many countries for which the results of war more than justified the costs. The Baltic states, Czechoslovakia, Finland, Poland, and Yugoslavia owed their very existence to the First World War: Romania's aggrandizement was more than adequate compensation for its efforts. For Japan and the United States, the war brought gains that they both could easily afford, and even in the colonial empires the efforts of wartime were recognized—somewhat ambiguously perhaps—by an awareness that racial suppression and unchecked exploitation no longer sufficed as the means and end of government, as the mandate system of the League of Nations clearly indicated. Such were the elements of gain, and no less clear was loss: for Austria–Hungary, Turkey, and Russia most obviously but also for Bulgaria and Germany.

But the real losers in the First World War were very different from those that most obviously spring to mind. Millions of very ordinary people wanting nothing more than to be left alone to live their lives found the latter ruined or impaired by wounds or widowhood. In postwar Europe, rickets was widespread, incest less obviously so. The personal human consequences of the war were awesome in terms of individual and collective suffering, but at another level the consequences of the war were no less traumatic. Europe emerged from the war as *le grand mutilé*, its primacy in the world shattered by a war that totally exhausted it other than in terms of exhausting the capacity of the defeated for hatred and the desire for revenge. The phenomenon of warfare itself should have been the loser of the war, and among the victorious major powers indeed it was, if only briefly: the pacifism and antimilitarism of the democracies in the interwar period was evidence that war itself was discredited. Until the First World War it was common to portray war in the most glorious and heroic of terms, but weapons of mass destruction ensured the destruction of the fittest. God, in 1914, may have matched His people with His hour, but the pain was too much and the old lie too great. But even in the democracies, though the irony of terms proved elusive, the "Great War for Civilization" did not destroy the will to wage war in the defense of civilization: Britain and France went to war in 1939 in order to ensure peace. In this action there was tragedy because in the interwar period Britain and France had managed to arrange their affairs in precisely the wrong order, given the situation that they had faced. In the 1920s France had sought to ensure against defeat and in the 1930s Britain sought to ensure against war: they were to go to war in 1939 having failed to provide for themselves against defeat.

In the vanquished countries war was less discredited, because the forces of change generated by the war assumed not a social but a national dimension: the revolutionary impetus associated itself with a frustrated, virulent nationalism that proved the main impetus in the unfolding of events in Europe between the wars. Herein, perhaps, one touches upon those aspects of the First World War that represent its greatest casualties. Though it saw the survival of parliamentary democracy in western and northern Europe, it did not result in its flowering elsewhere upon the continent. In the immediate aftermath of the war democratic principles were in the ascendancy, but the passing of time and the problems of peace showed that these, with the hope and optimism of the prewar world, were the real losers of the war. That prewar world had been full of falseness and injustice, but rising living standards, an easing of class antagonisms in most countries, and the increasing importance of law as opposed to order pointed to slow but real social and political advances to which even backward, poverty-stricken Russia was a party. Through the fanning of malevolent nationalism and the shattering of the unity of the

Labour movement, the First World War destroyed what should have been the bedrock of postwar liberal democracy throughout most of central and eastern Europe, while in the democracies

We think we gave in vain. The world was not renewed.
There was hope in the homestead and anger in the streets
But the old world was restored and we returned
To the dreary field and workshops, and the immemorial feud
Of rich and poor. Our victory was our defeat.[9]

In the immediate aftermath of the war constitutional government, the principle of representation, and universal suffrage were instituted in virtually every state in Europe. But the divisions of the Left, the evasion of the Right by its prewar and wartime responsibilities, and the social disruption, and seemingly intractable problems caused by war and brought by peace but apparently the price of liberal democracy ensured that Liberty and Hope were the real casualties of the First World War, their moment in its immediate aftermath a brief flickering before the gathering darkness.

* * *

How does one explain this darkness? So much has been written about Hitler's rise to power, and so much of the history of the interwar period is overshadowed by Hitler and Germany, that it is too easy to lose sight of two facts. Germany was by no means the first country to succumb to dictatorship; by 1936 there was no democracy east of the Rhine other than Czechoslovakia. Its eclipse was not a German disease; it affected virtually every country in Europe outside Scandinavia, the Low Countries, France, and the British Isles. Moreover, in the last free election in Germany the Nazis were denied a parliamentary majority. But, undoubtedly, the most important manifestation of totalitarian rule was that in Germany, for an obvious reason: even in defeat it remained potentially the most powerful state in Europe. It was its revisionist aims that affected the peace and stability of the continent, and more than any other single factor Nazism determined the manner in which the Second World War was fought.

* * *

The eclipse of democracy in Europe in the 1930s was clearly tied to the Great Depression, and the rise of Hitler to increasing unemployment in Germany but also to something more—to what has been defined as the "flight from freedom." The democratic form in Germany was under bitter attack throughout its existence, though these attacks were checked to some extent in the period between 1924 and 1928, when something akin to economic stability and a measure of prosperity prevailed. But from the birth of the Republic in 1918 it was saddled with responsibility for a lost war, and, perhaps far more importantly, it was assailed from the outset—specifically by elements that should have been its strongest supporters—as un-German, a cultural affront. One must be careful not to read the record backward and to attribute to Germany before 1933 thinking that emerged as state orthodoxy after that time, and one must be equally careful not to see Hitler as either inevitable or the representative of German thought. The determinist argument, for all its strengths, cannot be sustained.

But Hitler was not an aberration. Nothing he wrote or said was original, and in the striking fact that Hitler never developed any ideas beyond those that he had gathered in adolescence and immaturity, one notes that much of his appeal lay in the fact that he was able to tap widely held prejudice and to give it form and direction. He was acceptable to many Germans, particularly those in positions of authority and who perhaps should have known better, precisely because they shared many of his views; in no case was this more obvious than with the officer corps: it was Hitler's defeats to which the officers objected. But if the elements of continuity in German thought must be handled with some caution and with the proviso that this line of thought was but one at work in the German consciousness, one can identify six elements whereby Nazism was the expression of concepts deeply ingrained in German national perception, though one must note that the genuine endorsement that Hitler's rule was able to command by 1939 was in part practical—the result of the measures that were taken to cure the scourges of unemployment—and in part presentational.

The latter is a matter about which we as individuals, particularly those drawn from the Left, are reticent and not surprisingly so: Nazism was an appeal to the primitive that even the most committed libertarian cannot fully deny. "Based upon a crude irreducible atavism Nazism was . . . a black mass in borrowed vestments. . . . In the midst of a civilized world Nazism . . . was a harking back to a . . . pagan ancestry."[10] Nazism was an appeal to the black side of the soul, and its allure, through its enticement of an abdication of responsibility and reason, was persuasive in its comprehensiveness and its embrace of the individual within a collective identity. One defies any white male to deny the power of the Nazi image, specifically the sense of oneness and purpose that the rallies fostered and the emotional needs that this perversion of Christian values peddled. Nazism provided the fanaticism and crusading belief of a new religion, the opportunity for martyrdom and redemption and the intellectual escape clause: it had its tribe, complete with its supreme chief and totem, and it had its blood rituals and initiation ceremonies. Across the years, and in spite of our knowledge of the depravity of Nazism, the images of the Nuremberg *Parteitag*—the "licentious clamouring of the barbarians"—still make the flesh creep, the hair on the back of the neck tingle. Even at a distance of 60 years, Nazism tugs disconcertingly at the coattails of rationalism.

*   *   *

Of the six strands of thought within German political consciousness that Hitler came to embrace as his own, three need little elaboration: the exaltation of the state—specifically an authoritarian state that inevitably went alongside the vilification of democracy; a belief in the primacy of force; and the glorification of the Great Man. All were of long standing, reaching back over time to the early days of *Das heilige römische Reich deutscher Nation* and to Friedrich Barbarossa asleep in his cavern One matter, though, needs be noted. The creation of the German Empire in 1871 served to confirm German belief in the efficacy of war. Just as it seems that Germans have always experienced trouble in trying to work out why Man is plural and men are singular, so Bismarck's success served to blur the distinction between war and wars—and Bismarck, who understood, felt no compulsion to enlighten his countrymen. German unity was achieved in the course not of three wars but of three campaigns, each separated from the others by time and distance. The experience of the wars of national liberation between 1864 and 1871 completed the rout of liberalism but also served to stunt German political maturity. National unity was achieved without any realization on the part of German society of the role and limits of force within the context of power and of the limits of national power within the context of the existing international order. The passing of time, and the idea of struggle compounded and completed this process, for the obvious reason. The idea of struggle as the basis of the human condition, as the normal and not the occasional instrument of development and change, necessarily served to blur the distinction between war and peace; indeed, robbed them of their conventional meaning as Lenin, intellectually, and Hitler, instinctively, recognized very clearly. Within a context of permanent struggle war and peace were merely instruments—in fact the one and the same, or, perhaps more accurately, different sides of the same coin, to be pursued at one and the same time, with emphasis placed as circumstances dictated: they were not alternatives to one another. Perhaps such an idea is the last Darwinian legacy, since it would seem that this redefinition of struggle, war, and peace has survived the creeds that placed it at the heart of their ideological identities.

The remaining strands demand more considered examination. At the heart of Nazism, the core belief that explains much of German behavior in the Second World War was the *Volksgemeinschaft*—the concept of a racially pure society. To Hitler existence was governed by the struggle of blood and soil, and a people secured or lost its right to survival in racial war. Hitler saw the white races as superior to others and the Aryan as superior to all other whites, but within a concept that naturally assigned all progress as the product of Aryan achievement there had to be the converse. Racial nationalism thus identified an antithesis to the Aryan— a pollutant Jewry—and, as many observers have noted, the mixing of races was to Nazism what Original Sin and the expulsion from Eden was to Christianity. It is a matter of utter disbelief to this writer that in recent years certain revisionists should seek to deny that the Final Solution took place or that it took place without Hitler's knowledge and approval. Hitler, in a way that could not have happened in the Western democracies, was Germany, and nothing happened in Germany between 1933 and 1945 except at his behest. From the outset of his political career Hitler announced and prided himself as a systematic anti-Semite and declared his intention to complete the annihilation of Jewry. Given the critical, overwhelming importance of racial purity in the Nazi order of things, this was the primary task to be accomplished in the event at the expense of military necessity, and a policy central to Nazi creed was neither accidental nor unknown to Hitler. By its own terms of reference the Final Solution was Nazism's finest achievement even in defeat— especially in defeat.

* * *

Tied to the concept of Aryan superiority was that of *Lebensraum*, the two coming together in Hitler's belief that the German people's right to survive would be decided in a struggle to the death with the Slavs in the vastness of eastern Europe. The idea of the German colonization of eastern Europe is centuries old, but Hitler's ideas were clearly shaped by those of Kjellen, Mackinder, and Haushofer. Mackinder's famous heartland concept rationalized the twin imperatives of *Volksgemeinschaft* and *Lebensraum*. It provided the basis of ideas intended to provide the German people with the means of survival through the destruction of the threat presented by the Slavs and the acquisition of the resources of eastern Europe—grain, meat, wood, oil, and the various ores without which an advanced industrial economy could not function. Conquest and the annihilation of the *Untermenschen* was the basis of Hitler's thought, the premise of his personal leadership that was enshrined in the *Führerprinzip*.

The *Führerprinzip* is vital in an understanding of Nazism in large measure because it was so important in German defeat in the Second World War. It was the means by which Hitler sought to legitimize himself through the identification of himself as the *Volk* and the *Volk* incarnate in himself as the *Volksgeist*. Its importance in terms of Hitler's personal appeal to the individual is not to be understated. Nazism was in many ways a reaction against urbanization, industrialization, and the impersonal nature of twentieth-century existence, and one of Hitler's strengths lay in his personification of the ordinary man and the reduction of government to human proportions.

The ironies involved in such a presentation argue for themselves, but the basic point cannot be gainsaid. What was so critical in the unfolding of events, however, was that this union between *Führer* and *Volk* was undefined—indeed it could not be defined, and most certainly could never be institutionalized, any more than it could be limited. Hitler's leadership was personal, direct, and absolute, but his aversion to set forms of administration and jurisdiction, plus his personal disorganization and inability to work to any settled pattern, had immediate ramifications once the Second World War ceased to be a series of related campaigns and began to fulfill its name. The *Führerprinzip* contained within itself rejection of any means that might restrict the genius of the Great Man, but reality ordained that this war was too complicated to be directed by any single individual. The *Führerprinzip* allowed Hitler to divide and rule, and those convinced at the present time of the importance of joint warfare doctrine and organization, with its consequential concentration of power in single pairs of hands, should do well to consider that the *Führerprinzip* strangled the concept of joint warfare at birth; indeed, it was the means of escaping from its demands. The breaking of the institutional power of the individual services, the strengthening of central authority through the stripping the services of their organic functions, the primacy of theaters over service staffs, and the arbitration between theaters by an individual bereft of system were the more obvious structural changes imposed by Hitler in an attempt to ensure that he, and he alone, held the power of decision. In fact, the power of decision came as often as not to mean no decision. With no cabinet, no cabinet secretariat, and no permanent liaison committees between the services, the foreign office, industry, and research and development, there was no means other than Hitler to ensure the devising and, more importantly the supervision of the implementation, of policy. As the war entered its final phase, Germany was administered by force of habit but was neither led nor governed. Such were the direct consequences of the *Führerprinzip*. Hitler may not have been what so many German academics and intellectuals anticipated when they stressed the *Volksgemeinschaft*, the *Führerprinzip*, and the importance of force and power, but these elements were at the core of Nazism, the German historical experience, and defeat in the last war of the nineteenth century.

NOTES

1. V. K. Triandafillov, *The Nature of the Operations of Modern Armies*, transl. William A. Burhans (London: F. Cass, 1994), pp. 113–114.

2. F. Scott Fitzgerald, *Tender Is the Night* (New York: Charles Scribner's Sons, 1933).

3. John Ellis, *The Sharp End of War* (Newton Abbot, U.K.: Davis and Charles 1980), p. 37.

4. Friedrich Engels, quoted by William C. Frank, Jr., and Philip S. Gillette (eds.), *Soviet Military Doctrine from Lenin to Gorbachev, 1915–1991* (Westport, CT: Greenwood Press, 1992), p. 65.

5. Barbara W. Tuchman, *The Zimmermann Telegram* (New York: Viking Press, 1958), p. 139.

6. Georg Wilhelm Friedrich Hegel, quoted in Robert G. L. Waite, *Adolf Hitler. The Psychopathic God* (New York: Da Capo Press, 1993), specifically pp. 270–274, the sub-section entitled "George Wilhelm Friedrich Hegel," and generally chapter 4, "The Past as Prologue: Hitler and History," pp. 244–247; the first three sections of this chapter, "The First Reich 800–1806," "Germany without a Reich, 1806-1871," and "The Second Reich, 1871–1918," pp. 247-302, were consulted extensively in the preparation of this text. Also consulted two of the ageless histories: George H. Sabine, *A History of Political Theory* (London: Harrap, 1963), Chapter XXX, "Hegel. Dialectic and Nationalism," pp. 620–668; and George Catlin, *A History of the Political Philosophers* (London: Allen and Unwin, 1950), Chapter XV, "Georg Hegel," pp. 465–496. Also J. S. McClelland, *A History of Western Political Thought* (London: Routledge, 1996), Chapter 22, "Hegel and the Hegelian context of Marxism"; Azar Gat, *The Origins of Military Thought. From the Enlightenment to Clausewitz*" (Oxford: Clarendon Press, 1989), Chapter 7, "Clausewitz: The Nature of War," section 2, "Politics and War: The Ambiguous Transformation Clarified"; Sidney Hook, *From Hegel to Marx: Studies in the Intellectual Development of Karl Marx* (Ann Arbor, MI: University of Michigan Press, 1962); and Jacques Barzun, *Darwin, Marx, Wagner. Critique of a Heritage* (Chicago, IL: University of Chicago Press, 1981).

7. Oswald Spengler, quoted in Waite, *Adolf Hitler*, p. 289.

8. Bruce D. Porter, *War and the Rise of the State: The Military Foundations of Modern Politics* (New York: Free Press, 1994)—specifically chapter 5, "Total War and the Rise of the Collectivist State."

9. Herbert Read, "To a Conscript of 1940," *Collected Poems* (quoted in Paul Fussell, *Wartime: Understanding and Behaviour in the Second World War* (London: Oxford University Press, 1989), p. 131.

10. I would acknowledge as the basis of these comments the section on the nature of Nazism in Frank P. Chambers, Christina Phelps Grant, and Charles C. Bayley, *This Age of Conflict: The Western World—1914 to the Present* (New York: Harcourt, Brace and Company, 1943), p. 469.

3

A Reexamination of Interpretations of Aspects of the Second World War

In considering the historiography of the Second World War, one is convinced of the futility of being an historian. I served my apprenticeship with such writings as Michael Howard's *The Mediterranean Strategy in the Second World War* and *The Continental Commitment*, and these remain perhaps the best, most intelligent, single accounts of their respective subjects. But attendance at various conferences and listening to assorted papers on these and related themes left the distinct impression that no one else has ever read them. Indeed, such was the state of so much that was presented about the Mediterranean theater and Anglo–American military diplomacy with respect to Operation Overlord that I wondered which was worse: the exchanges that, amid mutual incomprehension and irritation, fashioned the strategic policy of the two Western Allies during the Second World War or the manner in which American and British historians have subsequently picked over the pieces and continue so to do. It was hard to avoid the conclusion that the historical portrayal and interpretation of these events have largely and unhappily followed an Anglo–American fault line and, in so doing, generated more heat than light. If I may be permitted to provide example, a lecture by an American on this very subject left this listener with two conclusions: that on the basis of the lecture American national mythology seemed alive and well and that, at least for some Americans, in terms of national demonology, Britain was, is, and seemingly always will be the real "Evil Empire." Indeed, one could go further with the suggestion that much recent American historical accounting invites the conclusion that the United States regrets having had Britain as an ally in two world wars and that Britain was politically embarrassing to the United States and both militarily inept and a liability that denied the United States the means and opportunity to win the Second World War more quickly than proved the case. Along with other aspects of history, specifically the nineteenth-century Irish dimension, one is tempted to believe that Britain and the British alone provide American history and prejudice with politically acceptable villains without fear of historiographic litigation.[1]

* * *

The Mediterranean theater in the Second World War demands examination of two sets of national mythologies, one British, the other American. For the British this theater was one of achievement in the face of adversity where Britain fought and won its last battles and campaigns even as the reality of greater U.S. and Soviet power took shape. No less importantly, it was a theater that played host to the last major war effort on the part of its Empire. Australian, Indian, New Zealand, and South African divisions fought in the Western Desert, and if the Australians disappeared from the order of battle after Alamein, the Canadians had taken their place by the time the war moved to the Italian peninsula.

For the Americans, the Mediterranean theater holds a very different place—as a theater that involved an unsought commitment which concentrated Anglo–American differences in a way that probably no other theater or issue achieved, with the possible exception of Burma. Mutual exasperation and displeasure characterized many Anglo–American deliberations, but the Mediterranean, particularly in early 1944, produced acrimony and discord of an intensity that served to prove only that relations between the U.S. and British high commands were characterized by trust and understanding. To borrow and slightly amend a famous comment, the Americans did not trust the British and the British did not understand the Americans.

* * *

The campaign in the Mediterranean theater lasted from June 1940 to May 1945, and only one power, Britain, fought throughout its duration: the only other major combatant involved for its entire length, Italy, served unwillingly as battlefield for its last 22 months. It was a secondary theater of operations. Italy lacked the power of decision to direct Axis policy in this theater, and as long as Germany was prepared to undertake only a limited commitment south of the Alps, there could never be any outcome in the Mediterranean other than an Axis defeat. But even if Germany had placed a higher priority upon this theater, it is doubtful that the Axis powers could have forced a favorable decision in the Mediterranean, in part because of their commitments elsewhere and in part because they could never overcome the three-fold problem of deploying and maintaining forces in that theater. These were the shortage of shipping needed to maintain the necessary flow of supplies across the Mediterranean; the very limited capacity of North Africa's ports; and the enormous difficulties involved in the movement of material from the main ports of entry, specifically Tripoli, to the front line. The Axis powers were never able to handle all three requirements at the same time, never over any extended period, and most certainly never when their armies were on the offensive beyond the El Agheila position. For the Axis powers, North Africa was always a defeat waiting to happen, and its timing was assured once their formations were halted on the Alam Halfa ridge in September 1942.

Nevertheless the defeat of the Axis powers in this theater was beyond British means. Indeed, for most of the time that Britain fought alone in the Mediterranean theater, its only army in the field proved unable to cope with one under-strength German corps and whatever wretchedly equipped Italian formations were added to its numbers. Alamein, indeed the campaign in Egypt and Libya, was small change. There were aspects of the British effort in this theater that were commendable, but the conduct of operations in the Western Desert can hardly be so dignified. Nonetheless, and somewhat perversely, the campaign in North Africa is one that has attracted inordinate British pride and attention in much the same way that a Scottish victory necessarily involves the annihilation of complete battalions other than commanding officer and piper. It was a campaign that provided Britain with two heroes—Montgomery and Rommel. For the British, the Western Desert was a gladiatorial contest between national champions that culminated at Alamein, and before that time it was no disgrace to have been worsted by a military genius. Cynicism suggests that when an army in wartime extols the virtues of an individual enemy as the cause of its defeats, something is very wrong with its system. Rommel's success coincided with the time when the U.S. military attaché code and the signals covering the British order-of-battle and operational plans sent from the Cairo embassy to Washington on a routine basis were compromised. This period of success ended when U.S. signals security was restored. If so much of his acclaimed tactical sense can be thus explained, what remains of Rommel's military reputation, which was never highly regarded in Berlin and Rome? One strongly suspects that just as in November 1917 the British military selected an unknown German officer to explain away the failure of the Cambrai attack, which was the result of their own ineptitude, so one suspects that the myth of Rommel's military genius, indeed the myth of German military proficiency in the Second World War, has been a cloak behind which the British army has long sought to hide its professional mediocrity in this period.

The pages of this chapter will not add to the already plentiful literature that encompasses perhaps Britain's most famous soldier of the Second

World War; rather, it will note the obvious. Moment and man came together, and in this fact lies the significance of Alamein. Contrary to the approved British version of the Second World War, the British victory at Alamein was not the turning point of this war. It was not a battle when victory, hitherto assured for the one side, switched its favors to the other. The war was not decided in North Africa. But the second Alamein, fought between 23 October and 4 November 1942, redeemed what otherwise was a disastrous year for Britain. It is difficult sometimes to realize how disastrous 1942 was for Britain. The prestige and authority of the lone defiance of 1940–41 was all but swept aside by the flood of humiliating defeats, but, at a time when Britain stood on the edge of eclipse as a great power, here was the victory that paid for all the defeats, won before dependence upon the United States undercut Britain's status and authority: Alamein was Britain's swan-song. But Alamein was also something else, because Fitzgerald was wrong: Alamein, not the Somme, was Europe's last great love-battle. This was the last battle involving Europeans with virtually no reference to outsiders, and somehow it seems both perverse and appropriate that with its fate to be decided by non- and extra-European powers greater than itself, Europe should have fought its final battle beyond its shores.

* * *

The American perspective of matters Mediterranean at the time was somewhat jaundiced: the passing of time has resulted only in the strengthening of the arguments that were used at the time against an expanded Allied commitment in the theater in 1942 and 1943. Both have their origins in the American belief in the primacy of the European theater of operations, and in recent years there has been an increasingly strident assertion within sections of American academe that the invasion of northwest Europe could have been accomplished in 1943. For the moment this remains a minority view, but it seems likely to be one that will gain ground, if only because it has been pushed with such fervor and conviction. The counterview, that an invasion of northwest Europe was not possible before 1944, is difficult to argue, lacks the simplicity of the other thesis, is staid, and does not boast the attractiveness of novelty and daring. Moreover, it lacks comforting assurance implicit in the 1943 argument that the war could have been won, and the whole course of postwar history changed, with the Soviet Union somehow excluded from eastern and central Europe.

* * *

Any examination of these conflicting claims must address two quite separate issues: conflicting Anglo–American policies with respect to the

Mediterranean and the unfolding of events in that theater, and the state of the Battle of the Atlantic and how that campaign affected strategic priorities and timings. To these could be added another consideration—namely, the state of German defenses in northwest Europe. The latter has been embraced by the revisionist cause, and in fact is one of its main arguments on the grounds that a 1943 offensive would have found the Germans less numerous and well prepared than was the case in 1944.

In order to consider the first of these—the conflict of Anglo–American attitudes and priorities in regard to the Mediterranean theater—one point must be cited at the outset. Accounts of this campaign and the arguments between the two commands invariably stress the extent of Anglo–American disagreement on most strategic issues, but, paradoxically, what is so often missed is the extent of agreement between the two sides. It was not a case of one side or the other having a monopoly on strategic wisdom. It was not that on occasion the British were right and on other occasions the Americans were correct, but that on many occasions both were correct—hence their inability to agree. For example, the basis of all American dealings with the British was contained in a four-part thesis: that the defeat of Germany could only be accomplished by the defeat and destruction of the *Wehrmacht* on the North European Plain; that the road northward up peninsular Italy was one that in strategic terms led nowhere; that Italy threatened only to be a liability to whichever side occupied it; and that once embraced, a Mediterranean commitment could not be limited but would divert resources and attention from the main theater of war. There is little doubting the essential correctness of these individual points: the U.S. high command grasped the fact that only through main-force action in the main theater of operations could the *Wehrmacht* be defeated. The latter, however, was not an obstacle to legitimate argument: the primacy of a northwest Europe endeavor did not preclude all other endeavors.

A very careful reading of the 1943 conferences reveals that the British high command never disputed the accuracy of the first two American arguments. The former sought a German defeat, not the defeat of Germany, in the Mediterranean theater, and, with regard to victory on the North European Plain, it saw the invasion of and subsequent campaign in northwest Europe as the means of completing the defeat of Germany. Herein is the basis of understanding British policy, but the basic problem associated with British policy in the Second World War stems from the assertion that British strategic policy has traditionally been peripheral and that in this war Britain sought to use naval supremacy to wear down a continental enemy by time and distance. One has also been told, often by American historians, that political considerations shaped British determination to prosecute a Mediterranean strategy. Certainly political considerations and the desire to use naval supremacy to wear down a continental enemy by time and distance by imposing costly but marginal obligations were arguments paraded by the British high command in its defense of the Mediterranean commitment. But the general comment lends itself to four observations.

First, what was called "the British way of war" does not bear serious scrutiny, as even the most cursory examination of British army battle honors would reveal. One can hardly find a less peripheral battlefield than Blenheim, and the battles of the Dunes, Namur, Ramillies, Oudenarde, Malplaquet, Dettingen, Fontenoy, Minden, Warburg, the 1794 campaign in the Austrian Netherlands, Walcheren, Waterloo, Ypres, the Somme, and Amiens share the common characteristic of being fought in the strategic heartland of western Europe. Throughout Britain's many wars between 1649 and 1940, a British field army of very respectable size and capability invariably went to the Low Countries or western Germany–northeast France to make the largest single British military contribution to the war in which Britain found itself. Over 30 years ago Michael Howard questioned the "British way of war" thesis, arguing that there was little evidence to support it. In reality the evidence points in the opposite direction, that the "British way of war" was the very opposite of what it was claimed to have been by such people as Bryant, Churchill, and Liddell Hart.

Second, in those wars in which Britain did not commit an expeditionary army to the main theater of operations in western Europe, the reason was simple. In the War of American Independence there was no theater of operations on the continental mainland. In the Napoleonic Wars the British involvement in Portugal and Spain stemmed from the defeat of its allies and Britain's patent inability to challenge French primacy in northwest Europe. Indeed, that Britain should have moved against France via the Iberian peninsula during the Napoleonic Wars was mute testimony to the desperateness of its position. As late as 1811, the anti-French cause in Europe looked hopeless, and no amount of victories won by the British south of the Pyrenees was ever going to break French domination of the continent. If Britain did indeed adopt peripheral strategies in the Peninsular and the Second World Wars, they were imposed upon it by necessity and weakness and not adopted by choice.

Third, the "British way of war" was inevitably associated with the notion of command of the sea. The problem therein is that it was presented as the alternative to the continental commitment, yet any careful consideration of British history would suggest that the two were intimately linked. Most certainly command of the sea and the continental commitment were never mutually exclusive, and for a country the security of which rested upon alliances, they could not be. Throughout British history the two elements have been complementary, at least in intention and policy if not in fact. Even at its greatest, Britain could never survive by sea power alone, most obviously not in the face of single-power control of the continent: recourse to a maritime strategy was invariably enforced by the failure of other means.

Fourth, there has been precious little attempt to define the alleged political considerations that the U.S. high command suspected at the time to be so important in shaping Britain's Mediterranean strategy in the Second World War. In the first 16 pages of Carlo D'Este's much acclaimed *Fatal Decisions: Anzio and the Battle for Rome*, a fine work which attracted much criticism on account of its alleged sympathy for the British position, there are five references to the political considerations that allegedly shaped British policy. Moreover, in these same pages is the comment, made with reference to an Allied failure, to "the inevitable fiasco that results whenever political aims take precedence over (sound) military practice."[2] Leaving aside this rather mysterious observation, never once were these considerations defined: a contemporaneous suspicion of the part of the U.S. high command of British motives was in itself proof of fact. Even more critically, the British chiefs of staff paper that read

Our final conclusion is that the Mediterranean offers us opportunities for action in the coming autumn and winter [1943–1944] which may be decisive, and at the least will do far more to prepare the way for a cross-Channel operation in 1944 than we should achieve by attempting to transfer back to the United Kingdom some of the forces now in the Mediterranean theatre. If we take these opportunities, we shall have every chance of breaking the Axis and of bringing the war to a successful conclusion in 1944.[3]

seems to have been omitted. The British reasoning was incorrect because German powers of recovery in 1944 were underestimated, but the error of the conclusion does not diminish the conspicuously military nature of calculation and argument. What is so often missed in any discussion of the Mediterranean strategy is the simple fact that as often as not strategic choice is illusory. One fights where one can, rather than where one would. The 1942–43 situation stemmed directly from the 1940 commitment when Britain had no choice but to fight in the only theater in which it was in contact by land with its enemies. No amount of U.S. earnestness was going to change this fact of life in 1942. If Operation Torch was justified in terms of the U.S. political need for U.S. troops to be seen to enter the German war in 1942, then the same was equally true for Britain vis-à-vis the Mediterranean theater. There was no way that the Mediterranean commitment in 1942 or 1943 could have been curtailed in order to provide for either Operation Sledgehammer or Operation Roundup. To put the matter a slightly different way—the mounting of an invasion of northwest Europe either in 1942 or 1943 would have involved Britain, by some mysterious and unexplained process, abandoning Egypt and with it the whole of its position in the Middle East. This, clearly, never presented itself as a practical proposition.

The British argument in favor of Torch was in part strategic and in part administrative—namely, that a cross-Channel operation in 1942 was impossible and Torch represented the best, indeed only, practical proposition open to the Western Allies in that year. The American argument in favor of Torch, or more accurately Roosevelt's decision to endorse it, was political, and in its final form the Torch plan included an ironic comment on the U.S. military that was so insistent on a cross-Channel operation in 1942. If a cross-Channel operation was so important in 1942, if it was so important for the German army to be brought to battle immediately, why did U.S. military leaders refuse to consider landings in eastern Algeria and Tunisia, and why did they have to be ordered by Roosevelt to include Algiers among the landing sites of the operation? The strategic logic that substituted North Africa for France can be understood. The operational logic that substituted Casablanca for Brest is harder to discern. Marshall wanted to invade France and get to grips with the German army, and the first operation that is mounted witnessed Marshall's reluctance to undertake a landing within 550 miles of Italian forces based at Palermo in Sicily. It is a little difficult to square Washington's rhetoric with reality.

* * *

Nevertheless, as the U.S. high command feared, this theater proved something of a black hole, and the overall military balance sheet of the campaign is difficult to calculate. Alexander's postwar assessment that the Italian campaign directly engaged or indirectly effected the deployment of 55 German divisions is mendacious since many of these were refitting or employed on occupation duties rather than providing against Allied amphibious operations. The lack of any clear objective in taking the war to the Italian peninsula, the confusion of aim in terms of seeking to impose attrition on the *Wehrmacht* yet at the time seeking advances into central and northern Italy that would ease its problems, the Dodecanese episode, the process whereby the opportunity to fight and win a battle of encirclement and annihilation against the German Tenth Army in summer 1944 slipped through Allied fingers, and Churchill's antics over the Istria–Vienna option obviously flawed the concept and conduct of this campaign. But whether this campaign really cost the Allies anything in terms of opportunity lost elsewhere is doubtful, except to those who believe that Operation Overlord could have been mounted either in either 1942 or 1943.

* * *

In terms of military merit, the 1942 argument deserves even less consideration than it was afforded at the time by the British high command, but the American demand in spring 1942 for a landing in northwest Europe during that year does invite four very real questions. The first is obvious. If Sledgehammer and/or Roundup was as critically important to the realization of U.S. national objectives as Marshall claimed, one is left wondering why it was that Marshall seemed quite unaware of the fact until the spring of 1942. The second is no less obvious: why, in April and July 1942, did Marshall and King press for a landing in northwest Europe in 1942 when King most certainly knew that lack of amphibious shipping would preclude such an operation? The third question arises directly from the second: given the lead-times for such an operation in planning and logistical terms, how could the U.S. service chiefs have contemplated an autumn invasion supplied over open beaches? Between 1 October and 28 February in any given year, the eastern Atlantic and Channel approaches average 76 days of Force 7 weather conditions and another 10 days of more severe conditions. With the Great Storm of 19–23 June 1944, when 13 merchantmen and over 800 minor craft were driven ashore, to serve by way of example, Marshall's insistence on a 1942 operation was hopelessly flawed, and it should be noted that the winter of 1942–43 proved worse than usual: Force 7 weather was encountered on 105 days, with another 15 days of even worse conditions.

The fourth question, however, is the critical one: what right has any nation to demand sacrifice of another? If the 1942 effort had been made, the British would have been obliged to provide most of the forces and losses when it failed. One wonders at the morality of Marshall in making a demand for which others would have paid the price, and those who argue that any defeat in 1942 could have been reversed by the greater U.S. power in 1943 miss the point entirely. The British had faced a similar problem before 1914 and specifically in August 1915. In the interwar period the likes of Liddell Hart argued in favor of limited liability—that is, the French taking the casualties and the British as little of a war as they wanted. In both cases, the British leadership made the right choice. The greater part of British military strength went to France in order to support an ally and to take its share of fighting and losses: that the 1940 campaign unfolded to a different conclusion does not reflect upon the original British decision. With respect to the events of 1942, it is difficult to resist the thought that the meetings of April and July 1942, when Marshall tried to force Operation Sledgehammer on an incredulous British high command, cost Marshall any respect for his strategic judgment on the part of the British service chiefs.

Inevitably, there is a plea of mitigation that has to be entered. The Americans had to deal with the demands of two separate but related efforts, but that hardly excuses a demand that was both unreasonable and unreasoning. There is, however, another explanation of Marshall's behavior, though one that is impossible to define and quantify. Undoubtedly Marshall's demand reflected a confidence born of unprecedented power: Marshall did not know what the United States was to produce in terms of war material over the next three years, but he knew that it would be sufficient to needs and more. Marshall's views reflected national power, but it is quite possible that they also reflected an ignorance and lack of imagination in terms of strategic geography that afflicted the U.S. and British high commands impartially in their dealings with one another. Certainly if one reads the British deliberations in 1944 with respect to the future British effort in the Far East, one is struck by the lack of any real appreciation of what would be involved, the lack of realism in many of the proposals that were examined, and a sense of unfamiliarity with the theater that is at very sharp contrast with British deliberations on European matters. And one is also struck by American flair and imagination in the devising of policy for the Pacific war and the way that on occasion it could be improvised. One could portray the British and the Far East and the Americans and Europe as mirror images of one another in terms of strategic imagination, but one could never prove the point.

* * *

The 1943 argument is less easy to dismiss. It is an argument that has obvious appeal and accords with what the American public came to assume to have been the national role in the Second World War. It has the attraction, noted earlier, of offering the prospect of German defeat without a Soviet victory, and it is explicit in the belief that an invasion of northwest Europe in 1943 would have proven easier than was the experience of 1944. The basis of this line of reasoning is the smaller number of German divisions in the western theater in summer 1943 than in summer 1944.

There would seem to be any number of very real objections to these three lines of argument. The case for an invasion in 1943 must rest upon the assumption that command of the sea was enjoyed, in terms of either the U-boats already having been defeated or the Battle of the Atlantic being illusory or overrated. Certainly there are some who subscribe to such views—witness the "pseudo-crises in the Battle of the Atlantic in

1942 and early 1943" that were the result of the "defects of British grand strategy."[4] Thus are the great issues of the day dismissed, a landing in northwest France and the ending of U-boat activities by the capture of their bases can be asserted, and the judgment of the U.S. high command thus vindicated. Such comments prompt the obvious rejoinder. If an invasion of northwest Europe was possible in 1943, then it must follow, given the lead-times involved in the planning and movement of forces and supplies, that the American effort and results attained in the Battle of the Atlantic in 1942 were critical. Between 11 December 1941 and 31 December 1942 U.S. naval operations accounted for six U-boats, and clearly this was the crucial contribution, the difference between victory and defeat, that provided opportunity where none had previously existed. If this is the case, those who would argue that an invasion in 1943 was possible, that the whole of the North Atlantic crisis was self-induced for the British, should devote their considerable talents to providing the answer to the question that has defeated decades of study, not least because people were obviously looking in the wrong direction: which was the U-boat sinking, by the U.S. Navy, that won the Battle of the Atlantic, and which should have marked the start of the end of the war? This is not a *reductio ad absurdum* of the 1942–43 theses: it is the argument that is absurd, not this rebuttal.

Moreover, the 1943 thesis would seem to be based on the implicit assumption that the technical capability of the U.S. Army in 1944 would have been available in 1943. That was not the case, and indeed the argument can be inverted. The technique of 1944 in terms of corps and divisional headquarters staffs, logistical capability, integration of air power into campaign planning, and generally good relations between Allied commanders would never have been achieved without the very commitment in the Mediterranean that the 1943 argument would deny. In addition, the 1943 thesis also seems to read the record backward in terms of an implicit assumption that the number of divisions available to the U.S. Army in 1944 would have been available in 1943. But with the main burden of a campaign in northwest Europe necessarily having to be shouldered by the Americans, does one really believe that Roundup's 30 divisions would have been sufficient to defeat the *Wehrmacht* in northwest Europe in 1943? In addition, one wonders, in light of what happened at Anzio in 1944 and the narrowness by which defeat was avoided in spite of possession of overwhelming naval and air superiority, how a landing in France would have fared in 1943, when such supremacy was not at Allied disposal and when the French rail system was still intact and German response times would have been much quicker than was the case in 1944. The thoroughness with which British and U.S. air forces prepared the way for a 1944 invasion could not have been registered in 1943.

The obvious counterargument, that an invasion in 1943 would have encountered a much weaker enemy than was the case in 1944, is irrelevant, its only aspect that possesses any merit being an ability to count. There were fewer German divisions in the western theater in summer 1943 than in summer 1944, but such percipience has little value. *Wehrmacht* numbers increased with every year between 1939 and 1944, and at the start of Operation Barbarossa in 1941 there were 59 divisions, with some 594,000 men, outside the Eastern Front: on 1 July 1942 there were 53 divisions with 971,000 men and one year later 75 divisions with 1,368,000. The increase in German numbers in successive years and in the west could not have been prevented. But, more importantly, any consideration of detail as opposed to numbers is revealing, as shown in Table 3.1.

An ability to count divisions would seem to be panacea strategy of the worst kind, ignoring as it does points about the divisions that were in theater which are too easily overlooked. Of the German divisions in the western theater on 5 June 1944, no fewer than 37 had been in theater for less than nine months and 18 for only five months or less. The 6 reserve divisions and the 9th Panzer Division, with only four tanks and partially motorized infantry, were for practical purposes nonexistent, and the 11th and 116th Panzer Divisions were scarcely any better. At least 8 allegedly good divisions were considerably under-strength, and 4 of the nominally strongest formations in theater were either reforming or being reequipped.[5] Yet the offensiveness of the 1943 thesis runs much deeper than this. By a simple concentration upon the number of German divisions in France in June 1944 compared to summer 1943, those who argue the 1943 thesis would divide what is indivisible—namely, three essential unities. There was a larger number of German divisions in the West in 1944 than in 1943, but by summer 1944 the *Luftwaffe* had been all but driven from the skies and the *Kriegsmarine* reduced to the occasional furtive success, they were more thinly spread than one year earlier because in 1944 the *Wehrmacht* had to face a Riviera threat and an internal security problem that had not existed in 1943, and their basic simplicity in terms of organization and chain of command had been lost, with their commanders at odds over the conduct of the forthcoming battle. The German divisions in the West in 1944 were aging: the average age of the German soldier in 1944 was 31.5 years, but in France in 1944 a quarter of all German troops were over 34 years of age, and in one division on the Cotentin peninsula the average age was 36 years. In many cases German formations in the west were wretchedly equipped— the Seventh Army in the Normandy and Brittany sectors possessed 92 different types of gun firing 252 different types and caliber of ammunition—and were on the defensive; they most certainly lacked the moral edge that they had certainly held in 1942 and probably held in 1943. The

Table 3.1. The German Deployment in the Western Theater on Selected Dates between 1 June 1942 and 1 June 1944

Type of division	In theatre on				Movement of forces to and from the theatre between 31 Aug. 1943 and 1 June 1944							In theatre on 1 June '44
	1 Jun '42	31 Aug '42	28 Feb '43	31 Aug '43	In	Out A	Out B	Out C	Out D	Out Total	+/-	
Panzer	3	3	2	2	8‡	—	1‡	2	—	3‡	+5	7
SS Panzer	—	—	—	—	5†	—	—	2	—	2	+3	3
Panzergrenadier	—	—	—	—	1*	—	—	1	1*	2	-1	—
SS Panzergrenadier	—	2	2	3†	1	—	—	—	3†	3	-2	1
SS Mountain Parachute	—	—	—	1	—	—	1	—	—	1	-1	—
Luftwaffe	—	—	—	—	3	—	—	—	—	—	+3	3
Field Infantry	—	—	3	4	—	—	1	—	—	1	-1	3
Light Infantry	22	27	18	15	12	4	—	4	—	8	+4	19
Bodenständig	—	—	—	—	1	—	—	—	—	—	+1	1
Security	—	1	6	11	6	—	1	—	—	1	+5	16
subtotal	25	33	32	38	37	4	4	9	4	21	+16	54
Reserve formations												
Panzer	—	—	—	2	1	—	—	—	3	3	-2	—
Infantry	—	10	10	10	—	—	—	—	4	4	-4	6
subtotal	—	10	10	12	1	—	—	—	7	7	-6	6
Total	25	43	42	50	38	4	4	9	11	28	+10	60

Data taken from B. Muller-Hillebrand, *Das Heer 1933-1945. Entwicklung des organisatorischen Aufbaues, 3: Der Zweifrontenkrieg, das Heer vom Beginn des Feldzuges gegen die Sowjetunion bis zum Kriegsende* (Frankfurt am Main: Mittler, 1969).

A: Movement of formations to the Italian front.   B: Movement of formations to the Balkans.   C: Movement of formations to the Eastern Front.   D: Formations disbanded.

‡ Returns include the *Panzer Lehr* Division, which was raised in theater in Nov. 1943, moved to Hungary in January 1944, and returned to theater in May.

† Returns of three *Panzergrenadier* divisions reorganized as panzer divisions after October 1943.

* Returns of one *Panzergrenadier* division reorganized as a panzer division after entering the theater in 1944.

1942 and 1943 theses, by stressing one aspect of German preparations, would destroy the basic unity of time, distance, area, and resources, counting ground forces at the expense of the essential unity of three services. They would consider numbers at the expense of qualitative and related aspects—organization, doctrine, and morale—that alone provide the basis of balanced judgment. There were more German divisions in the West in summer 1944 than in summer 1943, but the basis of comparison is not a 1943 absolute—it is relative to the Allies and against those elements of power other than numbers alone. The issues that are involved in the 1942 and 1943 thesis are too complicated to be resolved by mere assertion and ignoring those aspects of planning and preparation that do not accord with preconceived belief. The lack of freedom of choice in deciding the timing of operations existed because of considerations of weather and sea conditions, the lead-times involved in the preparation of plans and for preparatory operations, and the time that must be lost in the redeployment of forces and in their training. These and many more deserve better consideration that mere assertion of what would have been possible, alleged. Marijuana history, believable to those high on something other than historical substance, is all very well, for clowns: it is a substitute, not a replacement, for serious reflection. To repeat words written as long ago as 1968 and which have not lost their import: "An effective case still has to be made out, that there could have been any more rapid or economical way of winning the war."[6]

* * *

The bare facts of Operation Neptune of Tuesday, 6 June 1944, can be recounted with little difficulty. On that single day a total of 713 warships provided cover for the 4,218 landing ships and craft that put ashore a total of 174,320 troops, some 23,000 troops from three airborne divisions having been committed during the previous night. These facts provide the nail to one of the most pernicious myths about the Mediterranean theater and the Normandy campaign that the 1943 lobby has peddled assiduously—namely, that an invasion of northwest Europe in 1943 was possible because, as they say, the Allies put more men ashore on Sicily on the first day of the invasion of that island than they did in Normandy on the first day. The basis of this assertion would seem to be that at Operation Husky seven divisions were put ashore on the first day, compared to five at Neptune. The fact remains, however, that a 1944 amphibious assault division, with a standard establishment of about 25,000, was larger than its 1943 predecessor, and one formation, the British 50th Infantry Division, numbered 27 battalions and some 38,000 troops on D-Day. At best, it would seem that perhaps as many as 160,000 troops were embarked for the Sicily landing, and upward of 102,000 troops were landed in the first three days of the operation.[7] But the real comparison is not what numbers were landed on the first day or days of these operations, but what had to follow. For Husky, the Allies had to provide for a campaign on an island against an enemy that numbered two German and four Italian field and six coastal divisions. Certainly two, perhaps three, of the Italian field divisions were of dubious standard, and the coastal formations were no better and were known to be such: moreover, the Axis forces on Sicily could not expect reinforcement in the course of a campaign. For Operation Overlord, the requirement was against an enemy with 43 divisions north of the Loire, which could reinforce his formations around the beachhead. This is the first and perhaps the most important point that the 1943 thesis ignores—namely, that a cross-Channel attack was but the means and not an end in itself. What was required for an invasion of northwest Europe was not the capacity to conduct a landing but the ability to sustain a campaign. A landing in northwest Europe was not an end in itself but the beginning of a continental commitment.

The element of doubt that must be entered against the 1943 thesis extends beyond the number of divisions that might have been available on both sides. Four considerations lend themselves as legitimate cause for doubt. The first, noted previously, is the example of Operation Shingle and the fact that it was only by the most narrow of margins that the Allies avoided defeat at Anzio in February–March 1944. Would an Allied landing in northern France in 1943 have necessarily fared any better—and, indeed, would such a landing not have resulted in a victory that so narrowly eluded the *Wehrmacht* at Anzio? That the Allies were not defeated at Anzio can be attributed in major part to overwhelming naval and air supremacy, neither of which would necessarily have been available off and over Normandy and the Cotentin peninsula in 1943. This matter, in particular the question of the role of air forces, is one that the Sledgehammer/Roundup thesis signally fails to address. In Husky in July 1943 the air support afforded the assault was feeble. At Salerno in September 1943 air power was much more important and effective, while at Anzio in February 1944 air power, fully integrated into the plan of campaign, played its full, vital part in saving the beachhead from annihilation. The support that was available for Operation Overlord was possible only because of the Mediterranean experience, an experience that the 1942 and 1943 arguments seemingly would discount, as it would discount one other air power argument. The Allied offensive that secured air superiority in spring 1944 and which was so critically important in the ensuring the success of both Overlord in general and Neptune in particular was primarily American and could not have been registered in 1943 if only for one reason. The Americans could not have sustained the losses incurred in winter and spring 1944—422 Flying Fortresses and Liberators in April 1944 alone or the equivalent of losing

R.A.F. Bomber Command in six weeks—in spring 1943. The doubling of crew numbers available for duties with the 8th Air Force in the first six months of 1944 was concentrated in the period after April and, very simply, could not have been achieved at any time in the previous 18 months.

The second is the implicit assumption that underpins the 1942–43 assertion—namely, that the forces that should have come ashore in 1942 or 1943 possessed the Allied capability of 1944. This was not the case. The U.S. Army did not have its 1944 numbers available until 1944, and in 1942 and 1943 it most certainly did not have the technique it displayed in 1944. As Bradley noted in so many words, the combat experience of the army, corps and divisional staffs, and logistical capability could not have been acquired except in North Africa and Italy. Bradley could have added that North Africa and Italy were critical for the Americans in sorting out not just staffs and doctrine but also commanders. It should also be noted, moreover, that for the U.S. Army the learning process was obtained at the expense of the French, who most certainly did not merit classification as an enemy, and then weak Italian and a very small number of German formations. A raw U.S. Army in the Mediterranean theater did not have to face an intact, numerically powerful, single-nation enemy drawing on three years' combat experience, which was what it would have encountered in France had there been a landing in 1943.

Third, the question of technical readiness cannot be separated from moral readiness, and it must be noted that the Normandy invasion came only after a series of successes, when all the elements of choice lay in Allied hands and when the soldiers committed to the landings knew that everything had been done to ensure victory and minimize casualties. One wonders how the Allied troops detailed for these operations would have received news of their being committed to Sledgehammer in 1942 or to Roundup in 1943. In the summer of 1944 British prisons were packed with deserters, a fact that does not make the official histories. It is difficult to believe that a 1942 operation would have been regarded by those involved as anything other than a good means of committing suicide, and it is difficult to believe that for Roundup in 1943 the reaction would have been anything other than delicate. Perhaps American self-confidence may have carried the day, but optimism and ignorance would hardly seem to form the proper basis of a plan of campaign.

Fourth, and no less important, one wonders what might have happened if an invasion of northwest Europe had been attempted in either 1942 or 1943 without there having been 18 months of remarkably harmonious relations between U.S. and British field commanders. At the theater level one of the most important results of the campaign in the Mediterranean was the generally good Anglo–American relations that were established at theater, group, and army levels. The attention that has been paid to some of the unpleasant exchanges, such incidents as the Coningham–Patton clash, or the loathsome qualities of such individuals as Montgomery and Patton has served to obscure the fact that in the Mediterranean theater U.S. and British commanders learned to work together and in the process established a basic good faith. On the basis of such confidences, ruffled American feathers and British fur could be and were smoothed when the need arose. Could such harmony—uneasy harmony perhaps but harmony nonetheless—have been improvised in the course of a 1942 or 1943 invasion of northern France? Could such exchanges as the Coningham–Patton episode have been negotiated in the course of a Kasserine Pass fought around St. Lô in mid-1943? Herein may be perhaps the most important result of the Mediterranean commitment.

* * *

Of these four subjects, one would linger over just one before turning the page. The subject that would command a second consideration is the role of naval and air forces in ensuring the success of the landings in northwest Europe in 1944. Obviously the more immediately important of the two was the naval forces because without command of the sea there could have been no invasion; indeed, it is impossible to see how Britain could have sustained itself unless command of the sea had been secured. Herein is one point of difference between U.S. and British sea power. To state the obvious, the sea was critical to British national survival, whereas for an United States that could draw upon the resources of a continent, the sea provided the primary means of taking war to the enemy.

The critical point for Britain in terms of victory in the Battle of the Atlantic was that a major continental commitment could not have been undertaken until a full measure of command of the sea had been won, and herein lies the basis of common misunderstanding. I recall a conference in October 1991, held under the auspices of the Royal Air Force, in which we were told that the Battle of the Atlantic was won in May 1943. I was always under the impression that the Battle of the Atlantic was won in May 1945. The May 1943 claim subscribes to popular mythology: it has the attractiveness of the great event beloved by those intent on seeing war in such terms as "the decisive battle" or "turning points." Leaving aside the twin points that the idea of "decisive battle" is somewhat hard to reconcile to the reality of a war of six years' duration and that "turning points" in reality are milestones on a road, not a signpost where the road divided between assured victory and equally assured defeat, the May 1943 thesis is nonsense. At sea, battles and campaigns cannot be won in the sense that land battles and campaigns can be won.

There is no element of physical control conferred by victory unless the victories that are won are so overwhelming as to deny the defeated means of future resistance. Such successes are but seldom recorded at sea—perhaps only three or four times in the last three centuries. The very nature of the campaign against shipping precluded such a possibility in the Battle of the Atlantic: the victory that was won in May 1943—a victory in a single battle, not the campaign—had to be repeated in order to ensure that command of the sea was retained.

It cannot be disputed that the Allied success in the Battle of the Atlantic in May 1943 possessed singular significance. With 41 of their number lost, this was the worst single month of the war for the U-boats, and Dönitz ordered their recall on 24 May, two years to the day after the *Hood* had been lost. The dramatic quality of events in this month arises because crippling losses were inflicted on the U-boat service within two months of the worst month of the war in terms of Allied convoy losses and because of the apparently decisive intervention in the battle of land-based air power. This representation of events is misleading. The events of May 1943 conformed to a trend many months in the making to which the losses of March 1943 were very much the exception. If the impact of Liberators in May 1943 was exaggerated by German operational error, the fact was that land-based aircraft were beginning to inflict significant losses on the U-boats some months before May 1943. Additionally, Allied success in May 1943 was but one victory; it had to be complemented by the successes of July–August and October–November 1943, which, if lacking the dramatic impact of May 1943, were perhaps more far-reaching. These were victories won over a U-boat service reorganized, partially reequipped, and then deliberately committed to try to win back the initiative. In July 37 U-boats were destroyed, in August another 25; in October 26 were destroyed, in November 19. It was the combination of losses that broke the U-boat effort, and it was their being repeated in 1944 with the result that there was no resurgent threat that spelled Allied victory.

The trend to which the events of May 1943 conformed was a failing U-boat effort in terms of rate of sinkings of Allied and neutral merchantmen and rising U-boat losses. The trend had first become apparent in the second half of 1941, when the strengthening of convoy defenses in the eastern Atlantic resulted in significant U-boat losses. But the spread of the war to the western Atlantic cost the Allied cause six months and served to mask a pattern that the German naval staff nevertheless recognized at the time. After the introduction of convoys in the western Atlantic, the rate of sinkings by U-boats fell and U-boat losses began to mount as they were forced to concentrate in the central and eastern North Atlantic and to operate against increasingly well-protected convoys. After mid-1942, therefore, and when for the first time the U-boats amounted to sufficient numbers to mount comprehensive patrol lines in the North Atlantic, they were forced to operate against strength. The importance of this development is easy to underestimate. Of the 1,570 Allied and neutral merchantmen known to have been sunk by enemy action in 1942 no fewer than 962 were sunk while proceeding independently, 840 of this number being sunk by submarines. In 1943 the number of sinkings of independently sailing merchantmen to all forms of enemy action was 214, U-boats accounting for all but 25 of this number. Declining returns registered at the expense of unprotected shipping in part account for the fact that between August 1942 and April 1943 the merchantman–submarine exchange rate would have been as low as 2:1 but for German sinkings in the Arctic. As it was, the rate was 4:1, and this despite the massive German successes of November 1942 and March 1943. Moreover, in the last quarter of 1942 the rate of merchantman sinkings per U-boat in service per month fell below 0.5, and in January 1943, when the total number of U-boats in service exceeded 200 for the first time, the rate was 0.17. In simple terms, and noting that exceptionally severe weather conditions drastically limited U-boat successes in January 1943, the Germans needed 24 submarines in service in order to sink four merchantmen, and they would lose one submarine in the process.

Allied success in reducing losses among independently sailing merchantmen by extensive employment of convoys and the reduction of independent sailings was, however, only one part of the process whereby the U-boat effort was first curbed and then broken. No less significant was a strengthening of convoy defenses in terms of numbers of escorts allocated to individual formations, the increasing Allied ability to use set formations rather than collections of individual escorts, increasing air support, and an Allied operational superiority that exerted itself to ever greater effect during and after spring 1943.[8] The number of escorts afforded per convoy reached its wartime peak in April 1943, and with frigates and escort destroyers released from Torch entering the fray in considerable numbers for the first time after spring 1943 the advantage lay with the defense. New and much improved escorts, radar, radio locating equipment, improved sonar, new integrated weapons systems, and short-wave radio provided the basis of the estimate that, from a base of 100 in September 1939, whereas the effectiveness of the ocean-going U-boat had risen to about 125 by spring 1943, that of the escort had risen to about 400. The imbalance did not begin to be corrected until the use of the snorkel became widespread; that development conferred on the submarine some protection against detection and destruction but did not greatly improve offensive capability. The high-speed electro-boats, long delayed in development, entered service in the war's last months but in too small numbers to reverse earlier defeats. In terms of number and types of boat and sinkings of merchantmen, the U-boat arm, committed as it was to a stern chase of an enemy endowed with massive strength in depth, was always two years behind requirement.

* * *

The extent of the *Kriegsmarine*'s failure can be gauged by reference to the statistics of March 1943. In this month Allied and neutral losses totaled 120 merchantmen, and of this total 90 were sunk in, or after having straggled from, convoy. U-boats accounted for 72 of the 77 sunk while under escort—the highest number of convoyed merchantmen ever sunk by German submarines in a single month. U-boats sank 30 or more ships in convoy in one calendar month only six times during the war, and the seriousness of the losses for the Allies in March 1943 lay in the fact that the losses came at a time of unprecedented numbers of escorts. But in terms of "tonnage warfare" the Germans were already six weeks behind their 1943 schedule in March and this was the month when U.S. shipyards reached the peak of wartime production with the launching of 140 Liberty ships. March 1943 closed a quarter when for the first time since the outbreak of war new construction made good the losses inflicted by the U-boats. It was not until the third quarter of 1943 that new construction made good all losses incurred since September 1939, but the point was obvious. The U-boats needed to have quintupled their March 1943 sinkings of merchantmen in convoy in order to compensate for the decline in the number of sinkings of merchantmen sailing independently, if they were to offset new construction, and still reduce Allied shipping by 750,000 tons per month.[9]

Other factors were at work in ensuring the Allied victory in the Battle of the Atlantic in 1943, but lest this chapter become a summary of these factors, the basic point bears repetition: that the victory that was won was but a means, that it provided victorious sea power with the ability to take the war to the enemy at a time, in a place, and on a scale of its own choosing. A major continental commitment could not have been undertaken until the German challenge at sea had been broken. Command of the sea and the breaking of the U-boat threat enabled Britain to survive, and for the British high command at the time this was far more important than the military advantage thus conferred. This is seldom acknowledged, but critically it provides damning evidence against the 1943 thesis. Throughout the war the state of imports and reserves was a source of constant anxiety to the British high command. By the beginning of 1944 Britain, which had needed 60,000,000 tons of imports (plus oil) in 1938 to live and trade, was being sustained on 27,000,000 tons of imports a year, but on the basis of projected shipping resources would not be able to import more than 24,000,000 tons in 1944 and 1945. With some eight or nine weeks of reserves in hand, on import deficits of 3,000,000 tons in one year Britain could survive 1944 but not until the harvest of 1945.

Given such considerations, it is difficult to see how there could have been an invasion of northwest Europe in 1943. The slenderness of British administrative margins in 1944 was despite the curbing of the U-boat menace and shipping being available on an unprecedented scale. As it was, the danger explicit to British national survival by a continental commitment in 1942 or 1943 can be understood by reference to Jupiter, the 1942 plan for an invasion of Norway, and to Torch. The staff calculations that emerged in the course of the Jupiter planning indicated that it could be attempted only if there was a slowing and lengthening of the convoy cycle and the loss of 500,000 tons of imports—what would have been about 11% or 12% of Britain's reserve stocks in early 1944 but a larger percentage in 1942—was accepted. Torch, despite being in part supported directly from the United States, reduced the Royal Navy to one months' oil reserves, partly because of the losses sustained in the North Atlantic as a result of stripping convoys of escorts in order to provide for Torch. Over 1,000 ships with over 11,000,000 tons of supplies and equipment sailed from British home waters to the ports of French North Africa. To have undertaken an invasion of northwest Europe in 1942 or 1943 would have involved both a massive reduction of the scale of escort protection afforded merchant shipping and a slowing and lengthening of the convoy cycle on which Britain was totally dependent. If such relatively small undertakings as Jupiter and Torch carried such implications for the British import position, it is somewhat difficult to resist the perverse conclusion that had an invasion of northwest Europe been attempted before 1944, the only country that would have been brought to surrender would have been Britain.

* * *

The second part of this reconsideration of the elements that contributed to the ability to conduct and ultimately the success of a landing in northwest Europe in 1944 was identified as air power—and here one must consider four separate dimensions of the air war. The first, obviously, was the contribution air power made to Allied success in the Battle of the Atlantic itself, and it is difficult to understate the importance of air power to the outcome of this struggle. If nothing else, the effect of air power in 1943 in terms of U-boat sinkings is a reminder that no service is capable of handling by itself the responsibilities that fall within its area of competence.

British and U.S. air power, in the form of the close support afforded by
land-based aircraft, maritime patrols, and continuous support provided
by aircraft from ships—primarily escort carriers—accounted for 319 of
the 799 U-boats destroyed in the course of the Second World War; mines
laid by aircraft and the strategic bomber offensive accounted for another
89.50 units. In addition, various estimates indicate that the Germans
would have completed between 60 and 80 U-boats, had it not been for
the Allied bombing campaign. In terms of the invasion of northwest
Europe and the Normandy campaign, the contribution of air power was
no less critical—never more obviously than in the slowing of the German
concentration against the Allied beachheads. On 6 June 1944 the *Wehrmacht* had nine divisions between the Seine and the Cotentin peninsula.
Despite the attention of Allied air power and the activities of the French
resistance, by 30 June the Germans were able to bring no fewer than 16
divisions into the battle zone. Though some formations such as the 77th
Light Infantry Division were able to come against the beachhead quickly
and in good order, most were slow to arrive and the worse for wear by
the time they reached the front because of the attention they received
during their advance to contact. On 7 June alone the Panzer Lehr Division lost 5 tanks, 84 half-tracks, prime movers and self-propelled guns,
40 fuel trailers, and 90 soft-skinned vehicles in its move from Le Mans to
Caen. *Kampfgruppe Heintz*, drawn from the 275th Infantry Division, took
eight days to cover 140 miles to get into the battle. The Second Panzer
Division, just north of the Seine, was obliged to make a 160-mile detour
because of destroyed bridges, did not arrive in Normandy until 13 June,
and then required another week to concentrate. The Second SS Panzer
Division, fresh from Oradour-sur-Glane on 10 June, arrived from Tou-
louse between 26 and 30 June, and the First SS Panzer Division was not
able to reach Normandy from Brussels until 29 June. The slowness of
these forces' arrival in the battle zone and the harassment to which they
were subjected en route had two obvious effects. Any hope of the *Wehrmacht's* defeating the Allies at the water's edge or immediately inland
was destroyed; the second effect was scarcely less serious for the *Wehrmacht* because as its formations came into Normandy, the many gaps
along the front forced it to commit its armor piecemeal and defensively.
Whereas Allied deployment was deliberate, that of the Germans was
forced upon them, with the result that the defense was obliged to conform to the enemy's initiative and to fight the wrong type of battle. The
contribution made by air power was critical, both in the conduct of this
battle but also in denying the *Wehrmacht* the option of conducting a
mobile battle inland. Allied air superiority denied the German military
the ability to move *en masse* and in daylight, as the events of 29 and 30
June around Cheux demonstrated. On these days heavy bomber formations were committed to the destruction of the main German armored

counterattack of the Normandy campaign, and with its being broken, the last German hope of success of containing or eliminating the Allied beachhead disappeared.

The protection of ground and naval forces from significant attack from the air, the wrecking of German lines of communication into Normandy before the landing, and the harassment of enemy formations either making their way forward or on the battlefield were the main contributions made by air power to Allied success in northwest Europe in 1944. Without these contributions, whatever success the Allies commanded would have been much more dearly bought, and, indeed, it is doubtful if without command of the skies the invasion of France could have been attempted. This was all very different from the bailiwick of air power in 1918, though in terms of definition of missions, roles, doctrine, organization, and tactics air power had not really changed very much in the intervening years. Certainly air forces had established themselves as equal in importance to the other two services, even if recognition and status was denied in many countries. But the real point about air power and northwest Europe in 1944 lies in the line of analysis that suggests that "long-range fire and air strikes against reserves (have been) only one part of an overall scheme of combat operations in the past," the argument being that in the 1991 campaign these "were the primary means of achieving the war's aims . . . the trend away from close combat is clear."[10] It is not too much to argue that in the Normandy campaign air power demonstrated an ability that can be recognized in any consideration of the 1991 campaign, albeit at shorter range and to less effect than was the case in 1991. Moreover, in 1944 air power shared with artillery the responsibility and credit for the breaking of German offensive and defensive power: fire was not the monopoly of air power, and effective fire most certainly was not the preserve of air forces. But the wider point is clear. At the battle of the Somme in 1916 losses between the offense and defense were roughly equal, but at Normandy in 1944 the German defense incurred twice the losses of the Allies: the critical point was that the imbalance of losses reflected Allied material preponderance and ability to strike from the air.

But if air power was critical in the victories that were won on the ground and in the overall balance of losses saved lives, air power was to be dependent upon the ground forces in one area of operations. The clearing of France and most of Belgium had the effect of turning part of the German air defense system, and it brought to continental bases fighters and strike aircraft that could support the heavy bomber offensive against the German homeland. This offensive, after the distraction of the Normandy commitment throughout the summer, was resumed in full earnestness after September, and its scale is illustrated by the fact that between 1 January and 26 April 1945 the Eighth U.S. Air Force flew

55 thousand-bomber raids. Between 19 February and 4 March 1945 it flew nothing other than thousand-bomber raids, while RAF Bomber Command, with operations on 81 days and 100 nights, on average put 495 heavy bombers into the air in any 24-hour period.

The obvious question, which provoked bitter argument in the two decades after the end of the war, was what the strategic bombing offensive achieved. Extreme positions can be discounted, but in seeking to attempt to answer this question one is confronted by one very awkward fact of life. It is well known that German war production reached its peak in August–September 1944. What is less well known is that the peak of German distribution of war material was in October 1943. Given the fact that it was in that same month that U.S. heavy bombers met defeat over Schweinfurt and RAF Bomber Command had registered precious little real damage by that time, it is clear that the German distribution system was in decline even before the strategic bombing campaign began to inflict telling, cumulative damage on the German industrial, transportation, and social infrastructures. Much the same was true of the campaign against the Japanese home islands. The U.S. strategic bombing campaign began in June 1944 from airfields in southern China, but it was not until November 1944 that it started on any scale, and before March 1945 it was singularly ineffective. It was only after March 1945, when B-29 Superfortresses began to become available in significant numbers and the Americans adopted low-level area bombing, that this effort began to register telling results. Yet for the most part this effort was directed against redundant, surplus industrial capacity, because factories were already in end-run production.

Moreover, the one alternative to an offensive designed to destroy the enemy's capacity to make war—the enemy's willingness to make war—also obstinately fails to provide evidence of the effectiveness of the strategic bombing offensive. Neither Germany nor Japan showed any inclination to consider ending the war because of bombing, and in neither country was there any real sign of a collapse of civilian morale as a result of the Allied air offensive, though perhaps the wonder of this was not that it did not occur but that certain people had ever considered it possible in the first place. The totality of war, the knowledge that the issue at stake was national survival, and the conformity imposed upon German and Japanese societies on account of their political systems precluded the fragmentation of morale.

In an obvious sense, therefore, it is possible to portray the effect of the strategic bombing campaigns primarily in negative terms. The strategic bombing offensive clearly prevented German war production being greater than what it was: German industry functioned at about 10–12% below theoretical production potential because of Allied bombing. The strategic bombing offensive also imposed additional costs on production, and most definitely it warped the pattern of German war production by forcing concentration upon fighters at the expense of strike aircraft, and upon antiaircraft guns and communications equipment for air defense at the expense of vehicles, guns, and radios for field formations. But in another negative aspect the contribution of the strategic bomber offensive to Allied victory was immense, if impossible to quantify. The effect of this offensive in stripping fronts of fighter defense and ensuring that Allied armies operated under conditions of overwhelming air supremacy is widely acknowledged, but how long the war would have lasted and what cost would have been exacted had there not been a bombing campaign that by 1945 had reduced Germany to a transportation wilderness is debatable. What is remarkable about the defeat of Germany is how quickly it was achieved once the initiative had been wrested from its grasp. In August 1943 the Western Allies had yet to set foot on the continental mainland and German forces were still in the eastern Ukraine. In less than 21 months Germany had been destroyed. One wonders how long this process would have taken if the Allies not had to hand air power that razed the German communications system.

No consideration of strategic bombing in the Second World War can ignore the obvious finale: the use of atomic weapons against Hiroshima and Nagasaki. T. S. Eliot was correct: the world ended with a whimper, or thousands of whimpers, as unknown numbers died of cancer, leukemia, or as a result of radiation sickness. The use of atomic weapons against Japan remains a controversial matter—one that still can command intense passion, as the 1995 Smithsonian controversy demonstrated. It is an issue that lends itself to simplification and certainty, with all the intolerance thereby implied. Understandably and rightly, Allied troops who were to have mounted the invasion of the Japanese home islands entertain no doubts about the use of atomic weapons against Japan. But these people apart, the attacks on Hiroshima and Nagasaki in August 1945 prompt two observations and two questions. The first observation is simple. The use of atomic weapons undoubtedly sits uneasily alongside American claims upon morality as the basis of policy. Indeed, the strategic bombing offensives against Germany and Japan stained the morality of Anglo–American claims. But morality exists only in choice, and certainly in the period between June 1940 and late 1944 there was no choice, and hence there could be no immorality in the bombing campaigns directed against Germany and Japan. One does not need to subscribe to the Cromwellian dictum—necessity knows no law—to recognize that with no other means to take the war to the Axis powers, the strategic air offensives were wholly justified.

The Allies had no capacity and certainly no moral right to deny themselves the only means whereby they might force the enemy to conform to their will. If nothing else, to have done so would have represented a base betrayal of all those who lived under Axis occupation. But by 1945, when other means of taking the war to the enemy existed, the strategic bombing offensives become more difficult to justify other than under the terms of the obvious institutional escape clause. The means had been developed and could not remain unused, given the costs and the losses that had been sustained in the process, but that hardly represents just cause. Thus if the attack on Hamburg in July–August 1943 presents no moral qualms, the attacks of 1945—on Dresden in February, Dortmund and Tokyo in March, and some 60 Japanese cities thereafter—cannot be divorced from basic questions of morality.

The real point, and the first question, underlying the attacks upon Hiroshima and Nagasaki is one that seems to have been seldom considered. The attacks were presented at the time as the best means of bringing the Far East war to an end, quickly and without the necessity of an invasion of the Japanese home islands. The estimated casualty figures that were deployed to support this proposition were mendacious; no less clearly, the decision to use the bomb in July 1945 was based in large measure on possession: the bomb was not built not to be used. Moreover, as certain individuals involved in the policy discussions at the time argued, the decision to use atomic weapons against Japan was underpinned by calculations of the political and diplomatic advantages that were likely to be gathered as a result of the demonstration of this newly acquired power, specifically in dealing with the Soviet Union. But the question that the use of atomic weapons should provoke is whether the terms that were exacted from Japan in August 1945 could have been secured the previous month, and without the use of atomic weapons. Stripping away the emotionalism of the issue, the real question is whether the Japanese high command could have been induced to surrender in July 1945 on the basis of unambiguous undertakings given with regard to the person of the Emperor and to the imperial institution.

The argument would seem to be even-handed. The obvious rejoinder would seem to be that it was not the use of the atom bomb that brought the Japanese to surrender. Two bombs had to be used, and there was also the small matter of the Soviet entry into the war, but even this combination was not enough to bring the Japanese high command to the decision to surrender—it still needed the Emperor's personal decision to end the war. Yet weighty though this consideration is, the point is that those within the Japanese high command who opposed seeking to put an end to the war based their opposition on the defense of the imperial institution. In this context, the fact that Allied intentions toward the Emperor and the Imperial institution remained unclear was critically important. It may very well be that there were certain members of the Supreme War Council who could not have been brought to accept surrender other than by Imperial command, but the point would seem to be that Allied intentions toward the Emperor and the Imperial institution were never made clear to the Japanese. Given Allied intentions not to arraign the Emperor and not to destroy the throne, it is hard to understand the logic of the decision to use atomic weapons against Japanese cities. At very worst, the Americans might have been well advised to have defined what were and were not their intentions at the time of the Potsdam Declaration: a lack of response on the part of the Japanese would have clarified issues beyond all reasonable doubt. The counter to this argument, however, is that a statement of American intention might well have been taken as a sign that the Americans did not have the will to mount an offensive against the home islands. As it is, the use of atomic weapons against Japan in August 1945 will never be freed from a moral dimension and, if not censure, then considerable reservations, thus:

It is my opinion that the use of this barbarous weapon at Hiroshima and Nagasaki was of no material assistance in our war against Japan. The Japanese were already defeated and ready to surrender. . . . My own feeling was that in being the first to use it, we had adopted an ethical standard common to the barbarians of the Dark Ages. I was not taught to make war in that fashion, and wars cannot be won by destroying women and children.

When informed of the decision to use atomic weapons,

I had been conscious of a feeling of depression, and so I voiced . . . my grave misgivings, first on the basis of my belief that Japan was already defeated and that dropping the bomb was completely unnecessary, and . . . because I thought that our country should avoid shocking world opinion by the use of a weapon whose employment was, I thought, no longer mandatory as a measure to save American lives. It was my belief that Japan was, at that very moment, seeking some way to surrender with a minimum loss of "face."[11]

Such observations, with their confrontation of the moral issue—the first by Fleet Admiral William D. Leahy, chief of staff to Presidents Roosevelt and Truman, the second by Eisenhower—cannot be lightly discounted.

The second question that arises from the use of atomic weapons is whether an invasion of the home islands would have been necessary and, if necessary, what the costs would have been. The question is provoked by reference to Normandy. By the end of June the Allies had landed 929,000 men in the beachhead and had incurred a total of 61,732 casualties, 8,469 of them fatalities; in his memoirs Montgomery gives Allied casualties between 6 June and 19 August as 102,000 Americans and 68,000 British and Canadians. Between D-Day and the Liberation of Paris the Allies suffered some 227,000 dead, wounded, and missing, airmen included. A campaign on the Japanese home islands would have been different from the campaign in northwest Europe in one vital respect: home soil would have been at stake from the outset, and an Allied advance necessarily would have been into major built-up areas. But figures of between 500,000 and 1,000,000 casualties in an invasion of Japan that were paraded at the time as justification for the use of atomic weapons against Japan would seem to rest uncomfortably alongside three facts: the casualty estimates that were made by theater commands at the time were very different from these totals; it is difficult to see how losses could have exceeded the number involved in Operation Downfall; and it is hard to see how twice the number of casualties sustained in Normandy could have been incurred at the hands of an enemy much weaker in terms of armor, organization, and preparedness than German forces in Normandy.

The state of the Imperial Japanese Army (the *Rikugun*) in the home islands in summer 1945 bordered on the wretched. There were a number of good divisions, but the bulk of the classes of 1944 and 1945 were untrained, and most of the formations in the home islands were hopelessly underequipped in terms of communications, transport, and armor. Moreover, though the Japanese military had deduced the beaches where Allied landings had to take place both on Kyushu and Honshu, there were not sufficient good formations to cover them, and, in any event, the *Rikugun* faced an impossible dilemma in ordering a deployment. Divisions committed forward would be subjected to overwhelming fire and those held back would never be allowed to get into the battle because of American air supremacy and superior mobility. In addition, far from preparing for a people's war with the bulk of the population tasked to offer resistance, the *Rikugun* resisted demands for such a desperate expediency and actively tried to evacuate civilians from those areas where it anticipated that landings would take place. To have established themselves in southern Kyushu and to have conducted a campaign across the Kondo Plain and entered Tokyo would not have been lightly achieved, but one wonders at estimates that suggest that the powers of resistance of the *Rikugun* would have been so much greater than that of the *Wehrmacht* in Normandy. That there would have been slaughter in plenty cannot be doubted, but one wonders just how little of it would have been at Allied expense.

Yet there is another paradox beyond this comparison between what happened in Normandy and what never happened on the Kondo Plain—or, rather, its reversal: what did not happen in northwest Europe and what did happen to Japan. It is not idle speculation to consider what would have been the fate of Germany had the invasion of northwest Europe on that day miscarried. There is an off-the-shelf answer—that the Americans would have attempted another invasion. It is a rather unconvincing assertion. Leaving aside all questions of Allied morale after a defeat in Normandy, it is difficult to see how a failure in June 1944 could have been reversed later that same year, and, as noted elsewhere, it is equally difficult to see how the great Soviet offensives of that year and the Oder–Vistula attack of January 1945, would have been much affected by an Anglo–American debacle in Normandy. It is difficult to see, therefore, how the European war would not have ended in spring 1945 and how a second invasion might have been accomplished if Neptune had failed, unless the abandonment of the whole of the western theater in late 1944 by the *Wehrmacht* in order to shore up the Eastern Front had allowed a Roundup operation.

But if the ending of the European war did determine certain attitudes critical of events in the final phase of the Pacific war, and if the difficulties that immediately arose between the Western Allies and the Soviet Union with the defeat of Germany dictated an American desire to exclude the latter from the final stages of the Japanese war, there is another scenario that demands consideration. On 6 June 1944, of all days, U.S. heavy bomber strength in Britain reached 2,000, and one suspects that with two months of summer to assist the Allied cause and after defeat in Normandy the Americans not too worried about the distinction between precision and area bombing, Germany would have been seared from one end to the other as a series of Dresdens were inflicted upon it. And at the end, perhaps in the spring or summer of 1945, and if ready in time and if German resistance had proved more effective and protracted and the Soviets had still to take Berlin? If Hiroshima and Nagasaki saved Japan from an even worse fate had the home islands been invaded, perhaps the same—or is it the reverse?—can be said about Germany and its defeat in Normandy. Defeat in the west in 1944 saved it from a greater ruination from the air and from the east than was incurred.

Yet even this argument pales besides another—the second observation made possible by the fact of the atomic attacks. The clouds that rose over Hiroshima and Nagasaki wiped out eight years of war and responsibility: the Emperor's speech to his people on 15 August 1945 set out the basic theme that has become conventional wisdom, the national let-out, that Japan was the victim in the war. The attacks on Hiroshima and Nagasaki in a sense wiped the slate clean. The war that Japan waged in China was both brutal and appalling—as bad as anything that the Germans did in Poland and the Soviet Union. The Japanese army's capture of any major city, not just Nanking, was all but invariably accompanied by nightmarish scenes of mass butchery and rape; a pattern of atrocities was inflicted throughout the Yangtze valley through the systematic destruction of life and property long before "loot all, burn all, kill all" became standard *Rikugun* operational procedure in its conduct of counterinsurgency operations. For China the human cost of the war has been calculated at about 13,000,000, but given the fact that the fighting of 1937–38 created some 20,000,000 refugees in the Yangtze valley alone and that no one knows how many succumbed to malnutrition and exposure or were drowned when the dikes were opened in June 1938, one is left to ponder the accuracy of such an estimate. The routine murders, the use of biological weapons against civilian centers, the deliberate fostering of the drugs trade, the massive expropriation of property, and the deliberate manipulation of exchange rates in order to secure materials and goods at a fraction of their real value were the trademarks of the Japanese system of occupation that was to last until 1945.

The appalling nature of Japanese rule in east and southeast Asia has been passed over in silence by most Japanese accounts of the war; the Japanese official history's treatment of the Rape of Nanking drew protest from China because, according to it, it apparently never took place, any more than that some 120,000 Chinese were murdered at Singapore in the three months after the fall of the British base in February 1942. It is a matter of some credit, therefore, that certain honorable individuals—such as the historian Saburo Ienaga and Hiroshi Harada, the general director of the Peace Museum in Hiroshima—should have attempted to relate these matters to their compatriots, thereby to place what happened to Japan in 1945 into some sort of historical context. Their fate was to have been roundly abused by ultranationalists and right-wing groups intent on foisting their very selective interpretation of events upon their countrymen—witness the protests that attended the admission in May 1996 of the existence of "comfort women" in school textbooks. For the Japanese establishment, the only cause for apology about the conduct of the war was defeat, not the treatment Japan afforded its fellow Asians, which alone provides the context of what happened to Japan in the last six months of the war as its enemies gathered around it. The apology provided in 1993 by Morihiro Hosokawa, the first non-Liberal-party prime minister in more than 40 years, is not to be gainsaid, but the manner in which the war ended enabled Japan to avoid having to face the reality of its actions. As the Chinese saying has it, Japan has a long history and a short memory.

* * *

Examination of the ending of the Pacific war and the comparison between what happened and what might have happened in both Neptune and Downfall could lead to an examination of two quite separate issues—the first, Operation Market Garden, being another of the issues that had divided British and American historical perspectives. In reality, there should be no dispute, because any impartial and objective examination of this operation should lead to only one conclusion. If there was to have been an attempt to force the Rhine on a narrow front in September 1944, then it should have been made not by the British Second Army along the Eindhoven–Nijmegen–Arnhem axis but by the U.S. First Army in the direction of the Ruhr and across a road system considerably superior to the one on the line of the proposed British advance. But leaving aside this fact, the balance of argument would seem to suggest that the narrow-front argument was inherently flawed. By 1 October the there were 54 Allied divisions in northwest Europe, and if this number was adequate to deal with the 33 battleworthy German divisions in the line, the fact remains that in late September–early October 1944 the ability of Allied armies, with lines of communication that reached back to the beaches of Normandy and the ports of southern France, to have maintained 10 or so divisions beyond the Rhine was problematical. To have attempted an advance on Berlin, against an enemy with a nominal total of 71 divisions in the line by mid-October and 107 in the west by December, was nonsensical. For the Allied armies, the number of divisions available was never more than marginal to requirements until the last weeks of the war.

So much adverse attention has been paid to how long the Allies took to break out of the Normandy beachhead that it would be very easy to make the connection that the time that was required to break out cost the Allies the chance to end the war in 1944. The immediate answer to such a charge is that the postponement of Neptune from May to June in order to provide more amphibious shipping was probably more important, and that the achievement of the Allies, both in Normandy and in the western theater as a whole, in summer 1944 was rather remarkable. In 1944 Anglo–American forces established themselves on a 50-mile beachhead in Normandy by amphibious assault and during the next two months stocked that beachhead. At the same time they met and defeated an enemy that in numbers of divisions was always superior and on terrain that favored the defense and which the defense had held for four years. Thereafter they liberated most of France and Belgium and the southern Netherlands. In so doing they moved across a wrecked transportation system: 97% of the French rail system had been destroyed by September 1944. One gets the impression from some accounts of the 1944 campaign that the Allied performance was less than auspicious, and undoubtedly there were many failings, but one instinctively returns to one basic conclusion: that to assume on the premise of a June landing that victory could have been won that same year would seem to have little basis in terms of realities of time, distance, seasons, logistics, and numbers.

These realities underpin what should be the basic consideration about the other war, half a world away. The war in the Far East is unusual in the sense that states so mismatched as the United States and Japan normally manage their relationship accordingly and without recourse to war. No less obviously, the war that Japan initiated in December 1941 is unusual in that it was begun by a state that did not believe that it could win the war that it started. But it was also unusual in the sense that Japan chose to attack the only power that had the beating of it, and the United States defeated the only country in the Far East that it could defeat. One could also note that few wars better illustrate two truths, that "the final decision of a whole war is not always to be regarded as absolute. The conquered state often sees in it only a passing evil, which may be repaired in after times by means of political combinations,"[12] and that Allies are not necessarily friends.

Allies are not necessarily friends and never more obviously with the approach of victory: moreover, the power to determine and influence events may diminish with the reality of military victory. The Japanese war was in effect two wars, and the war on the Asian mainland was as important as the war in the Pacific, not in terms of the war's outcome, but in the shaping of subsequent events—and to ends very different from those that the United States would have wished.

* * *

The Second World War's significance in terms of the conduct of war is elusive and little understood. There is one obvious starting line for any consideration of this conflict and its place in the evolution of warfare, and that is *Blitzkrieg*. Herein one begins with perceived wisdom and seldom perceived problems. *Blitzkrieg* is invariably seen in terms of strategic application. Its champions—de Gaulle, Fuller, Guderian, Liddell Hart—are studied at military academies and colleges under the label "strategic thought," and the subject itself is presented as the attempt to overcome the tactical deadlock of the First World War. But *Blitzkrieg*—apparently not a term used by the German military—certainly never was a strategic concept, and if it was tactical, then it did not overcome strategic deadlock. *Blitzkrieg* might have been developed as a means of forestalling the possibility of Germany's being trapped in protracted war of attrition, but the simple fact of the matter is that the First World War lasted for 51 months, and in its European context the Second World War lasted for 68. If *Blitzkrieg* was the means of avoiding protracted wars of attrition, then it proved remarkably ineffective, indeed an obvious failure, and what is no less remarkable is the uncritical and highly selective acceptance of so many aspects of German military performance in this conflict in postwar Western historiography, but for a very obvious reason. Too many of the individuals concerned with events had too much invested in the propagation of myths for truth to have a chance. Those defeated in 1939–41 could stress qualities of conscious inferiority and helplessness induced by *Blitzkrieg* as mitigating factors in their defeat. German generals could stress its qualities in order to discredit Hitler's alleged lack of professional military judgment and thereby provide themselves with an alibi for defeats, and this was important as the cold war took shape. The need to rehabilitate the West German military and the demeaning of the Soviet military achievement in the Second World War were critically important as the confrontation between the United States and Soviet Union assumed substance.

The *Schlacht ohne Morgen* was an attempt to avoid protracted warfare, to restore tactical mobility to the battlefield, and its failure, when it became fact, was tactical, though it was realized mainly in other directions. Its ultimate failure reflected Germany's wider failure in the Second World War, and the latter cannot be divorced from Hitler's personality and decisions. But the German failure in the Second World War, in both wars for that matter, stemmed from a failure to understand the distinction between power and force, to realize the limitations of military force within the context of national power, to appreciate the limitations of force within the context of the international community, and to grasp the limitations of German national power. For states as different as Imperial Germany and Hitler's Germany to make the same basic errors suggests that failure cannot be explained away on the basis of personalities.

But this line of argument does not get very far and most certainly does not represent anything new—though the logical conclusion of this argument may be new and is perhaps startling: that Germany's failings in two world wars stemmed from a failure to understand the nature of war and, critically, to understand the differences between *war* and *a war*, and what distinguishes a war, a campaign, and a battle from one another. The real point of significance lies in the recognition of the lines of continuity that linked *Blitzkrieg* to the past. For all the acclaim, *Blitzkrieg* did not represent anything that was really new. It was politically inspired in that it reflected Hitler's ideas that stressed aggression, speed of decision, and destruction as the objectives of military operations. But *Blitzkrieg* was merely the application of an advanced technology to tactics of infiltration, penetration, and encirclement that had been developed in the form of *Der Angriff im Stellungskrieg* in 1918. In the final analysis *Blitzkrieg*, which had no theoretical basis and which was not committed to a field manual between 1938 and 1941, was the application of mobile fire power against a single point and thereafter, to borrow a phrase, "an avalanche of actions in which success sorted out the details"[13] during the attempt to move through the "spaces and gaps" in the enemy front in order to encircle and annihilate the mass of the enemy in the *Kesselschlacht*.

But in the final analysis, both the 1918 concept and *Blitzkrieg* were part of the process to which the First World War had seemed to be the climax—the inexorable growth of armies. The enlargement of mass was the product of both the changes of the late nineteenth century that enabled mass to be expanded and the deliberate search after 1871 for enlargement as the means of ensuring victory. The great irony about *Blitzkrieg* is that it seemed to offer the means of avoiding a precipitous, ruinous expansion of mass—indeed, that was the rationale behind de Gaulle's writing in the 1930s—yet in fact it did not. Armies were not smaller in the Second World War than in the previous conflict because of the mechanization of warfare. If anything, the reverse was the case: Britain, Germany, the Soviet Union, and the United States between them mobilized more men than were mobilized in the whole of the First World War by all the warring nations.

Appearances are deceptive, and none more relevantly than the British army. On a divisional count its size in the Second World War simply does not compare with its size between 1916 and 1918. In March 1945 the British army had only 17 divisions in its European order of battle, which included northwest Europe, Italy, and Greece; provision for the Indian army, support for dominion formations, and the proliferation of independent formations outside divisions meant that it had the equivalent of perhaps 30 or 32 divisions at the end of the European war. In the course of the First World War, the British army raised some 70 divisions—India raised 13 and the white dominions another 12—and at peak strength in November 1918 held 64 divisions on the Western Front, a total that is inclusive of Dominion formations. Given the vast expansion of supporting arms and services in order to maintain the armored–mechanized mass and the increased size of the divisional share of corps and army troops during the Second World War, the real numbers for the British army in two world wars are about the same. The overall number of men that were required to raise some sixty divisions in 1918 was about the same as that required to raise some 30 divisions in 1945.

The experience of the Second World War thus conforms to the basic pattern established in the course of the nineteenth century and which became synonymous with the First World War—namely, the growth of armies as part of a process whereby size was seen as the answer to military problems. In the course of the First World War this trend very literally drove the warring states of Europe into the ground, and in more ways than one: the search for victory through the *Vernichtungsschlacht* [annihilation battle] was ruinous for all concerned. But in very large measure this search for victory through the decisive battle of destruction and the employment of enlarged mass survived the First World War, and certainly in the case of Germany and the Western democracies in the Second World War produced armies that were raised and organized— with due allowance for the effect of mechanization—to fight this same type of battle and by the same means as in the previous conflict. In this very obvious sense, the Second World War was a nineteenth-century war.

The relevance of *Blitzkrieg* and the place that it occupies in the evolution of war, therefore, are much misunderstood. It was the product of the marriage of an aggressive, nihilistic ideology and a rearrangement of organization and tactics made possible by twin developments in the fields of mechanization and communications: it was not a strategic creature, and it did not herald a revolution in military affairs. German success in the 1939–42 period is usually associated with *Blitzkrieg*, the basic line of argument being that in this period the *Wehrmacht*'s superiority lay in its better understanding of the balance between the offense and defense than its enemies, its superior tactical ability, and the quality of its leadership and morale. Certainly some of this bears repeating, but German success in this period was as much if not more the result of political as military factors. Because of Hitler's ability to divide potential opponents, between 1939 and 1942 Germany fought a series of campaigns rather than a war—campaigns that were separated from one another by time and distance and were directed against individual states massively inferior to Germany in terms of population, industry, military power, and geography. Poland (1939) and Yugoslavia (1941) were all but surrounded and in terms of strategic geography beaten before they were attacked by a vastly superior enemy that held the initiative. In 1940 disparity of strength and the advantage conferred by initial choice in terms of the decision to attack provided the basis of German success in Norway, and in the attack in western Europe of that year the critical advantages that the *Wehrmacht* commanded was single-nation organization, as compared to disparate enemies with no common command organization, plan, and doctrine and the fact that France was denied allies of the scale of 1918. Certainly in 1940 in the case of France specifically military factors relating to the advantages of *Blitzkrieg* compared to other forms of tactical organization and doctrine—in this case the Methodical Battle—were at work. One must note also the critical advantages of air superiority and combat experience that the *Wehrmacht* enjoyed and the lack of any effective infantry antitank weapon that left the bulk of the French army hopelessly placed to resist the armored *Schwerpunkt*. But, critically, one would also recognize that in terms of morale and initiative the *Wehrmacht* was in a class of its own in these years.

The result was that the *Wehrmacht* in this period held overwhelming advantages over successive enemies that enabled it to conquer with little difficulty; it is certainly possible to assert that in all the campaigns between September 1939 and May 1941 Germany's enemies were defeated before the first shots of their respective campaigns were fired. But

Blitzkrieg could not square a circle. Hitler undoubtedly saw it as a means of avoiding protracted war, and for a time it was because of the very specific circumstances of the campaigns that were fought. But in the long term it could not do so, in large measure because Hitler believed in permanent war, struggle as a permanent condition of existence, and the system of organization of *Blitzkrieg*, indeed Germany itself, could not sustain such a requirement. Herein one encounters a basic problem of interpretation of why this was so.

There would seem to be three main lines of explanation—two that represent conventional wisdom and a third that has been gaining ground over the last two decades but which is very much the product of the 1990s. The first, and the obvious one, of these is the defects of Hitler's understanding of war and his conduct, or misconduct, of war. One could summarize all the points contained herein with the statement that Hitler broke the one and only principle of war: never get involved in a pissing match with a skunk, and, most certainly, not with two skunks at the same time. The Soviet Union and the United States might take offense at being thus described, but in terms of size, demographic and industrial resources, and the ability to mobilize this was exactly what they were in terms of mid-twentieth-century warfare. Hitler never understood these powers, and in 1941 by deliberate choice escalated the war in which Germany was engaged to an intensity that it could not sustain by taking war to two powers that were individually at least the equal of Germany. Perhaps that is to overstate the situation—perhaps the defeat of the Soviet Union was within the realms of possibility in 1941, or would have been had it not been Hitler's intention to destroy it. But that line of reasoning leads only into another circular argument. Suffice to note that quite obviously German failure in the Second World War and Hitler's direction of the national war effort cannot be separated.

The second line of explanation is quite obviously linked to and really is part of the first, but at a different level. Where the first is concerned with perceptions, and really with Hitler's view of will as the determinant of war, this second involves means and organization. It is a line of explanation and argument that develops the theme of the consequences of the decision to add the Soviet Union and the United States to Germany's list of enemies, and it is one that concentrates upon indices of production, an approach that threatens death by statistics and most certainly is exhausting long before it is exhaustive. Reference has already been made to one aspect of this argument: the Battle of the Atlantic and the German position in March 1943 are indicative of a wider pattern that embraced ground and air forces. This line of argument develops the theme that Germany's defeat was ensured once it entered a war of attrition that it could not win (just one table of statistics can make the point—see Table 3.2).

Lest the point be missed, between 1941 and 1945 U.S. factories produced over a million tons of airframe. At peak, in March 1944, they were turning out one aircraft every 294 seconds. Few statistics of the Second World War better make the twin points of difference between the two sides in terms of depth of resources and capabilities than these.[14]

But this line of argument is by definition materialist and determinist, and even if it is seldom expressed in such terms, it belongs to the *Vernichtungsschlacht* school: it forms part of the enlargement of fighting mass thesis that returns to late nineteenth-century developments and traces the direct link between those developments and this war.

The third line of argument is intimately related to this thesis—indeed, it is a development of and from it—namely, that the whole of *Blitzkrieg* concept was part of the *Vernichtungsschlacht* development and as such conformed to the perversion of the art of war that took place in the nineteenth and continued into the twentieth century, because it focused attention upon the wrong levels of war: upon the strategic and the tactical, rather than where it really mattered, which was the operational.

One cannot deny that Germany fought the wrong type of war between 1939 and 1945, and this became increasingly obvious in its latter stages, but it is quite another matter whether this can justify the portrayal of the nineteenth century in terms of "the mesmerization of military thinking with the archaic misconceptions of the Napoleonic experience [and] the long-standing failure to apply a systemic approach to the field of operational conduct throughout the nineteenth century and the first quarter of the twentieth led to the suppression of creative military thinking by a mechanistic mentality of attrition."[15] Certainly there is something in the question of why deployment and maneuver on the field of battle came to be dominated by the linear, and there is no doubting that, with one exception, the operational was the neglected area of military study, both in the nineteenth century and in the first half of the twentieth, not least because for the most part it was undiscovered. Moreover, one cannot be unaware of the power of such a thesis in that it accords with what has happened in Western military thinking over the last quarter of a century. For Western military establishments, the operational level of war was discovered in the 1970s, incorporated in the field manuals in the 1980s, and, as part of Maneuver Warfare, provides all the answers to the problems of the 1990s and the new millennium.

One entertains a certain skepticism about this thesis on two grounds: one could add that because it is associated with Maneuver Warfare, there are three grounds for objection. This line of argument would seem to belong to the Martin van Creveld production line of historical studies. Whatever just so happens to be the subject of this book provides the key to understanding everything that you ever needed to know about warfare; but, incidentally, in two years' time there will be another book,

Table 3.2. Aircraft Industries: Comparative Production

	Allied Countries				Tripartite Pact			
	United States	Soviet Union	Britain	Total	Germany	Italy	Japan	Total
Population	141,940,000	170,400,000	47,600,000	359,940,000	79,200,000	43,430,000	72,750,000	195,380,000
Work force	52,800,000	70,000,000	22,900,000	145,700,000	36,200,000	21,000,000	34,100,000	91,300,000
Steel (1937)	28,800,000	18,000,000	10,500,000	57,300,000	23,300,000	2,300,000	5,800,000	31,400,000
Coal (1938)	354,500,000	132,900,000	230,700,000	718,100,000	186,200,000	1,900,000	53,700,000	241,100,000
Electricity	116,600,000	39,400,000	25,700,000	181,700,000	58,300,000	15,500,000	35,000,000	109,800,000
% share of world manufacture	32.2	18.5	9.2	59.9	10.7	2.7	3.5	16.9
Number of aircraft manufactured								
1939	5,856	10,382	7,940	24,178	8,295	1,800	4,467	14,562
1940	12,804	10,565	15,049	38,418	10,274	1,800	4,768	16,842
1941	26,277	15,735	20,094	62,106	11,776	2,400	5,088	19,264
1942	47,836	25,436	23,672	96,944	15,409	2,400	8,861	26,670
1943	85,898	34,900	26,264	147,062	24,807	1,600	16,693	43,100
1944	96,318	40,300	26,461	163,079	39,807	—	28,180	67,987
1945	49,761	20,900	12,070	82,731	7,540	—	11,066	18,606
Total	324,750	158,218	131,550	614,518	117,908	10,000	79,123	207,031

Number of aero-engines manufactured

1939	n/a	12,499	12,499	3,865	n/a	n/a	3,865
1940	15,513	24,074	39,587	15,510	n/a	n/a	15,510
1941	58,181	36,551	114,732	22,400	n/a	12,151	34,551
1942	138,089	53,916	230,005	37,000	n/a	16,999	53,999
1943	227,116	57,985	334,101	50,700	n/a	28,541	79,241
1944	256,912	56,931	364,843	54,600	—	46,526	101,126
1945	106,350	22,821	129,171	n/a	—	12,380	12,380
Total	802,161	264,777	1,225,938	184,015	n/a	116,597	300,612

Weight of airframe produced (in lb.)

1939	n/a	29,000,000	29,000,000	n/a	n/a	n/a	n/a
1940	n/a	59,000,000	59,000,000	n/a	n/a	n/a	n/a
1941	81,500,000	87,000,000	168,500,000	88,000,000	n/a	21,200,000	109,200,000
1942	274,900,000	134,000,000	408,900,000	114,000,000	n/a	36,500,000	150,500,000
1943	650,600,000	185,000,000	835,600,000	160,000,000	n/a	65,500,000	225,500,000
1944	951,600,000	208,000,000	1,159,600,000	199,000,000	—	111,000,000	310,000,000
1945	429,900,000	95,000,000	524,900,000	n/a	—	70,000,000	70,000,000
Total	2,388,500,000	797,000,000	3,185,500,000	561,000,000	n/a	304,200,000	865,200,000

Data taken from R. J. Overy, *The Air War, 1939–45* (New York: Stein & Day, 1980).
Coal and steel output is given in tons, electrical output in mrd Kwh.

which will provide a different explanation—one that again will explain everything that is needed to be known. War does not lend itself to single-causal explanation, and the operational thesis would seem, at least in part, to be reading the record backward. More importantly, one can question the thesis in terms of such an assumption that, notwithstanding the possession of ample mechanized assets, the advanced European armies failed to develop operational patterns of maneuver in the course of the First World War. Moreover, one can question whether an operational solution was possible, either in terms of the level of technical capability of states in this period or in terms of what might have happened if such a solution had been available.

The first would seem to command an obvious answer: the mechanized assets of advanced European armies were far from ample in the Second World War, still less during its predecessor. It has been estimated that 85% of the *Wehrmacht* was horse-drawn in 1944, and in the Second World War only the United States had an industrial base that could provide for the mechanization of armies as a whole rather than selected formations. *Blitzkrieg* was an attempt to avoid this problem, and undoubtedly the German failing in the Second World War was partly the result of its being unable to compete at the strategic and operational levels in large part because mechanization was narrowly based at the expense of the mass of the army. But without an industrial base that could provide a general mechanization that would have bestowed operational capability, the argument that it was a mistake to recognize the importance of the operational concept per se would seem to have only limited relevance, even though this particular argument is undoubtedly correct. The success of *Blitzkrieg* was in very large measure the result of a German ability to bring overwhelming mass against a part of an inferior enemy force in relatively small theaters of operations. Its very success served to disguise the fact that no operational concept underpinned it—a fact that became increasingly obvious on the Eastern Front, in part because the size of the theater demanded an operational level of war, in part because of the fundamental German error of seeking victory in 1941 in a single decisive campaign, and in part because the principle of tactical concentration could not produce operational victories.

The second would seem to command an answer that is far from obvious: even though the phrase and concept would have not been recognized at the time on the part of its employer, there was an attempt to employ an operational concept to war-fighting, to evade the enlargement of mass, and it was an abysmal failure. The attempt was made by the Imperial Japanese Navy (the *Kaigun*). The "Strategy of Interceptive Operations" contained the paradox that the *Kaigun* believed in and sought "decisive battle," indeed it believed in decisive battle until it ceased to exist. In a sense it organized itself to fight decisive battle to the point where it could not fight anything else at the very time when it needed to be able to fight something else—namely, a war.

* * *

The real problem that the operational line of reasoning seeks to avoid is how wars that are worth winning can be won without attrition, how states with enormous reserves and powers of recuperation can be broken without protracted warfare. The present concept of Maneuver Warfare seeks to provide an answer, but arguably the evidence of the 1991 conflict points to the possibility not that attritional warfare can be avoided but that attrition can be inflicted on time scales that were previously unknown, such is the speed and accuracy of modern weapons, though an obvious care needs be exercised in making this point. But certainly in the period of the two world wars such a speed of decision was not within the realms of the possible, the 1940 campaign and the defeat of France being the one single exception and hence the unique significance of that particular campaign. But neither the *Kaigun* nor this campaign was the exception noted with respect to neglect of the operational art: the exception was the Soviet Union in the 1926–37 and 1942–45 periods.

* * *

Herein problems of understanding abound. The demands of Cold War conformity exacted their due toll on historical understanding and perspective until the late 1970s, but even today the extent to which Western ideas of Maneuver Warfare in the 1980s grew from the base of Soviet military literature in the 1930s is seldom fully appreciated and even less often acknowledged. More immediately, however, there is the problem of understanding the Eastern Front in the Second World War and to try to understand the place that the Great Patriotic War holds in terms of Russian perception and history. For example, how do we consider the Soviet Union's place in history—the 74-year interlude during which the otherwise remorseless process of Russian decline and fragmentation was halted? And where lies the significance of the Second World War—as the one episode that exacted so hideous a cost and left so crippling a demographic and emotional legacy that the process of disintegration, when it came, ensured that the rump successor state was left smaller than the Russia of Peter the Great?

* * *

Humor and war have proved inseparable, and, one assumes, for very obvious reason: humor has been the mental and emotional safety valve essential in the preservation of sanity in an insane situation. In writing about the Second World War, one can parody one's own country. Allies and enemies alike present themselves as worthy targets of mockery. Sister services inevitably are the butt of humor, or, in the case of the air force, would be if it ever appeared when needed. The insult is never more appropriate than in dealing with combat partners and opponents, and, to various degrees, the insult is not really meant nor offense fully taken, or at least one hopes that this is the case. Probably because of racial and cultural differences, Japan and the war in the Far East do not lend themselves readily to humor, but the Eastern Front is where humor dies. Who has ever read a book dealing with humor and the Eastern Front? This Eastern Front is where comedy, witticism, and parody pass quietly from the stage, to be replaced by unremitting horror. The Eastern Front was witness to a barbarity unseen in Europe, if not since Roman times, then certainly not since the Thirty Years' War, and perhaps the only basis of understanding it is by comparison with this war. The Thirty Years' War and the Nazi–Soviet conflict were Europe's last wars of religion.

Nothing in the Anglo–American experience can provide any inkling of what the Second World War must have been like in eastern Europe, specifically German-occupied Poland and the Eastern Front. To any western European or North American, the Eastern Front is all but incomprehensible. In 1992 a Russian historian stated at the 1942 fiftieth-anniversary conference at Caen that 33,000,000 Soviet citizens served in the armed forces during the Second World War, and of this total 31,000,000 saw services on the Eastern Front. He stated that in the course of the war the army lost 8,500,000 killed, 3,700,000 died of wounds, and 5,700,000 died in German hands. In addition, he cited 15,000,000 civilian deaths from causes directly related to the war. This would provide a total of 32,900,000 deaths, which is considerably in excess of normal estimates, indeed above even the "worst-case" demographic calculations. One has no way of commenting upon the accuracy of these figures, but with a population of about 170,000,000 (with 8,000,000 in the gulags at any one time between 1937 and 1953) and an imbalance of perhaps 10–15,000,000 between males and females in 1941, the Soviets must have mobilized just under half their total male population for this war and lost about half that number. The figures may be disputed, but in a sense whether they are accurate or not is not particularly important when set alongside the question of what it was that enabled Soviet society to survive such butchery and claw its way forward to final victory. One recalls all that one has read and been told about Russian fatalism, the sense of individual insignificance in the face of the harshness of climate and existence, of the immensity of the land. Let that land also tell us of the legacy of eastern despotism and the tradition of subservience before authority. In the music of Tchaikovsky and Borodin is a melancholy and sad languor that speaks of suffering that reaches back longer than Time itself can remember. One remembers that for centuries the farewell gift of a village to a peasant boy going into the army was his funeral mass, and that Tsarevich Alexis, dying of being impaled after torture, when one might reasonably expect that he would curse his father, curse God, or curse the woman who gave him birth, proclaimed only the right of the Tsar—his father, Peter the Great, who was responsible for his execution—to treat him thus. It does not make sense: the limits of understanding are reached long before any Westerner can begin to grasp the reality of the Eastern Front.

* * *

For the Soviet Union, the nature of the war on the Eastern Front was determined for want of any alternative. Such a comment explains everything and nothing, but it does at least provide some insight into one aspect of the Soviet effort. For Soviet society—in effect Russia, because that was what was left after the losses of the first three months—the war was fought, and losses were endured, because the enemy refused it the right to surrender. Slavery and death were all that the Germans could offer the *Untermenschen* of the east. German army planning before June 1941 envisaged the death of 30,000,000 Soviet citizens as a result of German military operations and requisition policies—and this, as it were, en passant and before the festering malignancy of Nazism settled on a conquered land. If such was the intention, or the casual expectation, of the enemy, then one entertains one thought, perverse perhaps. One wonders if the enforced collectivization of agriculture and the purges inflicted by the Stalinist state on its hapless, helpless peoples were not essential in preparing Soviet society for the ordeal that awaited it, the very awfulness of Stalin's rule being the essential discipline that enabled the system to keep going.

One knows why Russia fought. From the outset Nazism forced upon the Russian people a resistance in defense of a thousand years of national consciousness and future hope. Russians fought not with any real hope of personal survival, but in the belief that unborn generations might aspire to a better society that might yet emerge and in the knowledge that the enemy would destroy even these hopes. Ultimately the Russians were correct: the Stalinist abomination passed, and the Soviet system itself was consigned to the rubbish heap of history. A German victory in Europe in the Second World War could not have achieved such a result; the nature of Nazism precluded an evolution that would have allowed elements of human decency to emerge as the basis of social organization. There were no such elements within Nazi ideology, not even for the German people themselves—Nazism represented no intellectual or liberating force of the kind that had been the bedrock of the French Revolution. Much has been written along the lines that the Nazi and Soviet systems were as bad as one another. It is simply not true. Rather like U.S. presidential elections, Stalin and Hitler did not represent a choice as much as a dilemma, save in one critical respect. Stalin did not need to kill and certainly did not need to kill on the scale he did to achieve his objectives, but he was totally indifferent to killings—several millions more or less was an irrelevance. Hitler killed as policy. Policy was the destruction of certain peoples and cultures, and this is what makes Nazism unique in its frightfulness. The Stalinist state was a perversion of an ideology that was rationalist and humanist. The Nazi state was a perversion, and Nazism was an ideology of perversion that had as its base the most profound contempt for the whole of humanity and for the individual, whether Aryan or not. It was an ideology from which there could have been no redress, no concept of decency and enlightenment as the basis of social existence.

* * *

Any examination of the claims of the operational school, and especially its premise that the present concepts of Maneuver Warfare have as their base the idea of Deep Battle developed within the Soviet military in the late 1920s, must acknowledge as its starting point one fact: the Soviet concept was unique in the sense that the theoretical basis of doctrine preceded mechanization. In the German case *Blitzkrieg* was opportunist and improvised. In the Soviet case the main features of the Deep Battle idea were in place by the end of the 1920s, at which time the Soviet Union had about 90 tanks and the same number of armored cars. But much more importantly, the Soviet military were perhaps the first to recognize the operational dimension of war and to pay attention to the conduct of operations at this level as the means of unlocking an enemy defensive system. The Soviet military also moved away from the single-battle concept, arguing as early as 1926 that extended fronts—that is, the sheer mass of armies—made it impossible to destroy an enemy in a single battle, and placed in its stead the idea of successive operations that were closely related in time and space. Herein lay one of the two critical points of difference between Soviet and Western, specifically German, military thinking in the interwar period—the Soviet reasoning that systemic war, being total, could only be conducted by a series of campaigns and these campaigns by a series of offensives.

In each of these arguments the operational school is clearly on firm ground, and it must be conceded that in terms of the conduct of battle the operational school is correct in the assertion that it was in the 1920s that the Soviet military began to move into areas largely unconsidered by Western military establishments. These new Soviet concepts envisaged attacks across a broad front in order to disperse the enemy and deny depth to his defensive system. These attacks were to break into and through this system and to tie down enemy formations, most obviously reserves, and then to break into the rear of the enemy system. The attacks were to be conducted in depth with airborne, mechanized, and cavalry formations and organic air support being specifically moved into the enemy rear areas to paralyze the enemy system. The key to success was concentration of fire in breaking into and through an enemy defense system by attacks mounted by forces deployed en echelon, and herein lies what seems to be the kernel of these ideas: both at the point of contact and strategically, success was sought through successive offensive operations, very closely phased in terms of time and area.

With hindsight, it is easy to see the basis of these ideas. The First World War clearly pointed to the discrediting of standard military concepts; in no case was this more obvious than to the armed forces of a revolutionary socialist state. Moreover, the civil war and Intervention that followed the October Revolution of 1917 involved the Red Army in operations over hundreds, in some cases thousands, of miles and with force ratios that were very different from those that had existed on the Western Front. The desperate conditions of these wars necessarily pushed the Red Army in the direction of phased operations, and its offensives necessarily involved operations deep into enemy-held territory. Obviously both the factors that gave rise to the concept of Deep Battle and its details were very different from the broad outline of the contemporary Western experience. The concept of Deep Battle was bitterly opposed by a number of factions within the Soviet military in the 1920s, and, of course, *P.U. 36: Soviet Field Regulations* did not survive the purges. Soviet offensive operations after June 1944 bore certain characteristics of Deep Battle theory but were also distinctively different in other respects. One wonders whether some of the contemporary analysis of Soviet thinking was not mendacious, especially in searching for points of difference between it and Western ideas and taking refuge behind terminological distinctions that have little real basis in reality. There is no escaping the conclusion that the German offensive in the west in 1940 displayed most of the elements of Deep Battle, specifically with regard to a general offensive across a wide area, the deployment of the main attack formation in echelon, and the devising of clear operational objectives as the means of completing the strategic aim. The point of difference, of course, is that in 1940 the theater of operations and the forces involved were relatively small, with the result that a decision was reached in a single campaign that was divided into two quite distinct operational phases. There are points of similarity as well as of difference between Soviet and other developments, though in the final analysis it is indeed the latter that are the more important. Clearly the differences between *P.U. 36: Soviet Field Regulations* and the French army's contemporaneous Methodical Battle or German ideas are not to be explained in terms of scale and distance, but in terms of imagination.

* * *

In terms of the war on the Eastern Front, four matters command attention with regard to the conduct of war. The first is obvious, indeed, it is so obvious that it is usually missed: *Blitzkrieg* conformed to the law of diminishing returns. So much historical attention has been paid to the 1941 and 1942 campaigns that the progressive failure of *Blitzkrieg* is seldom properly appreciated. Certainly a number of factors went into the failures of 1941 and 1942, and in 1941 the wonder of the campaign is not that the *Wehrmacht* failed but that it achieved so much. Herein is a paradox in the sense that by any rational standard on 21 June 1941 there would seem to have been no way in which Germany could have destroyed the Soviet Union. If not on 22 June, then within a month or two, there would seem to have been no possibility of Germany not being able to complete the destruction of the Soviet Union.

But the German effort failed, and in failure is one inescapable fact. The *Wehrmacht* attacked the Soviet Union at a time and in a manner of its own choosing and held the initiative throughout the duration of Operation Barbarossa until the time that it met defeat outside Moscow in the first days of December. That the German plan of campaign failed despite the *Wehrmacht* having held such advantage suggests that the plan of campaign itself was flawed or that the German conduct of operations was amiss, or both. This is not to suggest that the Soviets were not in some way the agents of their own salvation. Clearly the Soviet conduct of the defense as Army Group Center closed around Moscow in November was very important in ensuring Soviet survival. But there cannot be any real doubting the basic point: the outcome of the campaign was the result of German failures rather than effective Soviet resistance. Why this should have been so is another question, and it remains debatable whether the failure was the result of the task itself being an impossible one.

But if the 1941 failure can be explained away, the failure of 1942 was more significant in that this was a much more deliberate affair and failure was far more fundamental. The conduct of an offensive at the most distant part of the front and where a decision could not be forced pointed to defeat being the product of a flawed plan of campaign, exacerbated by an abysmal conduct of operations, which left the potentially most important defensive sectors held by the weakest formations on the front. Western historiography has concentrated upon Hitler's personal responsibility in the misdirection of the campaign, the conduct of the defense at Stalingrad by the German Sixth Army, and the German counteroffensive at Kharkov. Despite the efforts of a number of distinguished scholars who have sought to examine the Soviet record of events, Western accounts have paid very little attention to the extent of the Axis defeat in the south in the period between November 1942 and March 1943. Manstein's much-vaunted counterattack at Kharkov provided no compensation for the destruction of the German Fourth Panzer and Sixth Armies, the Romanian Third and Fourth Armies, and the Italian Eighth Army, and the ground that had been lost in the process. Even more important, especially in light of the tendency to portray Soviet success in terms of sheer numbers, it needs be remembered that the two most important battles of the war for the Soviet army, in front of Moscow in December 1941 and in and around Stalingrad in November 1942, were fought without superiority of numbers in the immediate theaters of operation. Whatever numerical superiority the Soviets commanded at Moscow and Stalingrad was the result of their local concentration of formations and the dispersal of their enemies.

This point is the second of the four matters that command attention in terms of the conduct and evolution of war, and the third is its reverse: numerical superiority was critical in the outcome of the 1943 German summer offensive, though the extent both of Soviet numbers and success in the Kursk–Orel salient are seldom properly appreciated. The extent of the Soviet commitment at this battle can be gauged by reference to the 375th Rifle Division, which was in the line in the southern sector of the Kursk position, just to the north of Belgorod. At this time the artillery establishment of a rifle division was twelve 122-mm howitzers, thirty-two 76-mm field and fifty 45-mm antitank guns, and twenty-one 120-mm and eighty-three 82-mm mortars. The 375th Rifle Division mustered, in addition to its standard establishment of sixty-one tanks, no fewer than eighty 76-mm and thirty-five 45-mm antitank guns and one hundred thirty-four antitank rifles, in addition to its howitzers and mortars. At the various points of contact at the opening of this battle German divisions enjoyed a 7:1 advantage over Soviet formations deployed in depth, but it was this depth of the defensive system that ensured that the main German effort was broken within a week and without any single German attack registering an advance of more than 40 miles.[16] Herein, of course, was evidence of the limitations of *Blitzkrieg* and its decreasing effectiveness against an enemy that was able to survive its first disastrous impact. In 1941 the *Wehrmacht*, with some 30 armored and motorized divisions in its order of battle, attacked across a frontage of 1,000 miles and achieved penetration of Soviet positions to depths of 500 miles in the direction of Leningrad, 600 miles toward Moscow and some 900 miles in the south, where Rostov-on-Don was captured on 21 November. In 1942 the German effort, with two panzer armies in the line, was concentrated between Voronezh and the sea, a distance of some 320 miles, and, in the Stalingrad sector, it recorded a maximum advance of 350 miles. In July 1943, and with 49 first-class divisions committed to an offensive across a front of some 115 miles, converging German offensives against Kursk were halted more than 60 miles apart.

The Prokhorovka action—the clash on 12 July between II SS and XXXXVIII Panzer Corps and the Fifth Guards Tank Army—is perhaps the best-known episode in this battle. In this one action the Soviets lost about 500 tanks and were forced to abandon the battlefield, but in accounting for about 300 German tanks they denied Army Group South the means to continue the battle. The real significance of this action, indeed the Kursk battle as a whole, lies, however, in two other directions. First, the Soviet counterattack at Kursk against Army Group South opened on 3 August, the day after Manstein had declared that there could be no Soviet offensive in the Kharkov area for weeks, and was led to the reconstituted Fifth Guards Tank Army. Second, Kursk dominates 1943 historiography—nothing compares in terms of losses and significance. But German armored losses in 1943, indeed in the period between July 1943 and May 1944, make very interesting reading, not least because in June 1943 the war most obviously held its breath, as shown in Table 3.3.

What is most striking about German losses is the extent by which front-line tank strength declined between July and August 1943 and never recovered until 1944—indeed, it was not until April 1944 that front-line German tank strength exceeded the January 1943 total. No less striking is the fact that the July 1943 total of German losses was exceeded in April 1944, while losses in August 1943 and in each of the months between November 1943 and January 1944 were not appreciably lighter.[17] The scale of German losses in this 10-month period between August 1943 and May 1944 is notable. This is a period not prominent in Western histories of the war because of the very limited commitment of Anglo–American armies in these months. After the clearing of North Africa and of Sicily, the landings in southern Italy were followed by the six-months' stalemate on the Winter Line. But in terms of Western treatment of the Eastern Front, this is a period that has been written off as strategically sterile; the overall impression given in the U.S. Army's official history is the "drab pointlessness" of operations.[18] The underlying reason for so dismissive a treatment of this period is obvious: it was a period deprived of battles of encirclement and annihilation and lacked the clear-cut results of previous and later campaigns. Be that as it may, the fact remains that this period was most certainly neither drab nor pointless in terms of strategic balance and results. On 1 July 1943 the *Wehrmacht* deployed a total of 276 divisions, of which 186 were deployed on the Eastern Fronts, with another 7 with the Finns and a further 14 in Norway. Yet by August such numbers were not sufficient to secure the initiative, and in December 1943, at a time when there were 38 German divisions in the West and 12 in Italy, of the 151 German divisions on the Eastern Front 10 panzer and 50 infantry divisions were officially described as *abgekämpft* [burnt out]. In other words, the number of *abgekämpft* divisions on the Eastern Front was greater than the number of divisions in the two western theaters. Such a writing-down of German strength would hardly seem to merit the operations of this period being dismissed as pointless.

What is surprising about this period and its events is suggested by the figures of German losses and production. After losses in 1941 and 1942 that ran at a rate of about 235 a month, losses more than doubled in 1943 but showed no great increase in 1944. With due allowance for the February 1943 figures, which in part must represent a cumulative loss over several weeks, what these figures suggest is the battles of 1943 could not have been significantly smaller than the better-known battles of 1944. Given the fact that the Soviets were not able to complete a battle of encirclement and annihilation in this period, the obvious questions that present themselves from so basic a consideration of German figures are what was happening at the front at this time and, less obviously, what was happening to German production and the panzer divisions in this same period because clearly something was very seriously at work.

It was in the year 1943 that Germany lost the war in the sense that it had to win it or go under, but it was the only year between 1941 and 1944 when German tank losses exceeded production. One would admit that in one sense the German tank losses were inflated: 2,962 of the 6,362 tanks lost in this year were Mark III and earlier versions and they were replaced by qualitatively superior tanks, but they were lost nonetheless. German sources give the older tanks as having been lost, not phased out and scrapped. This, in itself, is significant in that it reveals the extent to which in 1943 the *Wehrmacht* was dependent upon its earlier tank marks. Reading accounts of German armored operations in 1943 and 1944 always leaves the impression of Panthers and, to a much lesser extent, Tigers, but at Kursk–Orel in July 1943 there were no fewer than 141 Pzkw III Mark J and 432 Pzkw III Mark M, 155 Pzkw III Mark N and 41 flame-thrower Pzkw III tanks with Army Groups Center and South. Even allowing for the fact that the Pzkw IV was a very good tank and that its appearance in numbers in 1943 was a major factor in eliminating the Soviet qualitative advantage that had existed in 1941 and 1942, it is perhaps surprising to note that as many as 748 of the German tanks in Normandy in June 1944 were Pzkw IVs. Such a formation as the *Panzer Lehr* continued to use Pzkw IVs, the newly raised 116th Panzer Division used the Pzkw III Mark F, and the 21st Panzer Division included Czech-made tanks in its orders of battle. It is a matter of some amazement to

Table 3.3.   German Armor: Production, Front-Line Strength and Losses, 1941–1944

		Production		Strength at front		Losses		Eastern Front	Other theaters
		Tanks	Assault guns	Tanks	Assault guns	Tanks	Assault guns		
1941	total	3,256	540	—	—	2,758	95	—	—
1942	total	4,728	788	—	—	2,648	330	—	—
1943	Jan.	257	130	4,364	1,155	431	30	Stalingrad, Don, Voronezh	Tripoli
	Feb.	320	144	4,261	1,244	1,596	253	Stalingrad	Kasserine Pass
	Mar.	370	207	3,177	1,116	502	135	Third Kharkov	—
	Apr.	306	312	2,540	744	416	43		Tunisia
	May	689	405	2,504	1,048	306	14		Tunis
	June	496	305	2,900	1,470	19	36		—
	July	522	308	3,453	1,737	645	207	Kursk–Orel	Sicily
	Aug.	478	296	2,547	1,814	572	143	Fourth Kharkov	—
	Sept.	591	355	2,672	1,955	353	224	Smolensk	Salerno
	Oct.	662	407	2,986	1,887	450	208	Advance to Dnepr	Advance to the Winter Line
	Nov.	561	167	3,227	2,018	524	243	Kiev, Dnepr	
	Dec.	757	376	3,355	2,054	546	189	Western Ukraine	—
	total	6,009	3,406	—	—	6,362	1,704	—	—

1944							Eastern	Western
Jan	718	416	3,544	2,120	531	291	Relief of Leningrad	Anzio
Feb.	641	500	3,868	2,300	339	159	Nikopol, Cherkassy	Anzio
Mar.	704	506	4,207	2,803	191	280	Bug, Dnestr, Uman	—
Apr.	750	594	4,856	2,814	690	348	Odessa, Ternopol	—
May	792	629	4,923	2,977	226	139	Crimea	Winter Line
June	831	797	5,481	3,524	528	198	Vyborg–Petrozadovsk, Byelorussia	Rome, Normandy
July	840	832	5,807	3,960	1,068	1,056	Byelorussia, Lvov–Sandomiercz	Normandy
Aug.	865	792	5,486	3,571	769	430	Iaisy–Kishenev, Warsaw	France
Sept.	720	750	5,605	4,055	775	523	Baltic States, Bulgaria	Market Garden
Oct.	679	876	4,594	4,409	546	551	Petsamo–Kirkenes, Belgrade	—
Nov.	800	1,012	4,793	4,649	254	210	Debrecen, Mohács	—
Dec.	821	978	5,423	5,239	517	225	Budapest	Ardennes
total	9,161	8,682	—	—	6,434	4,490	—	—
Total	22,704	13,416	—	—	18,202	6,619	—	—

Data taken from B. Muller-Hillebrand, *Das Heer 1933–1945. Entwicklung des organisatorischen Aufbaues, 3: Der Zweifrontenkrieg, das Heer vom Beginn des Feldzuges gegen die Sowjetunion bis zum Kriegsende* (Frankfurt am Main: Mittler, 1969).

note that some of the very first Pzkw IIs, produced in 1936 and 1937, remained in front-line service into late 1943 and active on secondary fronts until the very end of the war. What is very clear about the German production figures is the extent to which, like the operations of the *Kriegsmarine*, German tank output was perhaps two years behind requirement. It was not until May 1944 that output of the Panther exceeded that of the Pzkw IV for the third successive month, and what is most striking about German armored production was its proliferation—six different types of tanks in 1943—and the changing balance of production between tanks and much cheaper, more easily built assault guns. In 1941 the latter accounted for just 14.22% of German tank and assault gun production, in 1942 only 15.55%. By 1944, however, these figures had risen to 48.66%, and in the last four months of that year assault gun production in fact accounted for more than half of tank and assault gun production.

But what is so significant about the period between August 1943 and May 1944 is the nature of Soviet operations and the sharp contrast that exist between this period and what was to follow. After June 1944, 14 major encirclements saw the annihilation of 96 Axis divisions and 32 brigades, but after Stalingrad a year was to pass without any Soviet offensive resulting in a major encirclement and annihilation of Axis formations. With most of the 1944 successes being registered after June of that year, the contrast of Soviet operational capability and success between these two periods is very marked; clearly, therefore, there is a need to address this issue.

What represented the difference between the Soviet military performance before June 1944 and thereafter is the fourth and last of the matters that demand attention in any consideration of the Eastern Front. One aspect of the answer is quite obvious: in relative terms the German defense in 1944 was considerably weaker than it had been in 1943. After November 1943 the *Wehrmacht* was confronted with the reality of a three-front war, and it had to divide its forces accordingly. The German definition of the western theater as having priority over the Eastern Front predated the landing in Normandy by seven months. Increasingly in 1944 it was obliged to spread itself as the tide of war threatened to engulf Germany, and on neither of its two main fronts was it able to meet its enemies on a basis of equality.

The real point of difference, however, was that by summer 1944 the Soviet army had acquired the means to complete offensive operations deep into the rear of an enemy position, whereas previously it had lacked both the means and the willingness to undertake such an effort. Before summer 1944 a lack of mechanization—specifically a lack of mechanization of the logistical support available to mobile formations—went hand-in-hand with a very real fear of German armor on the part of a Soviet high command that was only too aware of the fate of its Kharkov offensives in March–May 1942 and February–March 1943. In the course of its first summer offensive, therefore, the Soviet high command sought a series of deliberate offensives in which the depth of advance was subordinated to the need to secure a river line along which a defense could be organized and behind which Soviet armor could be reconcentrated. Soviet offensives were usually characterized by attacks across a broad front but with the main effort concentrated, the general result being enforced German withdrawal over a wider sector in order to prevent turned formations from being trapped. Under these conditions it was all but impossible for the Soviet army to complete encirclements, but in any case such battles were beyond formations that, because of their limited supply lines, could not penetrate an enemy defensive system to any depth. With a radius of action that was perhaps as low as 50 miles and certainly not more than 80, Soviet advances could not encircle and drive back the main part of the enemy over distances too great for an effective breakout or sortie to relieve. With the Stalingrad exception, throughout 1943 and the first half of 1944 the Soviets completed a series of encirclements, but in every case trapped Axis formations were able either to hold their ground until they were relieved or to break out.

Herein is the answer to the allegation and criticism of lack of finesse in the Soviet conduct of operations in this period between Kursk and Operation Bagration: the Soviet army did not attempt finesse, either operationally or tactically. It fought primarily at the strategic level, switching the point of attack in order to evade German armor, and it fought, on the basis of its material advantages, battles of attrition. The nature of this intention is perhaps best summarized in an account of an episode within the STAVKA (Soviet military headquarters) in August 1943, when, as Soviet armor and infantry began to become separated even before Kharkov was taken and German resistance hardened around the city with the arrival of armor from the Mius and Donets sectors, Stalin was responsible for a change of orders in an exchange that was recorded thus:

After this there was a pause while Stalin collected his thoughts. Then . . . a whole paragraph was dictated: "The urge to attack everywhere and capture as much territory as possible without consolidating success and providing sound cover for the flanks of the assault groups amounts to a haphazard attack. Such an attack leads to the dissipation of forces and material and allows the enemy to strike at the flank and rear of our groups which have gone far ahead and not been provided with cover for their flanks."

The Supreme Commander stopped for a minute and read what I had written over my shoulder. At the end of the phrase he wrote in his own hand, "and to slaughter them piecemeal." He then went on dictating.[19]

Here was the concern for the flanks on the part of an individual not noted for an aversion to the shedding of blood, and here, too, is an explanation of the nature of the Soviet effort in the period between Kursk and Minsk: a very deliberate assault characterized by close control and proper investment against surprise and counterattack.

In the final phase of the war, however, the Soviet army was able to move to a conduct of operations that was very close to the concepts that had been defined in *P.U. 36: Soviet Field Regulations*. It was able to do so for one basic reason—the mechanization of the logistic facilities of its seven armored and mechanized armies. This was made possible by U.S. Lend-Lease, U.S. factories and shipping being responsible for the supply of some 420,000 four-wheel-drive trucks, which put the Soviet army on wheels. The scale of this effort can be understood when it is remembered that this total was greater than the number of motor vehicles in Britain in 1939, and the United Kingdom was second only to the United States in terms of automobile production. Where, however, the concept of Deep Battle continued to elude the Soviet army was in the lack of overall mechanization, since the vast majority of Soviet infantry remained on foot and hoof, of a genuine deep-strike air force, and of adequate airborne forces. As a result the Soviet army, like the German army, was unbalanced, with quality concentrated and narrowly based. Its success in the final period of the war was much to do with superiority of numbers and technique. The superiority of Soviet resources, not of manpower but of tanks and artillery, was critical to success. But no less important was the fact that by 1944 Soviet commanders and staffs had acquired the experience that ensured that these advantages could be used to the full as the Soviets deliberately sought to ensure massive operational superiority and to fight at a level at which the German defense could not respond effectively. By staggering formations in echelon, what were only marginal manpower advantages throughout most of 1944 at the strategic level were translated into pronounced operational and overwhelming tactical superiority, which more than offset any advantage that the *Wehrmacht* retained at the tactical level in terms of leadership, technique, and individual weapons systems. With the bulk of what was a relatively poorly equipped and trained army committed to holding operations that were designed to deny the defense freedom of action, the Soviets sought to overwhelm a defensive system at selected points and to reach into rear areas in a series of offensives. By the end of 1944, however, Soviet superiority in numbers and technique permitted simultaneous offensives and destruction of the enemy in depth and across the frontage of attack.

What both phases meant in terms of operational technique can be understood by reference to artillery practice. Reference has already been made to the gunnery establishment of the 375th Rifle Division at Kursk in July 1943, but the fact of the matter was that the Soviets put emphasis on artillery reserves rather than upon the provision of strength at divisional level. In November 1942 artillery divisions were formed, each with two gun, three howitzer, and three antitank regiments and a total of 168 pieces. In April 1943 the Soviets embarked upon the raising of artillery divisions with six brigades and a total of 356 guns, howitzers, and mortars; the creation of rocket artillery divisions began at the same time. By the end of 1943, breakthrough artillery corps were raised by merging different types of artillery divisions, with the resultant concentration of 496 guns, 216 mortars, and 264 rocket launchers in a single command, and this at a time when the Soviet army mustered 6 artillery corps, 27 artillery divisions, and 7 rocket launcher divisions. With such numbers, the Soviets were able to achieve enormous concentration and margins of superiority. In front of Vyborg in June 1944 the maximum Soviet concentration was 800 pieces per mile of front, and in the Vistula–Oder offensive in January 1945 over 46,000 guns, heavy mortars, and rocket launchers provided operational shock at the point of intended break-in. In this offensive certain German divisions broke under artillery attack before being subjected to assault. Interestingly, the Soviets also employed mass artillery deliberately as a deception, to mislead the defense as to where their effort was to be made.

The extent of Soviet success in such operations as the Byelorussian, Lvov–Sandomeircz, and Vistula–Oder offensives (June–July 1944, July–August 1944, and January 1945, respectively) and the depth of penetration registered in such offensives as Iaisy–Kishinev (August–October 1944) and Manchuria in 1945 could not have been achieved by an army lacking impressive technical capability. In the first days of the Lvov–Sandomiercz offensive, for example, the First Ukrainian Front passed two tank armies, a couple of mobiℓ ⁻ ⁻⁻ ̗ ̗, and an infantry army— perhaps 2,500 tanks plus other arms—through a four-mile breach in the German defenses in three days.[20] In the Vistula–Oder offensive the First Ukrainian Front on the first day broke through German defensive positions to a depth of 10 to 12 miles across 22 miles of front. In the offensive as a whole, the Soviets committed four army groups to an attack across a 310-mile sector, and in 19 days they registered a maximum advance of some 350 miles, destroyed 35 German divisions, and inflicted 60–70% losses on another 25 divisions. In this same operation the Third Guards Tank Army, in an attempt to force the German evacuation of Upper Silesia, was diverted from its western axis of advance to the south in two hours and on a single radio order, and thereafter advanced some 80 miles in three days in pursuit of its newly defined objectives. The contrasts with Operation Goodwood, the largest armored offensive ever undertaken by the British army, and with Patton's much-acclaimed countermove during the Ardennes offensive needs no elaboration. In the

Manchurian offensive the main Soviet effort, by the Sixth Guards Tank Army, involved an advance that was equivalent to one from Caen in Normandy to Milan. With holding forces committed to containing Japanese formations on the main axes of advance, the Sixth Guards Tank Army advanced through mountain passes considered by the defense to be impassable for armored formations and reached Changchung and Mukden in 11 days. This was a formidable achievement by any standard, except the standard foreshadowed by the manner in which the Japanese war was to end.

* * *

This chapter has concerned itself with tyranny—the tyranny that arose to cause the Second World War and that perished in its course, and the tyranny of historiographic orthodoxy. It is an essay that has concerned itself with perspectives, specifically Anglo–American perspectives, of their role and the greatest war in history. One would admit quite freely that over the last two decades there have been changes in Anglo–American accounting of this conflict; many of these have concerned themselves with special interests, such as women, minorities, and other similar subjects, but there have been changes in other areas of study more pertinent to an understanding of the Second World War. The increased attention paid since the 1970s to the Soviet dimension of the war is an obvious example, the reevaluation of the role of intelligence in light of revelations about ULTRA another.

Yet what is very striking about interpretations of the Second World War is how little they have changed since the first decade after the war, when a host of memoirs and the first official histories set out terms of reference for our understanding of this conflict. Certain historical reputations have been diminished over time, issues that were simple have become more complicated, but for the most part our perspectives of this war have remained much the same, no one more obviously than in three critically important fields. There remains a largely uncritical admiration for the German military, and Normandy is a case in point. German resistance in Normandy is always cited as example of the *Wehrmacht*'s resilience and professionalism—and the clock is stopped in the last week of July, when the Normandy battle ended and the northwest European campaign began. The Soviet dimension remains undervalued—though not demeaned, as it was during the cold war. Our understanding of the Pacific war remains wedded to an interpretation that casts most of the blame for the outbreak upon the behavior of the *Rikugun*, which pushed Japan down the road to war despite the protests of a moderate, cautious Imperial Navy. It was, of course, the *Rikugun* that demanded an end to the naval limitation treaties in the 1930s, was primarily responsible for the move into Indochina in 1941, insisted that a war with the European empires in the Far East had to begin with a strike on Pearl Harbor, and began its mobilization in June 1940. With 18 months needed to mobilize, one is left to wonder what situation the *Kaigun* anticipated it would face in December 1941, when its third construction program would be all but complete. If, as was the case, the exhaustion of foreign reserves would have meant Japan having to stop trading in spring 1942, then what was the significance of the American trade embargo of summer 1941? By the least exacting standard, it would seem that the die had been cast before the United States imposed sanctions on Japan in July 1941. In summer 1941 Japan faced a "go-now-or-never" dilemma of its own making, and responsibility for this situation rested as much on the *Kaigun* as on its sister service.

* * *

There remain many aspects of the Second World War in need of reevaluation, but having set out a view of Anglo–American perspectives of this conflict and stated the need for fresh interpretation, the writer is presented with a double irony. The theme of this book is resistance to conventional wisdom, the need to look beyond standard terms of reference. Yet this chapter has dismissed one of those new interpretations— the 1942–43 invasion thesis—and ends with a repudiation of a second revisionist argument that has emerged in recent years and seems to attract ever wider support. This argument asserts that British interests would have been better served by striking a deal with a victorious Germany than by continuing the war after the fall of France in 1940. Clearly underpinning this argument is a muted anti-American sentiment and implicit racism. It is an argument that has gained ground with the ebbing of British national power and the growing awareness of decline in status and wealth relative to the defeated powers of the Second World War. To have made such an argument at the time, as did the majority of the Conservative members of the War Cabinet in summer 1940, was perhaps understandable. To make the claim today is contemptible and inexcusable, if for no other reason than it is an argument that would rob the British decision at the time of its essence and context. With the evidence of the genocide programs so obviously available, the issue of the war cannot be disguised. It was not about standards of living, disposable income, about how the British have mismanaged their affairs since 1945 while the Germans have done so well. The issue of war was basic human values and about resistance to a depraved regime unique in its vileness and malevolence. Any attempt to suggest that Britain should have sought an accommodation with Germany in 1940 would deny Britain its real achievement in the Second World War, because it was in the period of German triumph that Britain made a contribution to final victory that was incalculable. It was Britain that provided refuge to the flotsam of Europe that would fight rather than submit to tyranny: it was Britain that maintained the cause of freedom when it was extinguished on Europe's mainland and until the time when its cause could be rescued by stronger hands. At war's end arguably the greatest and most prestigious of British institutions were the BBC and parliament, the one on account of its reputation for truth and honesty and the other obviously for a somewhat different reason. Churchill's dismissal from office in July 1945 was proof, if any was needed, that for all its many imperfections parliamentary democracy worked. It was, perhaps, the British system's "finest hour" of the Second World War, and herein lay both the real basis of British offering to the Allied cause and the answer to the very familiar accusation that is born of the reputation of *perfidious Albion*. In the four great wars that have gripped Europe in the last 200 years— the French Revolutionary, the Napoleonic, and the First and the Second World Wars—only one state fought in every war and, depending on the date one gives the outbreak of war, from the first day to the last. Britain never deserted any ally, and in 1940 it never deserted the defeated nations of Europe. At war's end only one country, Poland, could consider itself aggrieved, but there was nothing that Britain could have done to have prevented that country reassuming its role as the Christ nation of Europe, destined to suffer crucifixion between two thieves. To have struck a deal with Germany in 1940 would have given proof that Britain merited the description perfidious, and it is to its credit that at the test Britain was true to itself. The issue was never so well put as in one editorial leader, all the more impressive for its having been written in *The New York Times* in the summer of 1940: "Is the tongue of Chaucer, of Shakespeare, of Milton, of the King James version of the Scriptures, of Keats, of Shelley, to be hereafter, in the British Isles, the dialect of an enslaved race?"[21] It seems to be a summary of choice quite beyond the comprehension of those who would contend that Britain should have sought an accommodation with Germany in 1940. A people who never surrendered to the French and Spanish, who were gentlemen, does not surrender to the rubbish collected from the gutters of Munich and Milan, and in so refusing to treat and in denying Germany victory ensured, in the long term, the redemption of Europe from a darkness that it could not lift for itself.

NOTES

1. With grateful acknowledgment to Michael H. Coles and his letter of 5 July 1997 for an argument that the author could not articulate for himself.

2. Carlo D'Este, *Fatal Decisions: Anzio and the Battle for Rome* (New York: HarperCollins, 1991), p. 6.

3. Michael Howard, *The Mediterranean Strategy in the Second World War* (London, Weidenfeld & Nicolson, 1968), p. 37, and *History of the Second World War. Grand Strategy.* Vol. IV, *August 1942–September 1943* (London: Her Majesty's Stationery Office, 1972), p. 419.

4. Robert W. Love, Jr., *A History of the U.S. Navy.* Vol. II, *1942–1991* (Harrisburg, PA: Stackpole Books, 1992); see chapter 4 and, specifically, chapter 5.

5. The German order of battle is based on the movement of German formations given in Burkhart Muller-Hillebrand, *Das Heer 1933–1945. Entwicklung des organisatorischen Aufbaues, 3: Der Zweifrontenkrieg, das Heer vom Beginn des Feldzuges gegen die Sowjetunion bis zum Kriegsende* (Frankfurt am Main: Mittler, 1969), specifically the orders of battle in the western theater between June 1942 and June 1944.

6. The sentence that concluded Michael Howard's *The Mediterranean Strategy in the Second World War.*

7. To the best of the author's knowledge none of the official histories gives a total for the number of troops put ashore on the first day. The figure of 160,000 troops involved in Husky is taken from David Woodward's article in Purnell's *History of the Second World War*, Vol. 4 (London: Purnell, 1966), p. 1489. The figure of 102,000 troops landed is an estimate using the totals given for individual beaches in the Admiralty staff history; the problem is that not all the beaches are cited and the totals that are given are not standardized in terms of day/days of disembarkation.

8. In the latter category one would identify intelligence; routing, diversion, and tracking; operational research; and, critically, the growing imbalance of experience. Dilution and heavy losses—the latter concentrated among the more aggressive and successful units—meant that from 1942 the U-boat arm was having to send units to sea with officers with perhaps only two or three missions to their credit. With escorts taking relatively few losses, the Allies held advantages of experience and technique that became ever more pronounced with the passing of time.

9. It was a measure of the failing U-boat effort that in 1943 and 1944 only one in seven convoys in the North Atlantic was subjected to attack. It shows the strength of national and service prejudice that when this point was made at a service conference in 1991, it elicited from U.S. naval personnel present the comment that it confirmed the correctness of the view that the Battle of the Atlantic was overrated. The speaker stated that if so few convoys were attacked, then they could have been stripped of escorts, losses accepted, and naval forces freed for offensive purposes. Further comment is unnecessary.

10. Major General I. N. Vorob'yev, "Tactics of the Long-Range Battle," *Vioennaya Mys'l*, October 1992.

11. Gar Alperovitz, *The Decision to Use the Atomic Bomb* (New York: Knopf, 1995), pp. 2–3.

12. Carl von Clausewitz, *On War*, Book I: *On the Nature of War* edited by Anatol Rapoport (London, Penguin, 1968), p. 108: Chapter I. "What is War?" Section IX. "The result in war is never absolute."

13. Quoted by Shimon Naveh, *From Vernichtungsschlacht to AirLand Battle: The Evolution of Operational Theory*, doctoral thesis, King's College, University of London, 1994, chapter 4.

Table 3.4.   Front-Line Strengths

	U.S.A.	Britain	Germany
1942	6,610	7,400	4,207
1943	20,185	6,026	5,536
1944	32,957	8,395	6,297

14. U.S., British, and German front-line strengths and losses are shown in Tables 3.4 and 3.5.

15. Naveh: two statements made in the thesis abstract.

16. At enormous cost. David M. Glantz and Jonathan House, *When Titans Clashed: How the Red Army Stopped Hitler* (Lawrence, KS: University of Kansas Press, 1995) pp. 296ff., give Soviet losses at Kursk as 70,330 killed and 107,517 wounded, plus 1,614 tanks and self-propelled guns and 3,929 artillery pieces destroyed in the defensive phase to the end of July 1943; 112,529 killed and 317,361 wounded, plus 2,586 tanks and self-propelled guns and 892 artillery pieces destroyed in the Orel counteroffensive (12 July to 18 August); and 71,611 killed and 183,955 wounded, plus 1,864 tanks and self-propelled guns and 423 guns destroyed in the Belgorod–Kharkov counteroffensive to 23 August. The whole action, therefore, cost the Soviet army 256,470 killed and 608,833 wounded, with 6,064 guns and self-propelled guns and 5,244 artillery pieces destroyed. What is appalling about these totals is that the number killed or missing is modest relative to overall Soviet wartime losses; on the basis of average daily losses, in the 45 days represented by these actions Soviet dead would have totaled more than 850,000.

17. There is an obvious element of catch-up in the accounting: clearly the figures for April reflect some of the March losses when the Soviet army recaptured Uman and the German tank workshops in that city.

18. Earl F. Ziemke, *Stalingrad to Berlin: The German Defeat in the East* (Washington DC: Center of Military History, 1966), p. 196.

19. S. M. Shtemenko, *The Soviet General Staff at War*, trans. Robert Daglish (Moscow: Progress, 1985), pp. 182–183.

20. Thus it is all the more important to note two matters relating to these two periods of Soviet offensive operations—the watershed between them being June 1944 and Operation Bagration—that might otherwise be missed. The first period,

Table 3.5.   Wartime Losses

	U.S.A.	Britain	Germany
Bombers	9,949	11,965	21,807
Fighters	8,420	10,045	48,804
Totals	**18,369**	**22,010**	**70,611**

Table 3.6. Soviet Losses

Offensive	Original strength	Killed & missing	Wounded	Tanks/SP guns lost	Artillery pieces lost
Defensive phase *17 July–18 Nov. 1942*					
Stalingrad	547,000	323,856	319,986	2,436	13,716
to Feb. 1945					
Byelorussia	2,441,600	180,040	590,848	2,957	2,447
Lvov–Sandomiercz	1,002,200	65,001	224,295	1,269	1,832
Iaisy–Kishinev	1,314,200	13,197	53,933	75	108
Baltic States	1,546,400	61,468	218,622	522	2,593
Belgrade	300,000	4,350	14,488	53	184
Debrecen	698,200	19,713	64,297	n/a	n/a
Budapest	719,500	80,026	240,056	1,766	4,127
1945					
East Prussia	1,669,100	126,464	458,314	3,525	1,644
East Pomerania	996,100	55,315	179,045	1,027	1,005
Berlin	2,062,100	81,116	280,251	1,997	2,108

Source: Glantz, *When Titans Clashed*, pp. 294–295.

between the counterattack at Kursk and the end of the western Ukraine offensive, may have been strategically sterile or characterized by drab pointlessness, but the destruction of German defensive capacity was essential and was achieved primarily by the Soviet army and only at immense cost. Soviet success in such undertakings as the Byelorussia and Lvov–Sandomiercz offensives was dearly bought. If the successful defense of the Kursk salient was bought at relatively light cost, the price exacted in the five major Soviet offensives that followed between July and September was enormous. The totals were 429,890 killed, missing, and wounded at Orel; 255,566 at Belgorod and Kharkov; 451,466 at Smolensk; 273,522 in the Donbas; and 427,952 at Poltava. In addition, 8,339 tanks and self-propelled guns and 3,288 artillery pieces were destroyed in these offensives. The five offensives in the south in the first half of 1944 cost the Soviets 1,430,710 killed, missing, and wounded. Such was the massive human cost in the essential attritional phase of operations on the Eastern Front, but amid the acclaim that has attended the Byelorussian, Lvov–Sandomiercz and Iaisy–Kishivev offensive, strengths and losses involved in these and other operations need be noted (Table 3.6). Soviet losses in the offensives that really mattered were therefore very considerable, even in the period of greatest success and impact, and certainly the losses in the Byelorussia and Lvov–Sandomiercz offensives do support the Soviet case that failure in front of Warsaw in August 1944 was the result of losses and local defeat. But two other sets of figures are of interest—the first in 1945 and the defensive phase between 17 July and 18 November 1942 (Table 3.6).

21. William Stevenson, *A Man Called Intrepid. The Secret War* (New York: Ballantine, 1976), p. 127.

4

The Destruction of Values, 1945–1974

The concept of the "revolution in military affairs" is one that has come to occupy center stage in military thought over the last decade and specifically refers to the changes set in hand in the early 1970s, though, as noted elsewhere in these pages, historians and commentators have identified various "revolutions in military affairs" at different times in history. The set of events presently selected to constitute a fundamental change in the conduct of war thus has predecessors and rivals to any claim upon such recognition. Again, as noted elsewhere, one would submit that any and all of these claims are necessarily flawed. The changes that have occurred have invariably been evolutionary in nature, and however startling or dramatic any single change may have been, its impact was inevitably limited and did not affect the conduct of war in its entirety. Herein, perhaps, lies the basis of the most important objection to the very concept of the revolution in military affairs, particularly the current version: this revolution is not one in military affairs but is technological in terms of relevance to the military. The present concept represents a confusion of war and warfare, of the nature of war and the conduct of war, and it places primacy upon the conduct of operations by the military, whereas in reality war is a political not a military activity.

Nonetheless it is difficult to resist the conclusion that the atom bomb did represent a fundamental change in both the nature and the conduct of war and, more than any other predecessor or rival claimant, did indeed constitute a "revolution in military affairs." Obviously it was evolutionary in the sense that the atom bomb was developed over several years—Einstein's famous letter to Roosevelt was dated 2 August 1939—and, no less obviously, it did not touch every aspect of warfare.

Yet in terms of its implications and consequences the atom bomb profoundly altered war and wrought major changes in three respects. These
weapons were not revolutionary in terms of an ability to destroy whole
societies, since such ability had been long vested in humanity—any
change in this field of activity was merely of scale, time, and effort
expended—but from the first acquisition of these weapons deterrence
emerged as the alternative to defense. Deterrence had always been a part
of war and the conduct of states in their dealings with one another;
individual services had long been regarded as serving a deterrence role
as well as existing for the defense of the state. But after 1945 the existence
of such power of destruction, apart from entailing massive restraint
upon use and even the threat of use, imposed upon military establishments double roles of deterrence and defense that were largely separated from one another. Such unprecedented power of destruction
inevitably meant that the avoidance of war, and of the use of these
weapons, assumed critical significance that was more important than the
waging and winning of wars: as such, deterrence and defense diverged
because the means of deterrence were not those of defense and the
means of defense counted for little in terms of deterrence capability.

No less importantly, atomic and nuclear weapons and the emergence
of deterrence as the primary objective of such states as the United States
and the Soviet Union carried with it implications in terms of preparation
and readiness that were unprecedented, or, as N.S.C. 20–21 of August
1948 stated the need

to consider more definite and militant objectives toward Russia even now, in
time of peace, than it was ever called upon to formulate with respect either to
Germany or Japan in advance of actual hostilities with those countries.

Deterrence policies could work only under conditions of permanent
readiness, and only if the interests that were to be protected were properly defined, if the party that was to be deterred made aware of the fact,
and if the penalties likely to be exacted for transgression were deline-
ated. But the real basis of deterrence lay in technical capability. For
deterrence to be effective, available force had to be permanently at hand,
and in this fact deterrence was to lead to what was perhaps the ultimate
absurdity: the existence of permanent standing alliances with strategic
forces on a round-the-clock footing for the purpose of not making war—
indeed, for ensuring that war did not occur. This was, by any standard,
a somewhat strange state of affairs.

Moreover, the development of atomic and nuclear weapons came to
reinforce the tendency of the first half of the twentieth century with
reference to the indecisiveness of war as an instrument of state policy,
and for very obvious reasons. By forgetting to patent the weapon, the

Americans ensured that their monopoly of possession was lost, and in this respect the atom bomb went the same way as other "potentially decisive" weapons: shared ownership meant that the element of possible decisiveness or advantage was lost. Such a development, however, was inseparable from context—the context of the Cold War, which was very largely the product of one set of circumstances. The absence of any real cause of rivalry between the United States and the Soviet Union ensured no point of agreement. Once it had assumed substance and form, however, the Cold War produced issues and rivalries that would divide the two great powers, but in this period whatever element of decisiveness war had possessed was very largely lost.

* * *

The development of atomic and nuclear weapons affected war and military establishments at three levels: deterrence made essential the pursuit of policies aimed at avoiding strategic confrontation and with it the danger of escalation; deterrence also made essential the definition of forms of warfare below the atomic-nuclear threshold; and there was a search for forms of warfare whereby the struggle between the superpowers and their respective alliance systems could be continued "by other means." In some ways the last of these was perhaps the most important, for two reasons. Atomic and nuclear weapons, and the resultant strategic stalemate, reinforced a trend already identified in terms of nineteenth-century development. This was to narrow and blur still further the distinction that had existed between war and peace because, in a very real sense, strategic deadlock and ideological hostility produced struggle as the permanent factor in the relationship of the superpowers. With no real basis for either an agreed reconciliation of differences or the military victory of one side or the other, the relationship between the two superpowers became one characterized by a permanent low-grade militarization that was all the more dangerous because of the implication that deterrence carried with it. It involved the primacy of science and the emergence of an intellectual aristocracy. These were equally dangerous since deterrence, in the long term, involved the subordination of the decision-making process to technique, because the logic of deterrence was self-generating. The need to sustain the deterrent involved the subordination of the political process to this purpose—witness the American decisions to proceed with MIRV in 1967 and the Trident decisions in 1971–72. Even allowing for the fact that these decisions were not wholly mechanistic, in a very obvious sense nuclear weapons and deterrents were and remain profoundly undemocratic.

This may seem an absurd statement, but it cannot be disputed. At the level of society there is an acceptance of responsibility for the soldier. Servicemen, ships, aircraft, individually and collectively, belong to society, to "us," but nuclear weapons, because of their awesomeness and the frightfulness of the prospect of their employment, belong to "them." The reasons for this recognition of responsibility for the conventional but not the nuclear battlefield are twofold. As individuals, we cannot conceive of our own deaths, and we cannot conceive of either the total annihilation of all societies or of a society with no future. Nuclear weapons inhibit us in terms of imagination: we cannot envisage something the size of a tennis ball, weighing about 10 kg, killing perhaps 100,000 people in less time than it takes a heart to beat, and we certainly cannot imagine what failed deterrence would involve in terms not of hundreds of thousands but hundred of millions of people slowly dying of radiation sickness.[1] Such concepts are beyond us as individuals—a reflection of Einstein's comment that the splitting of the atom had changed everything except human modes of thinking. As General George L. Butler put it, faced with such moral problems, to think about the unthinkable, justify the unjustifiable, rationalize the irrational, ultimately we contrived a new and desperate theology to ease our moral anguish, and we called it deterrence.[2]

But at the level of the state and society, the impact of deterrence was undemocratic in another sense, not simply because of the self-fulfilling nature of deterrence but because of the demands that it placed upon the state and the changes it wrought as a consequence. Deterrence, and with it a state strategy for survival, necessarily involved the orchestration of all aspects of social existence as part of the process whereby the superpowers came to confront one another and a fusion of the component parts of power as instruments of state policy in a manner and to an extent that was without precedence. The inevitable consequence of nuclear weapons and deterrents was the politicization of every aspect of social existence, and every aspect of life formed part of this confrontation. Aid programs, educational and training schemes, preferential terms of trade—these and many other matters formed parts of the process whereby the superpowers bid against one another for the support and allegiance of others. While many examples of this process could be cited, perhaps the most obvious was sport, in which respect 1936 cast a long shadow. It was not mere chance that the Soviet bloc developed so formidable a sporting reputation and achievement, that East Germany took as many or more medals at games as did the superpowers. The sporting achievement of the Soviet bloc was part of a very deliberate policy of projecting a virile, clean-cut, benevolent image; holding the Olympic Games in Moscow in 1980 was endorsement of the Soviet regime and its policies, an indication of approval and respectability.

This orchestration of aspects of government within a coherent national security strategy necessarily involved the growth of state power, the latter being inevitable given the commitment of the state to the social market and welfare programs after 1945. It was also part of the process of an ever-increasing concentration of power at the upper reaches of government, the general trend of improved communications in the course of the twentieth century having been an ever-greater capacity of superior authority to control and supervise rather than the encouragement of decision-making at the lower and more relevant levels of administration. Critically, however, this orchestration of the various elements of state and social existence as part of national policy involved a profound alteration in the perception of mutual exclusion of the political and military in their respective areas of competence and authority. Of course the two were never properly exclusive, but with means of instant communications at their disposal, restraints upon the use of force, limits on even the threat of the use of force, and strict control of the extent and severity of force when used, the elements that become essential as part of the process of crisis management and the prevention of an escalation of local conflicts could not but erode the professional exclusiveness of the military, though the latter was under threat from two other directions.

The development of atomic and nuclear weapons necessarily involved the primacy of science, though this conformed and reinforced a trend that had been increasingly important since the industrialization of Europe and North America. The trend had provided a divergence between the services in the sense that whereas in navies and air forces men service weapons, in armies weapons support men, though with future developments armies are likely to fall in line with their sister services. But more importantly, the increasing importance of scientists and engineers to the military went hand-in-hand with an increasingly important civilian contribution to military thought. What is very noticeable about military thought before 1945 is its domination by the professionals and almost an absence of a civilian input. Persons such as Corbett were exceptional, and were accepted—barely—on sufferance: they rationalized what the professionals could not articulate and were a substitute for, not an encouragement to, thought. Military professionalism was jealously guarded and largely exclusive before the Second World War. Deterrence, however, witnessed the intrusion of the civil and political upon military exclusiveness, partly because of the sheer difficulty the military encountered in dealing with so many problems in the decade immediately after the Second World War and partly because deterrence necessarily involved a definition of morality: this was not a matter that the military could determine.

Because it involved a definition of the interests that were to be maintained under the auspices of this policy, deterrence had to be shaped by the civilian authorities. Over time this was to be provided by the policy of containment and later by the concept of Limited War, but more immediately the questions of morality and civilian authority presented

themselves at a different level of warfare. The Second World War produced the crisis of the imperialist system, for very obvious reasons: the
Second World War released forces of change, specifically nationalist and
revolutionary aspirations on the part of various peoples who lived under
Western colonial rule. This was most evident in those colonies that had
been unwilling battlefields during the Second World War, but the implications of the Atlantic Charter of 1941, the formation of the United
Nations in 1942, and the promise of postwar Indian independence that
same year were not lost upon subject peoples. For the most part, however, the European colonial powers were slow to appreciate the expectation that had been implanted by war, yet in the reconstruction of their
own societies the more democratic their institutions and practices became, the less could they meet those expectations. After 1945 the deeper
the entrenched democratic practice within metropolitan homelands, the
more difficult it was to justify imperialism. The colonial power could not
be democratic at home but in the empire hold down peoples by force and
deny them rights that were established in the homeland. This point was
only recognized slowly in various imperial countries. With regard to
Britain, the contradiction was recognized in the 1950s in the case of the
campaigns in Kenya (1952–60) and Cyprus (1955–59), but it was not
until the 1960s that the European empires began to act upon its logic.
It should be noted, however, that the immediate cause was provided in
the recognition of the force of "the winds of change" within colonies
rather than the implications of changes within homelands, as Macmillan
in his speech to the South African parliament in February 1960 clearly
acknowledged.

* * *

The failure to recognize and act upon the logic of developments, to
resolve the contradictions inherent between ideas and reality, was very
natural: in the parallel area of deterrence there were two similar failures
at this time. First, the emergence of the concept of Limited War during
the 1950s was not accompanied by the realization that, in the final
analysis, such wars could only be fought by a nation that, rather than
escalate to a level at which victory could be won, had to be prepared to
lose the war that it intended to limit. The point was obscure and did not
become apparent until the second half of the 1960s. Moreover, the emergence of the concept of Limited War during this period was not attended
by any realization of another set of implications that involved the explicit repudiation of the *sine qua non* of warfare as it had come to be
conducted over the previous 50 years. The conduct of Limited War
demanded public understanding and support, which by definition had
to be both rational and consciously given, and could not involve the
Clausewitzian elements of popular passion and commitment. As the

Vietnam War was to demonstrate, what was rational and consciously given could be rationally and consciously withdrawn: rationalism and commitment were not synonymous. Second, at this same time the expansion of strategic nuclear arsenals was justified on the basis of ensuring security—that somehow or other survival would be ensured by adding to a destructive power already sufficient to destroy all life on the planet—while the defense of moral values was to be ensured by policies that involved "demographic targeting." By any standard, the morality of deterrence was somewhat odd, but what was no less strange was the manner in which developments in the colonial empires became entangled with a confrontation that developed over Europe. With the onset of the Cold War and faced with a struggle with a superior opponent, the Soviet Union sought to encourage anti-imperialist aspirations as the means of weakening the associates of the United States. To a Soviet Union that could not directly challenge the United States, what is now known as the Third World provided the basis of an alternative form of struggle.

The reality of deterrence and confrontation provided the context of revolutionary struggle in the two decades after the end of the Second World War. The concept of armed revolutionary struggle that was to be so important in this period was provided by Mao Tse-tung and represented a fusion of two distinct elements—a concept of guerrilla warfare provided by the example of history and a concept of revolutionary socialism derived from the writings of Marx and Lenin. Maoist concepts contained little if anything that was new, the main element of novelty being the manner in which the different strands were brought together, the purposes to which the revolutionary and military aims and means were to be put, and the context of struggle within the colonial empires. The extent of the novelty presented by Maoist concepts can be gauged by the fact that the book that for some three decades provided perhaps the most authoritative analysis of military thought, Edward Mead Earle's *The Makers of Modern Strategy: Military Thought from Machiavelli to Hitler,* published in 1943, contained but four references of trifling importance to guerrilla warfare in its 520 pages.

Revolutionary guerrilla warfare was of minimal importance before 1945, which is somewhat strange given the fact that guerrilla warfare is so old and revolutionary wars can hardly be deemed uncommon in the last two centuries. There are references to guerrilla warfare by Sun Tzu. It seems likely that some of the actions related in the First Book of Samuel contain a substantial amount of guerrilla warfare. The Romans, their legions beaten by Hannibal, employed guerrilla warfare under the leadership of Quintus Fabius Maximus to destroy the power of Carthage. The Annamites in the tenth century employed it as a means of resisting Chinese attempts to conquer their country. Revolutionary warfare, similarly, can trace its antecedents back over the centuries. One tends not to consider the Peloponnesian Wars as revolutionary, but it is difficult to believe that Athens' attempt to raise a slave revolt in Sparta as a means of destroying its enemy can be classified as anything other than an early indulgence in revolutionary warfare. Certain of Europe's religious uprisings and wars must be considered examples of revolutionary warfare, while the eighteenth century provides at least one case of revolutionary guerrilla warfare—the employment of guerrilla tactics and techniques in pursuit of a revolutionary objective—in the form of Greene's campaign in the Carolinas in 1780–81, though the War of American Independence as a whole witnessed this same phenomenon. Both revolutionary and guerrilla warfare, therefore, reach back over hundreds, thousands, of years, and even in the twentieth century pre-date Maoism: Lawrence and the Arab Revolt between 1916 and 1918 and Collins and the war against British rule between 1919 and 1921 provide evidence of guerrilla warfare's political dimension in the twentieth century before Mao's concepts of revolutionary warfare came to center stage. What was novel within Maoist concepts of revolutionary guerrilla warfare was threefold; that guerrilla warfare was systematically and deliberately employed as a means to conduct internal political disputes as well as fulfilling a role in the conduct of international affairs; the circumstances peculiar to the post-1945 world; and the *Leitmotiv* of communist policy. The latter was that the loss of the colonies, involving the loss of raw materials, sources of energy, and markets, as well as of population and of a position of geopolitical advantage, would prove disastrous for the capitalist system.

Mao Tse-tung wrote about revolutionary warfare at three distinct levels. To the mass of his following Mao wrote a practical do-it-yourself guide, a Jominian checklist governing personal behavior. In so doing, he provided comment on the state of China in the interwar period, when it was the victim of a series of civil wars and Japanese aggression. His instruction to Communist soldiers not to steal property and food, not to rape and murder, was comment on the normal behavior of soldiery in China at this time, and in so instructing his soldiers Mao defined the basis of what was to distinguish the Communists from their enemies. At a higher level, Mao explained the three stages of revolutionary warfare, starting with a phase of preparation in less accessible areas, the prosecution of guerrilla warfare, and a final conventional campaign. This three-fold division of revolutionary warfare has often been defined as the kernel of Maoist warfare, but, at the third level, any careful consideration of Mao's writings would reveal that the basis of revolutionary struggle lay in the subordination of the military aspects of war to political considerations, specifically the rendering of military effectiveness dependent upon the level of political commitment of the population. This allowed unindustrialized and primitive societies, lacking modern arms and equipment, to adopt a militant political philosophy based on armed struggle. From this fundamental premise Mao developed a military doctrine that would enable the poor and weak to adopt a form of resistance even when confronted with the militarily superior forces of an highly industrialized and technologically advanced enemy. In so doing Mao Tse-tung set down time, space, and will as the basis of revolutionary war, and through a dogged, unwavering adherence to principle and method brought his party to victory in 1949 after 22 years of civil and foreign war.

The Maoist pattern of revolutionary warfare was based on the countryside and popular support, and it sought to use time and space to overturn the advantages of technological sophistication. Time was the equalizing factor between the rich and the poor; dragging out war to a point where it becomes politically and economically unacceptable to the enemy was the basis for the Communists' faith in ultimate victory, no matter how long a war lasted. The prosecution of war over an extended area was no less important in that in a revolutionary war

its operation is according to the surface. The greater the surface and the greater the contact with the enemy's army the greater will be the effect of arming the people. Like a slow gradual heat it destroys the foundations of the enemy's army [because] a people's war possesses on a grand scale the peculiarity that the principle of resistance exists everywhere but is nowhere tangible.[3]

The words may belong to Clausewitz, but the concept of war prosecuted over great distance in order to destroy the physical and moral resources of the enemy is Maoist, especially when the interdependence of time, space, and will as the determining factors in the conduct of revolutionary war are identified. Space bought time and time brought the opportunity to ensure popular endorsement because

without a political goal guerrilla warfare must fail, as it must if its political objectives do not coincide with the aspirations of the people and their sympathy, co-operation and assistance cannot be gained. . . . Because guerrilla warfare basically derives from the masses and is supported by them, it can neither exist nor flourish if it separates itself from their sympathies and cooperation. . . . The moment this war of resistance separates itself from the masses . . . is the precise moment it dissociates itself from hope of ultimate victory.[4]

The three factors of time, space, and will, the essence of the Maoist concept of rural insurgency, whether singly or together, provide the basis of examination of the major insurgency campaigns fought between 1945 and the mid-1960s. With the single exception of the Hukbalahap Rebellion in the Philippines between 1946 and 1954, China stands apart from all other campaigns in that it was wholly indigenous; the other campaigns that were fought in this period were directed against colonial authority. Moreover, in its final stages the Chinese Civil War was fought on a scale that eclipsed all other revolutionary wars—indeed, all wars fought since 1945. More importantly, it can be argued that its outcome was decided before 1945 in that the end of the Second World War found the Nationalist regime at Chungking beyond salvation. Its endemic corruption, the lack of any radical program to address the country's many ills, its evident failure in the Japanese war, and its sheer incompetence had robbed it of credibility. Such was the state of China in terms of the ravages inflicted upon it by the appalling combination of Kuomintang misrule and Japanese rapaciousness that the communists had been handed causes with which to build a basis of rural support without any major need for coercion and intimidation: terror was to come after victory. In military terms, the Japanese surrender led to the dispersal of Kuomintang armies and their being exposed to defeat as the countryside overwhelmed the towns. In Manchuria, where the Nationalist armies were too weak to occupy such important cities as Harbin and Tsitsihar, the Kuomintang was able to hold the southern areas throughout 1946, but their garrisons became increasingly isolated in the course of 1947, when full-scale civil war was resumed. Throughout the course of 1947 the Manchurian pattern established itself throughout northern China, and even the Nationalist success in reducing the communist stronghold in Shensi served only to aggravate the Kuomintang's problems of dispersal and weakness. Beginning in October 1947 the Communists were able to move into the third phase of conventional operations throughout southern Manchuria and northern China. With Shensi recovered in spring 1948, the summer saw the progressive reduction of Kuomintang positions north of the Yellow River, with the Communist field armies routing two Nationalist army groups on the Kaifeng–Suchow line between November 1948 and January 1949 in the Battle of the Hwai Hai. With the fall of Mukden and Peking at this time marking the end of the campaigns north of the Yangtze, that river was crossed by Communist armies in April, followed by the progressive Kuomintang collapse throughout the south. With the fall of Chengtu in December the Kuomintang abandoned the mainland and established itself on Formosa.

The Maoist concept of revolutionary warfare invited imitation. Throughout southeast Asia the legacy of defeat was the emergence of forces of national independence with which the returning colonial powers had to contend. Three major campaigns were to be fought in this area between 1945 and 1960, and if three colonial empires disappeared in the process, the course and outcome of these campaigns differed greatly. The demise of the Dutch empire in the Indies was primarily the result of American pressure. The Dutch had secured control of Java by December 1948, and their position on the outlying islands had been more or less secure by the time the United Nations resolution of January 1949 ordering the granting of independence undercut Dutch efforts. Independence was conceded in November 1949, after which time the new state of Indonesia descended into a decade of domestic violence and strife as separatist forces unsuccessfully sought to assert themselves.

In Indochina and Malaya, however, the positions of the colonial authorities were somewhat different from that of the Dutch in the Indies. Both the British and the French possessed substantial military forces and the status of great powers, and were not expendable in terms of *Realpolitik*. Careful consideration of the Indochina and Malaya campaigns reveals four critically important factors at work that largely shaped the outcome of these campaigns, which differ profoundly from each other—factors that worked to British advantage and to French disservice. Malaya was isolated from outside support and supply, whereas after 1949 the French faced an impossible problem presented by the Communists' victory in China, which provided the Viet Minh with sanctuaries, base areas, and logistical support. In both campaigns the Communists sought to conduct revolutionary warfare in rural areas according to the Maoist formula. But in Malaya the inaccessibility of most of the interior and the concentration of the battlefield on either side of the main road running the length of the country meant that the insurgents could not trade space for time and allowed the British to concentrate in a manner denied the French in Indochina, where population distribution ensured that the campaign was fought across the whole of the three Annamite provinces. On the basis of comparative areas of operations and the numbers of troops committed to these campaigns, the British in Malaya were some 14 times more numerous on the ground than were the French in Indochina. In Malaya the British were faced with an insurgency campaign conducted by a minority community within a racially divided society, and they were able to assume the hostility of the greater part of society to the communist endeavor; this situation repeated itself in Kenya, where the Mau Mau Rebellion was essentially drawn from the Kikuyu and was resisted generally and by certain groups, such as the elders and the Christians, within that tribe. In Indochina the French possessed an empire that encompassed various nationalities with long histories of mutual antagonisms, but while this did provide bases of support from among the smaller communities, it did not alter the fact that the challenge to the French position on the peninsula was mounted within the majority Annamite community. Even though the latter was divided, most obviously along religious lines, the contrast between the British position in Malaya and that of the French in Indochina was very sharp. The British on their peninsula were faced by an insurgency campaign that was opposed by the majority of the local population and was confined to about one-tenth of the land area of the country. The French were faced with a rural insurgency over most of Tongking, Annam, and Cochin China that was supported by the greater part of the population. Perhaps the least acknowledged but most important is the fact that the British and French difficulties differed in terms of the nature of their effort. In Malaya the British problem was to secure control of rural areas—specifically first the squatter camps and then the new villages in which lived that part of the Chinese population that supported the Malayan Peoples' Liberation Army. In Indochina the French had to recreate a basic governmental structure and administration as the essential prerequisite for the conduct of a rural campaign. The significance of this difference cannot be understated. The French faced the problem of having to reconstruct the basic institutions of government in the middle of a losing war. The British fought a campaign in Malaya on the basis of an intact administrative machine at federal, state, and local levels. Moreover, with the exception of a single village for a matter of a few hours, the British in Malaya never suffered the collapse of administration in any single area at any time during the emergency. At various times British control in certain areas was tenuous, but there remained the basis of government on which to build. Throughout Indochina, the French were obliged to create where nothing existed.

*   *   *

This basic problem was one that the French faced not once but twice in the decade after the end of the Second World War, and the second time with far more serious consequences than in Indochina. The second occasion was in Algeria, where after November 1954 the French faced a nationalist insurgency that brought together three disastrous influences: the determination of the French military to prevail at all costs; the lessons that the French military had drawn from the Indochina debacle; and the governmental and parliamentary weaknesses of the Fourth Republic. The result was a campaign that ended in self-induced defeat and in the breaking of the French military, which is without parallel in Western history since 1945.

The irony of this lay in the fact not that the French suffered military defeat in Algeria, as had happened in Indochina, but that the French military was successful in Algeria—indeed, it was so successful that the French army had to be broken by the French state in order to ensure its own preservation. In a very obvious sense the French army learnt the lessons of Indochina only too well—not the wrong lessons, but the right ones, which was even more dangerous—but the real problem that emerged for France in the course of this campaign stemmed from the legacy of defeat endured by the French army after 1940. In less than one generation the army of du Guesclin, Bayard, Condé, Turenne, Villers, Saxe, Foch, not to mention Napoleon, for centuries the greatest army in

Europe, suffered a series of humiliating defeats. The worst of these was in 1940, and it was a defeat that, with the creation of the Vichy state, forced the French military to chose between soldierly virtues. Pétain represented duty, obedience, service, but de Gaulle something much worse, *l'honneur*. It was to Pétain that the overwhelming part of the army pledged its allegiance, and it was de Gaulle who was vindicated by events; but in 1945, when the French army stood in desperate need of peace in which to try to heal the wounds of wartime division, it found itself committed to wars that ended in defeat in Indochina in 1954, in Morocco and Tunisia in 1956, and, disastrously, at Suez, also in 1956.

If the French army had returned from the Suez fiasco saddled with a crisis of confidence, then scarcely anyone would have been surprised; in reality the Suez affair had no such effect but reinforced a belief within the French army that this defeat was not its responsibility. The gut reaction of the professional military was that the defeats incurred over the previous 16 years were attributable not to the French army but to a democratic system, specifically to a series of weak governments that had failed state and army. If there was some truth to this, at least with regard to Suez, the evidence of Indochina suggests otherwise: the French military, not the despised politicians, had made the decision to stand at Dien Bien Phu, and the defeat had been military, not political. Admittedly, the lack of support from the homeland and the sense of isolation and abandonment felt by the French military in Indochina were very real and part of the reasons for defeat, but, as certain middle-ranking officers within the French regular army appreciated, the cause of the defeat in Indochina had been identified by Clausewitz more than a century before it happened:

The first, the grandest, the most decisive act of judgement which the Statesman and General exercises is rightly to understand [the nature of] the War in which he engages, not to take it for something, or wish to make of it something, which [it is not and] it is impossible for it to be.[5]

In these lines lay the rationale of *La Guerre Révolutionnaire*—recognition that in Indochina the army was defeated because, in failing to understand the nature of that conflict, it fought the wrong war.

The need to fight the right war posed problems to many French officers unwilling to accept the assertion that the only way to combat revolutionary warfare was for counterinsurgency to present itself as a mirror image of its enemy, as Jean Lartéguy noted in *Yellow Fever*:

The Viet Minh have created a remarkable type of army, a total army, in which every soldier is at one and the same time a propagandist, a schoolmaster and a policeman; every officer an administrator, a priest and an agronomist. To tackle an army like this would have required an army of the same type, a sort of military order, otherwise defeat was inevitable. I don't like being defeated or being commanded by incompetent leaders but I should dislike it even more if I had to become a monk–soldier or lay-preacher of some new doctrine or other.[6]

But if many French officers found the idea of becoming knights templar committed to a militant counterinsurgency credo repugnant, *La Guerre Révolutionnaire* embraced the notion as it set down a doctrine that sought to reverse Maoist concepts of revolutionary war, substituting a three-part program. It envisaged the destruction of insurgent forces and infrastructure, the creation of a counterinfrastructure, and the provision of political leadership and aims that could ensure popular endorsement and support. If the very fact that these ideas were committed to paper in the form of a coherent concept or doctrine of counterinsurgency was in itself very unusual, it need not have carried serious, still less sinister, implications. These ideas could have been lifted straight from the example of Malaya, where the British, empirically, had stumbled across most if not all of them. What made them so dangerous, however, was the willingness of certain French officers to consider it their duty to provide political leadership and aims in the event of the legally constituted authorities either failing to do so or providing leadership and aims of which they disapproved. At the very lowest level within Algeria the infringement of the military on the political began from the outset. Much of the mountains and interior had never been under formal administration; it had been ruled via traditional tribal structures and approved headmen. From the beginning of this campaign the military was obliged to provide village administration and aid programs and to explain France's purpose in Algeria. The experience of Viet Minh prison camps had introduced many French officers to the potency of indoctrination, and with a recognition of the importance of psychological operations, the French army began to set the political agenda of the counterinsurgent effort within Algeria.

But the real danger implicit within *La Guerre Révolutionnaire* lay not so much at the local level but in the challenge presented to the state itself. What made the danger explicit was the army's desperate determination to win in Algeria, to halt a humbling sequence of defeats, for reasons of national greatness and of its own raison d'être, and for reasons that were tied to the circumstances of the Indochina defeat. In 1954 the French army was obliged to abandon peoples who had supported it to the tender mercies of the Communists. With the evidence of the savagery of the Algerian nationalists to serve as warning of what would happen if it was defeated, the army was determined that never again would it desert the people who looked to it for protection and security. Moreover, Algeria was home soil, and in a combination of these factors is the explanation of the sheer ferocity of the French army in its dealing with the Algerian insurgency. Admittedly, the army had not shown much in the way of moderation in such campaigns as the one fought in Madagascar. In one year the number of deaths attributed to French military action was in six figures. But Algeria was different. In a campaign in which an estimated million people died, the depths were reached with the Battle of Algiers (September 1956–August 1957) when, on the French military's own admission, about 8,000 people died under interrogation. Nationalist claims suggest the real total was three times that number.

By a policy of frightfulness, the French army broke the challenge presented by the Algerian nationalists within Algiers, and with a three-part program it broke the back of rural insurgency. By a policy of forced resettlement, often conducted with great brutality, the French army cleared border areas; by means of extensive barriers and free-fire zones it effectively sealed off the insurgents from the outside world. Within the country the French army used conscripts on garrison duties, specifically to allow the concentration of elite forces for mobile operations in the interior and mountains. With helicopters used on an extensive scale for the first time in an insurgency campaign, the French fought a highly mobile campaign, but one with a consequence that further strengthened French military intransigence. The majority of French casualties were sustained by units that were the most estranged, those that felt the humiliation of past defeats most deeply. In early 1958, as Paris began for the first time to acknowledge the significance and ramifications of what was happening in Algeria, it was among such units that there emerged the determination to set the terms of reference of the French national effort in Algeria, even if this meant bringing down the government of the Republic. At its acid test in May 1958, the French military engineered the downfall of the government and the recall of de Gaulle to power, and did so on the assumption that the latter would provide the leadership that would ensure *Algerie française*.

In power, however, de Gaulle had to face the basic problems that the Fourth Republic had begun to face in its last days: the war crippled France politically, economically, and diplomatically. He came to see that rather than a won campaign in Algeria being proof of French greatness, the Algerian commitment was the obstacle to such status, and he realized that as long as the war in Algeria lasted, the army would always be exposed to the temptation to bring to heel the one institution that it did not control—the government of the Republic itself. Very slowly and cautiously de Gaulle began the process of reasserting civilian authority over the army and moved toward a recognition of the principle of Algerian self-determination, which, in effect could only mean independence. Within three months of coming to power, the budget of the Cinquième Bureau (formed in November 1957 as the army's department dealing with psychological operations) was slashed, and a policy of selective postings of officers known to be deeply implicated in the events of May 1958 was begun. Moreover, the referendum of September 1958 that confirmed de Gaulle in power and paved the way for the inauguration of the Fifth Republic saw Moslems in Algeria—women as well as men—vote on the same basis of equality as the *pied noir* settler population, with obvious implications for the future. Within two years the ceding of independence to France's other African possessions rendered the Algerian effort increasingly anachronistic and meaningless, and, having crushed a *pied noir* revolt in January 1960, de Gaulle spoke for the first time in November 1960 of *Algerie Algerienne*.

Realization of the drift of events prompted the Generals' Revolt of April 1961, in which selected regular army units staged a coup within Algeria in a desperate attempt to bring down de Gaulle and forestall Algerian independence. The coup was broken, largely because its leaders mistook their considerable personal popularity within the army for promises of active support: the vast majority of the army waited on events. With France preparing for civil war, de Gaulle broke the back of the revolt with an appeal that was a desperately ironic comment on the events of 1940: with the revolt basing its appeal on *l'honneur*, de Gaulle's appeal for support from the nation and the mass of the army was to duty, obedience, service. In so confronting the army, de Gaulle ensured that it would be broken. As its conscripts began to sabotage equipment, arrest suspect officers, and refuse orders, and as wavering individuals and units confronted the concept of loyalty and made their choices, the coup collapsed.

* * *

Few campaigns illustrate better than the Algerian war the danger presented to liberal democracy by insurgency in terms of military encroachment upon the prerogatives of state power, the principle of civilian authority, and the political decision-making process. The Algerian campaign politicized the French military to the point that for the French state defeat was more welcome than the continuation of war, and defeat was the means whereby it might reassert control of an army that had sought to determine the national interest. *La Guerre Révolutionnaire* failed because it was successful—indeed, so successful that it had to be destroyed. Expressed another way, the state had to accept defeat in war because the army won the campaign. A dozen more years were to pass before another European army faced a dilemma that was very similar to those faced by the French army in May 1958 and April 1961, but in April 1974 the Portuguese army insisted on ending wars in colonial territories that it recognized it could not win. In order to free the state and itself of impossible open-ended commitments, the Portuguese army broke the

Caetano dictatorship and, after two years of confusion, initiated constitutional and representative government.

* * *

The common point between the example of France in 1958 and that of Portugal in 1974 was the move by the military against the incumbent regime. In neither case was the military defeated in the course of the campaigns that provoked these crises. These campaigns were fought in overseas territories considered part of the metropolitan homeland, but they were nevertheless distinctive, and both were fought by nationalist forces, using Maoist methods and doctrine, which enjoyed considerable external support. Indeed, the internationalization of these campaigns was a critical factor in their outcome, both in terms of ensuring that the counterinsurgent effort was subjected to mounting political and diplomatic pressure. These same factors were at work in deciding the outcome of another campaign, again one that ended with the defeat of counterinsurgent forces, but on this occasion in a context very different from that of either Algeria or the Portuguese overseas territories. This campaign was fought on home soil between indigenous forces, not against a colonial authority, but it was not fought on Maoist principles. As such, this insurgency came to present itself as an alternative to Maoist concepts of revolutionary warfare, and it was to form the basis of a series of insurgency efforts in the 1960s. This campaign, fought in Cuba between December 1956 and December 1958, resulted in Castro's coming to power in January 1959.

* * *

The Cuban revolutionary war was to provide an alternative to Maoist concepts because it seemed to offer an escape from Mao's fundamental premise, that revolution had to be broadly based and preparation and organization alone provided the basis of success. It was this seductive argument that made the Cuban example so attractive to many Latin American revolutionaries, and in large part the series of defeats they incurred in the 1960s can be attributed to their having accepted far too willingly a concept of revolutionary war allegedly drawn from the experience of the Cuban revolutionary war by one of Castro's principal lieutenants, Guevara. In his writings about this war Guevara drew three conclusions: that the experience of Cuba showed that revolutionary forces could defeat security forces; that revolutionary war was primarily rural, the countryside was the natural area of revolutionary activity; and, critically, that revolutionaries, rather than awaiting an opportune moment, could generate their own success through direct action. While there seemed good evidence for these conclusions, they were, by narrow margins, erroneous, and with their uncritical acceptance of

Guevara's thesis the revolutionaries of Latin America in the 1960s made the disastrous error of adopting a revolutionary strategy that had never worked in Cuba and had little relevance in the totally different conditions of the mainland.

The first of Guevara's theses, that revolutionary forces could defeat security forces, was the one that seemed the most obvious and the one with which there could be no quarrel. Indeed, it seemed so obvious that the casual reader may well wonder why anyone should wish to dispute a self-obvious conclusion. Guevara's argument, however, was a call to arms by assuring would-be revolutionaries of the certainty of victory. Since the time that Latin America had won its independence from Portugal and Spain, the armed forces of the various states had attained an aura of invincibility, and proven American willingness to intervene in defense of its various interests in the Caribbean and in Latin America had only added to this luster. Before Cuba, the established social order throughout the continent seemed secure, and there appeared to be very little reason for revolutionaries to embark on courses of action doomed to defeat. Armies were generally popular. In caste-ridden societies they provided one of the very few means of social mobility and advancement, and the military's claims to be the arbiters of the constitution in the event of failure or abuse by politicians were generally conceded by society. Very few countries had any record of established democratic practice. Countries such as Bolivia and Venezuela were synonymous with instability and military intervention in politics, and until the 1960s not one democratically elected president of Venezuela had ever served a complete term. Politically and socially the armies of Latin America had always seemed so much in control that only those with a very pronounced death-wish harbored notions of testing their aspirations in battle. Cuba changed this. In Cuba the army was beaten, and the most important aspect of the Cuban revolution was precisely the destruction of the myth of invincibility enjoyed by Latin American armies. Armies, it appeared, could be beaten and this was the point that Guevara was trying to get across to his followers.

The truth of the Cuban revolution was somewhat different. There is no disputing that the army was defeated and its defeat led to the toppling of the Batista regime. But such a view is simplistic and fails to confront the special circumstances involved in the Cuban revolution. The army was untypical of Latin American armies. It had none of the prestige, status, or authority enjoyed by most of the latter. Cuba had been freed from Spanish rule by the Americans in 1898, and given U.S. rule and intervention thereafter, the army never secured a significant standing within society. Moreover it lacked a homogeneous officer corps identified with a ruling-class interest, as was the case in most Latin American countries. In fact, by the 1950s the Cuban officer corps was badly polarized between supporters and opponents of the Batista dictatorship, and this basic lack of unity within the army and its relative alienation from the rest of society was crucial in its defeat. In Cuba the army commanded little respect, and what it did possess was eroded disastrously as a result of its excesses in the course of anti-Castro operations. But more than that, in the course of the insurgency it deployed a total of about 30,000 men with a peak strength at any one time of about 20,000, yet in the course of two years of operations it lost about 200 dead before it collapsed. This might well suggest that an army that disintegrated with less than a 1% loss rate over two years owed its defeat more to it own internal weaknesses, lack of morale, and utter lack of professionalism than to enemy action. The fact was that the army was incompetent and racked by political favoritism. Any enthusiasm or ability on the part of the rank-and-file were all but nonexistent, and there was a marked distaste for action in many units. In all these respects the Cuban army was as dissimilar to the other Latin American armies as Cuba and its society were untypical of Latin America. When the revolutionaries on the mainland attempted to emulate the Cuban experience, they found far more formidable opponents who did not give them a chance to recover from defeats at the start of operations. In Cuba the army let Castro off the hook at the outset, and with the passing of time it became demoralized by its own failure. In the 1960s Latin American armies were alert, better trained, and far more determined than Batista's army had been, and these considerations, plus the social standing these armies enjoyed, were vital in their defeat of rural insurgency.

This, naturally, leads to the second of Guevara's theses—namely, the rural nature of revolutionary insurgency in Cuba. Once again a strong argument could be made out that the Cuban revolutionary war was a rural conflict. Castro spent the entire campaign in the Sierra Maestra in eastern Cuba, and right until the end the insurgents failed to take any significant town. These facts could not be disputed, but their recounting failed to take into account the fact that Castro and Guevara either never realized, or were never prepared to admit, the extent to which their final victory depended on support they obtained from all sectors of Cuban society, especially from the towns. Castro was to draw his celebrated conclusion that the towns were "the graveyard of revolutionaries and resources," but the truth was that the towns were crucial to his success. From them he drew a steady and growing stream of supporters who were forced out of the cities by the counterterror program unleashed by Batista. From the urban areas he drew the human and material resources that enabled him to win, and insurgent activity within the cities was important in dividing the Batista forces' attention. It was only in the last months of the war, after Castro's belated attempts to win over the peasantry of eastern Cuba by a "hearts and minds" campaign, that

Castro's forces began to achieve results, but in fact it was the combination of rural and urban support that gave Castro his victory.

For a variety of reasons this second thesis, even if it had been accurate, would never have worked in Latin America generally. Throughout the continent in general, but in the Andean states in particular, land and the question of agrarian reform were not explosive or even major social and political issues. In Bolivia, where Guevara made his disastrously inept attempt to raise the standard of revolution in 1967, reform had already given the peasantry more land than they could efficiently use, and here, as elsewhere along the mountain chain, the Indian peasants were themselves a built-in ingredient of social stability. Flight from the land to the burgeoning cities was a factor in preventing the pressure on the land becoming acute, but the reality was that the Amerindians were probably the least suitable raw material for social revolution to be found anywhere in South America. Their habitual obedience to authority and low standards of expectation dulled the impact of revolutionary appeals. Marked xenophobia and distrust of strangers compounded the problem, fatally for Guevara in Bolivia in October 1967. Latin America in the 1960s was not revolutionary, least of all in the countryside.

But it was the third thesis, the belief that revolutionaries did not have to await favorable circumstances but could generate their own momentum to success, that aroused the most adverse comment at the time it was set down. In ideological terms it represented a direct challenge to Leninist and Maoist revolutionary theory and practice. Guevara set out an elitist concept that stressed that revolutionaries could, by armed action, produce the social and political conditions needed for victory. Guevara's was a purely mechanical concept of a small, fast-moving, but hard-hitting guerrilla force, acting without a political base, which did not tie itself to the peasantry, producing through the momentum of its own military success the social, political, and military conditions necessary for its ultimate triumph. The *foco* concept aimed to produce a "revolution within the revolution", or, more crudely, a bandwagon effect.

Again it was a case that the facts of the Cuban revolution could be construed in such a way as to confirm the validity of this thesis, but this was a grotesque distortion of reality. The fact was that the conditions for successful insurgency were present even before Castro landed in Cuba. The Castro revolution did not need a long period of preparation and organization, because it had already been provided. Castro's very real achievement was to bring the various anti-Batista elements together under his own leadership, but this was very different from creating the conditions for revolutionary success. What had happened in Cuba was that Castro was able to tap into a deep and profound disenchantment with government on the part of a cosmopolitan, sophisticated population. The large and powerful middle class was divided in its loyalties, but in the main it had little time for Batista, who had come to power in a coup. The normal bastions of the established order, Church and Army, were weak, and all sections of society turned against a dictatorship that became increasingly violent and less discriminatory as its position worsened.

Latin American societies were nothing like as volatile as Cuba's had been, and in the 1960s revolutionaries throughout the continent came to grief in trying to spur into revolutionary activity social groups that were uninterested in insurgency. In urban centers the threats of unemployment and underemployment in a surplus labor market pressed caution on the workers. They, like many middle-class members, were prisoners of the cost-of-living index and had little inclination to engage in activities that could see them on the employment scrapheap. Moreover, in the 1960s the very example of the Cuban revolution, through its subsequent identification with the Soviet Union, served to confound the revolutionaries. Polarization did take place, but against the revolutionaries, because people regarded the choice not as between the established order and social change but as between the status quo and Communism. In this situation the overwhelming part of society chose to stand by the existing order. Even the local Communist parties had little interest in direct action. They were committed to constitutional action and were the only substantial group in society that might have provided the revolutionaries with the manpower and organization needed for any chance of success. Their standing aside from the various revolutionary efforts in the 1960s was a major factor in the success of the security forces.

Moreover, the physical conditions of campaigning in Latin America worked against the realization of the *foco* idea. If in Cuba the insurgents operated in the manner that Guevara claimed, they did so because terrain and vegetation were in their favor. The mountains were broken but not too difficult, and cover was freely available, as were sources of food and supplies for the insurgents. On the mainland conditions were very different. The jungle could provide cover, but at the price of mobility, while the mountains and fast-flowing rivers posed often insurmountable problems to insurgents whose fieldcraft, in many cases, was poor. The Guevara expedition in Bolivia, for example, seems to have spent most of its time lost, losing men at river crossings and hacking its way through jungle—the very antithesis of a mobile, hard-hitting force. Throughout the Andes the paucity of communications and the ruggedness of the terrain worked to the advantage of the security forces.

In setting out the reasons for the defeat of Batista in Cuba in the 1950s and of the revolutionaries throughout South America in the 1960s, one factor has not been mentioned, and it was critical to both. In part Batista's fall can only be explained in terms of American failure to support him. The United States remained unaware of the seriousness of the situation within Cuba at the time, and when it awoke to Batista's plight, it was too late to do anything. American opinion, moreover, was divided about Batista, and this served to prevent the incumbent Republican administration from formulating a coherent policy toward Castro's insurgency. After Castro's success, however, American resolution was never in doubt. In the aftermath of Castro's victory, the Kennedy administration was determined to show its resolve throughout Latin America as the Cuban threat to the stability of the continent emerged. With the intensification of the Vietnam War, this American commitment in Latin America deepened in order to ensure stability. American aid programs, particularly in the form of military equipment and training facilities, were important in preparing the Latin American armies for the revolutionary challenge in the 1960s. It was no coincidence, for example, that the Guevara expedition in Bolivia lasted less than two weeks after the Bolivians committed the last elements of their one and only U.S.-trained Ranger unit to his force's destruction. The American position in both failing to support Batista and then backing established governments was absolutely critical in the fluctuating fortunes of the revolutionaries. In a very obvious sense, the Cuban revolution invited both emulation by admirers and defeat at the hands of enemies alerted by its very example.

* * *

The collapse of the revolutionary movement in Latin America in the course of the 1960s was to have enormous consequences for revolutionary warfare, but its immediate importance lay in the fact that the continent remained, at least for the moment, stable at a time of massive upheaval and change. In terms of the color of maps, the 1960s saw what amounted to the demise of empire: virtually everything that remained under colonial rule at the end of the 1960s had been served notice of forthcoming independence. The Portuguese and Spanish overseas territories were different, but for the most part that phase of revolutionary warfare that had witnessed the Maoist concepts of rural, protracted war harnessed to the cause of national self-determination was all but spent. Henceforth the great part of revolutionary endeavor would be very literally home-grown, and revolutionary wars would be fought on the single issue of legitimacy.

This change, with its implication that future insurgency would be fought on home soil from which there could be no withdrawal, however, was, or at the time seemed to be, of small value when set alongside other, much more important developments. The 1960s, which opened with the Paris summit of the four great powers, witnessed the ebbing of European power relative to the United States and Soviet Union, which, with the first use of the term "superpower" in this decade, emerged in a class of their own—wholly mismatched but unable to be realistically compared except to one another. This decade saw the Soviet Union acquire an ability to strike at the continental United States with such strength as to ensure that henceforth a condition of mutually assured destruction existed. The decade saw Japan and Germany surface from the shadow of defeat in the form of industrial and financial performance that rendered their equaling Britain and France in terms of real power if not status, and China test its first atomic weapon. If the diffusion of power has been one of the most important features of the international community in the course of the twentieth century, then the 1960s represents the single decade when most change occurred. In 1938 there were perhaps only seven major powers; most of the population of the world still lived under European control. On 26 June 1945 the United Nations' Charter was signed by delegates from 48 independent states in the world; in 50 years the membership of the U.N. has all but quadrupled. Even allowing for the fact that in 1945 there were perhaps as many as 70 states in the world, the significance of the 1960s in terms of the end of the colonial empires is obvious. In real terms one year, 1960, saw independence conceded by colonial empires to more new states—19—than in the 14 years since the end of the Second World War. By the mid-1960s the period of wars of national liberation was clearly drawing to a close; the process of decolonialization after the 1960–63 period was settled and largely peaceful and orderly, errors and omissions excepted.

But the 1960s as a whole came to be dominated by one war—Vietnam. There were other wars, other events, but Vietnam was different. In part the difference lay in the fact that it was the first television war, and in part in that the greatest power in the world was humbled by a fourth-rate state in southeast Asia. The war cast a shadow over American power that was not to be lifted for a generation and then at a hidden cost: in July 1994 the number of American dead in Vietnam was exceeded by the number of suicides from the ranks of its veterans. There are good wars: Vietnam was not among them.

* * *

Vietnam proved so traumatic for the United States chiefly for two reasons. First, it was a war of uncertainties. It has often been said that the United States, by the fact of its distance from the theaters of operations, can only export war in crusades and when clear moral issues are involved. The Mexicans and Plains Indians might have some observations on this matter, but the point is well made. The Cold War was a period of massive certainty. It was this certainty that had underpinned the British effort in Malaya and had impregnated *La Guerre Révolutionnaire* in terms of the French military seeing the Algerian war as part of the Cold War struggle. Yet for the United States certainty dissolved in southeast Asia. Despite the fact that the enemy was avowedly Communist, this war divided American society, and in so doing it provided Maoist concepts of revolutionary warfare with continuing validity, even as various developments seemed to suggest that rural insurgency might be overtaken by events. The Vietnam War proved that rural insurgency remained the weapon of the poor, and that its relevance remained in terms of providing the basis of political and military resistance even in a war with the most powerful state in the world. By the time the United States came to the realization that the ideas that underpinned the type of war that it had intended to wage in southeast Asia were flawed, there was nothing that it could do about this situation. In Vietnam the United States found the bottom line of the concept of Limited War: the only war a power could limit was a war that, in the final analysis, it had to be prepared to lose.

* * *

The kind of war that the United States had intended to wage in southeast Asia shared a basic characteristic of that form of warfare of the eighteenth century with which it shared its name—the deliberate practice of restraint in the conduct of war—though they differed in that Limited War of the eighteenth century died with the emergence of ideological warfare, whereas after 1945 the context of Limited War was provided by ideological confrontation and struggle. In its post-1945 guise, however, what set the terms of reference for Limited War was the existence of atomic and later nuclear weapons.

After 1945, the emphasis of U.S. military planning was upon the prevention of war; as the confrontation with the Soviet Union assumed substance, so the United States in effect adopted a policy of Massive Retaliation, even though the formal doctrine was not coherently articulated until January 1954. The policy was simplicity itself and based upon U.S. strategic invulnerability: Soviet aggression would be met by attacks on the Soviet homeland with strategic weapons. The creation of an independent air force in 1947 was part of this process. As the Americans assumed responsibility for a western Europe that was wholly unable to provide for its own security and defense, Massive Retaliation was all that it could ever be as far as the European members of NATO (formed in April 1949) could have wished. Massive Retaliation provided guaranteed security in that any attack on them would be met by an American strategic response, and the European states did not have to contribute to the process. In effect, Massive Retaliation was a Medicare guarantee to western Europe, with the Americans having paid the insurance contributions.

The strength of deterrence lay in the combination of overwhelming U.S. strategic advantage and credibility. The American homeland was invulnerable to Soviet attack until the late 1950s, and the United States possessed the weaponry, means of delivery, and forward bases from which to carry out a strategic offensive against the Soviet Union. Moreover, the United States had used atomic weapons, and there was very little doubt that it would use such weapons again if the need arose. Indeed, at least before 1949, when the Soviet Union tested its first atomic weapon, there were individuals highly placed within the Truman administration who urged the waging of a preventive war against the Soviet Union; it was not until 1954 that the idea was formally discarded. In a period marked by mounting antagonism and increasing certainties, Massive Retaliation, whether formalized or not, possessed and represented assurance. The whole concept of Massive Retaliation fitted the pattern of "all-or-nothing" war, the concept of total war, that had been set in place by the two world wars, and it rested upon rationalism: an aggressor, faced by the realization of the destruction that would be incurred in the pursuit of a given objective, would abandon intention.

What deterrence and Massive Retaliation could not provide, however, was an answer to what would happen in the event of war if that war did not directly involve the parties to deterrence. The period immediately after the end of the Second World War was one of major upheaval for the U.S. military establishment, involving as it did demobilization, the formation of the Department of Defense and an independent air force, and the Admirals' Revolt. By 1949 just one armored division remained with the U.S. Army, and in the context provided by running down conventional capability, Massive Retaliation in effect became a substitute for policy. The United States would use strategic weapons in the event of a war with the Soviet Union because, in effect, it had no other means of waging war. The real policy, of course, was deterrence, but Pearl Harbor had proved the weakness of a policy of deterrence that was not backed by an adequate defensive capability. In the fraught circumstances as the Cold War took shape, this basic weakness in the U.S. strategic posture was largely obscured, but it moved to center stage with the outbreak of the Korean War in June 1950.

* * *

The demise of the Soviet Union and the opening of its archives has cast new light upon this conflict, though a thorough reevaluation lies in the future. What we do know from what has already emerged, however, is not that the war began as a result of the Soviet Union's having endorsed North Korea's planned aggression, but that Stalin's decision was reluctant and given only after much procrastination and evasion. If nothing else, it would seem that this conflict illustrates the extent to which the great power was the prisoner of its client, which it could not repudiate and in the end had to support. In the origins of this war there would seem to be a case of the proverbial tail wagging the equally proverbial dog, and a similar problem was to present itself in the American conduct of this war.

The Korean War had its origins in one fact and one miscalculation on the part of the North Korean leadership. The fact was a wholly unnatural division of Korea at the 38th Parallel as a result of being occupied by U.S. and Soviet forces at the time of Japan's surrender. Historically, there was no precedence for a division of Korea, and in fact neither side on the Korean peninsula regarded the existing division as either right or permanent. The miscalculation was the North Koreans having taken Washington at its word.

The months immediately before the outbreak of the Korean War were extremely difficult for the United States in terms of the formulation of a coherent national security strategy. The creation of NATO came at the time when the civil war in China reached its peak, when the Communist insurgency in the Philippines assumed serious proportions, and when Britain and France found themselves committed to major counterrevolutionary undertakings in southeast Asia. In this situation the United States hesitated, for obvious reasons. After all the trials and tribulations of Sino–American relations over the previous decade, the defeat of the Kuomintang was not a cause of much grief for the Truman administration, within which there was an awareness that Chinese and Soviet interests were very different and that American interests in China were not dependent on what type of regime existed in Peking. The real problem besetting such foresight and rationality, however, was an increasingly vociferous Right within the United States ever more loudly beating the anticommunist drum: within a matter of months the Truman administration was obliged to try to devise national policy against the background of an increasingly partisan congress and the charge of its having "lost" China—not that China had ever been the Americans' and still less the Democrats' to lose.

As 1949 passed into 1950, certain choices were made as United States sought to distance itself from the Chinese civil war. The Truman administration made it clear that there would be no American intervention in the event of a Communist invasion of Formosa, and Secretary Acheson publicly defined U.S. national interests in the western Pacific area and excluded South Korea in the process. The consequences of this latter decision became apparent with the North's invasion of the South on 15 June 1950. The immediate issue was whether America was *bundnisfähig*, as American failure to respond to aggression would undermine American credibility worldwide. But with those worldwide interests, and particularly the importance to the United States of its dependent allies in western Europe, went a conventional weakness that could not but circumscribe the U.S. response to the North Korean attack. The United

States had to fight initially with what was available, and, as this war began to lengthen, with what could be deployed when other more important priorities were met. During the course of this war, more U.S. troops made their way to Europe than to Korea, and the United States deliberately chose to meet both sets of demands without the mobilization of its economy and military manpower, fighting the Korean war with a little less than 10% of its available army manpower and less than 8% of its total service personnel.

From the outset, therefore, the United States limited the scale of the Korean War in terms of resources, and as the war lengthened, it chose to limit its scope in three other directions. The outbreak of the war, and specifically the Chinese intervention in October 1950 as U.S. formations approached the Yalu, resolved Washington's difficulties in the formulation of policy with respect to China: the Korean War committed the United States to the defense of Formosa. But just as this commitment was accompanied by the determination to prevent any Nationalist attempt to resume the civil war on the mainland, so the Americans, intent on avoiding a general land war in Asia, chose not to exercise the right of hot pursuit of Communist aircraft in Chinese air space, not to carry the war to the cities of Manchuria and China, and not to use atomic weapons either on or outside the Korean peninsula—the latter in spite of demands in Congress within a week of the outbreak of war.

Restriction upon the use of force in terms of scale and individual weapon systems came to be one of the main ingredients of the concept of Limited War, but it was to be the *cause célèbre* of this war for the U.S. high command. Conventional wisdom, handed down over many years, has always held that the decision not to use atom bombs in Korea was basically the result of the United States having relatively few such weapons at the time and its concern to preserve what it had in order to underwrite western Europe. Recent research has indicated that Truman was not unwilling to use atomic weapons in Korea but was not prepared to vest such power in a commander such as MacArthur, and it was precisely over the combination of two issues—the conduct of the war and the prerogatives of civilian authority—that the real battles of winter 1951 were fought. At issue—which MacArthur sought to conceal with his claim that "there was no substitute for victory"—was the right to direct U.S. national policy, and Truman broke MacArthur's attempt to secure for himself that power without its attendant responsibility. To Truman there most definitely were substitutes for victory—far more important than victory was avoidance of the use of nuclear weapons.

MacArthur was dismissed from his command in April 1951, at a time when the fighting in Korea had settled roughly along the starting lines from which the North Koreans had begun their offensive 10 months earlier. The war was to continue for another two years, and with two points of note. The battle line took the form of the Western Front of the First World War, complete with trench systems and deadlock, and the war lasted for another two years primarily because the United States refused to consider the Communist demand for the forced repatriation of prisoners as a condition for ending the war. Morality is often confused in and by war, but here was example of the moral dimension of war ensuring continuing hostilities long after the futility of proceedings was recognized by all concerned. Yet the real point of these events lay in their confirming one more ingredient of Limited War. In this period of hostilities, the Americans came to accept limitations of aim.

The authorization of U.S. action in Korea had been provided by the United Nations and was restricted to the support of South Korea. After their counteroffensive and clearing of the south, the Americans in effect abandoned these terms of reference, indeed the whole policy of containment, in favor of rolling back Communism with an invasion of North Korea. With Chinese intervention, the defeat and retreat of United Nations' forces, and then the stabilization of the front, renewed realism spelled a return to defensive, limited objectives.

The context of Limited War, however, is more difficult to define. The concept arose from the Korean conflict, which was fought with no script. Limited War was improvised by the U.S. high command, and it was from this war, and from their own study of history, that such individuals as Brodie and Osgood began to impose some form of intellectual discipline upon confusion after 1952. The definitive statement of Limited War was to await the New York conference in December 1957, but the essential characteristics of Limited War were present from the start of the U.S. intervention in Korea in 1950. The trend in warfare over the previous 100 years had been toward totality, and total war had undergone a military transubstantiation from its Second World War form into Massive Retaliation. Limited War returned to the distinctions between combatant and noncombatant that had existed since the time of Aquinas and ideas of proportionality and discrimination that lay at the heart of the concept of *jus in bello*. Total war had involved mass—mass mobilization, mass hatred, mass death. Limited War sought to restrict all three, though in the context of the Korean conflict one caveat must be noted: noncombatant casualties in this war greatly exceeded military losses as intention and reality diverged.

But if the concept of Limited War represented an attempt to reverse a process whereby "the greater and more powerful the motives of the war, by so much closer would the war approach its absolute form" by a deliberate observation of restraint, the fact was that the element of choice explicit in an acceptance of limitation was possible only in the absence of a war involving the issue of national survival or independence and by the conduct of war on soil other than one's own. In a very real sense, the concept of Limited War that was developed in the 1950s was designed for export by a great power: states fighting on their own soil and for national survival lack the luxury of choice. Yet, paradoxically, there are examples of Limited Wars being fought on home soil, and herein may be the exceptions that prove the rule. The Indo–Pakistan war of September 1965 was limited for the very simple reason that neither India nor Pakistan possessed the capacity to fight total war. But the conflict of December 1971, which resulted in the dismemberment of Pakistan and the independence of Bangladesh, was most definitely and deliberately limited by India from choice, and it sought no gain for itself from this conflict: the last Indian troops were withdrawn from Bangladesh within three months of the end of the war. As it was, this particular conflict accorded with the concept not merely of Limited War but of Just War, specifically *jus ad bellum*: the exhaustion of all other means of resolving the problem and the recourse to war as the last resort. Restraint in the use of force and the latter's employment for defensive purposes, good intention in terms of the pursuit of peace and reconciliation, plus just cause and respect for noncombatants, were the hallmarks of the Indian national effort in this war.

* * *

The formulation of the idea of Limited War in the course of the 1950s coincided with changes that provoked the New Look ordered by Eisenhower during his second term. The Soviets' launching of the first earth satellite, deployment of cruise missiles on submarines, and development of a nuclear arsenal clearly pointed to the deterrence having to undergo profound change. With the loss of American invulnerability to strategic attack clearly foreshadowed, such individuals as Brodie, Kissinger, and Wohlstetter in the period between 1959 and 1961 argued that the essence of the United States deterrence had to lie in scale and diversity in order to ensure a "secure second strike"—that is, the ability of the U.S. nuclear arsenal to survive a preemptive attack and still devastate the Soviet Union. The 1960s, therefore, was to see an immense increase in the number of land-based Inter-Continental Ballistic Missiles, the relative decline of the U.S. Air Force and Strategic Air Command, and the development of an invulnerable retaliatory capability vested in the submarine force. But no less seriously, the loss of strategic invulnerability forced the United States to confront the problem that it had to consider how to wage war, not simply to deter. Thus began, at the very end of the Eisenhower administration, a search that was to lead to the doctrine of Flexible Response, under which terms NATO would seek to fight a conventional battle in the European theater of operations with the intention of avoiding strategic escalation. However sensible such a policy was—and it certainly made no sense to remain committed to a concept of

Massive Retaliation that provided the United States with an all-or-nothing choice and would ensure the one thing that deterrence sought to avoid—the implications of the move to Flexible Response were not lost upon western Europe, not least because U.S. Secretary of State Herter in April 1959 stated quite openly that he could not envisage a U.S. president committing the United States to all-out nuclear war unless it was directly threatened itself. European reluctance and misgivings prevented the new doctrine's formal acceptance by NATO until December 1967, some five years after being adopted by the U.S. administration. The Gaullist *force de frappe* was partly an insurance that flexibility would not involve a nonresponse—politically, the French strategic nuclear forces were directed against the United States and provided against Europe being abandoned by the Americans—but, scarcely less significantly, Flexible Response contained a series of paradoxes. In 1961 the Americans had about 2,500 nuclear warheads in Europe, but by 1966 this total had risen to about some 7,200, and this at a time when it was committed to Flexible Response and the raising of the nuclear threshold in an attempt to delay or prevent the use of these weapons. But many of these warheads were vulnerable, and possessing them would involve the "use-them-or-lose-them" dilemma, when NATO was confronted by the "no first use" dilemma in addition to the fact that it made little sense for the alliance to fight with tactical nuclear weapons within West Germany. Moreover, militarily the concept of flexibility demanded the conduct of a defensive battle in mass and in depth, but politically the NATO area had to be defended forward and any Warsaw Pact offensive had to be broken in the border area by a defense that lacked mass and depth. Given the fact that Flexible Response seemed to differ only marginally if at all from the concept of Limited Nuclear War that had been touted in the 1950s, European NATO's lack of enthusiasm for the Kennedy administration's embrace of Flexible Response was palpable. It was not until the 1970s, however, that the inconsistencies and dilemmas at the heart of the new doctrine really began to become apparent.

The New Look also initiated change in two other directions: a new interest in conventional capabilities and, with General Maxwell Taylor as chairman of the Joint Chiefs of Staff, refinement of Limited War doctrine. Under the definitions supplied at the December 1957 conference, Limited War involved the exercise of restraint in the definition of aim, self-denial in terms of resources, and restriction in geographical area with respect to the prevention of the spread of conflict. Under Taylor there was one minor change in that limitations under the headings of resources and weapons were separated from one another—the two had tended to be run together throughout the 1950s—and there was one major change: force and "coercive diplomacy," as originally conceived by Kahn as part of nuclear escalation, became part of the doctrine of the 1960s. In a very obvious sense force and "coercive diplomacy" had always gone together, but under Taylor the concept of Limited War came to embrace the deliberate employment of force for specific political purposes: to show resolve, to warn, to induce a desired response. Just as nuclear deterrence had come to embrace such notions as Kissinger's Limited Nuclear War and Kahn's 44 rungs on the "escalation ladder," so Limited War came to be expressed in terms of graduated response in order to fulfill certain desired aims in ways that translated themselves into formulae, graphs, statistical tables, and God knows what other forms of visual representation.

As one rereads some of the things that were written at the time about how force might be used within the context of Limited Wars, some of which seems quite incredible even today, the real cause of wonderment is too easily missed. It is not so much that the ideas themselves were somewhat unreal, but that the assumption that underpinned them was wholly unrealistic: that the United States could set the terms of reference of any war in which it found itself, that it could always fight as it chose. What underwrote American assumptions at this time was a national self-confidence that held that there was nothing that the United States could not achieve, that there was no limits to national power and capability. This was the time when America was young. Wherein lay the reasons for the American failure in Vietnam? Was it in the assumption that the United States had the means to ensure that the war would be fought on its terms of reference, in a way of its choice and to an end that it desired? That this same impatience and restlessness, this same desire to take the battle to the enemy and destroy him in the shortest possible time that had characterized U.S. policy in the European context in the Second World War, was the one that was applied so disastrously to Vietnam? Wherein lay the basis of the Somalia debacle, but in the victorious 1991 campaign?

At best, this can only provide a partial explanation of what was to follow. Vietnam proved what was both obvious and unappreciated— that there are always limits to national power. But there would seem to be at least two other matters that must be considered in any assessment of the American failure in Vietnam. The first is perhaps somewhat quixotic: that the U.S. military was singularly unfortunate in that in Vietnam it had no experience of failure on which to draw. It is one of those very curious aspects of the military psyche that victory is regarded as the basis of military tradition—but it is no more so than the test of a great power is the winning of wars. Great powers are those that lose wars and keep going: it is defeat and failure and the reaction to failure and defeat that are the measure of a great power, not victory. Outside the very special circumstances of civil war, the U.S. Army, unlike any European army, has never been pitted against a superior enemy or forced to fight at a time when it was not ready. It has no experience of fighting defensively on its own soil and having to improvise in the midst of defeat and failure. The U.S. military has had its defeats and failures, but for the most part it has been able to wage war in strength and with success. Korea apart—and this war could be discounted because of "special circumstances"—the U.S. military, and specifically the army, has never had to recast itself, its organization, and its doctrine in the middle of a losing war to accommodate failure. In Vietnam it could not, and throughout the conflict its response to failure was to seek to bring "more of the same" to the battlefield.

But if this inability to recast doctrine was a factor in the American failure in Vietnam, the second matter is more substantial but no less contentious, since it touches upon one aspect of the war that continues to ruffle American plumage. The argument that the United States could have won in Vietnam had it used air power against Hanoi, the Red River dykes, and other strategic targets of major importance within North Vietnam has been consistently advanced since the 1975 debacle and continues to occupy pride of place in certain quarters. It is an argument that demonstrates a continuing failure to recognize the one matter critical to any understanding of the Vietnamese war. This war was not America's to win, and what was a U.S. failure in Vietnam was primarily the result of the inability, like that of the French a decade earlier, to recognize the nature of the war. Clausewitz's observation, cited in our examination of the French failure in Indochina, sums it up:

The first, the grandest, the most decisive act of judgement which the Statesman and General exercises is rightly to understand [the nature of] the War in which he engages, not to take it for something, or wish to make of it something, which [it is not and] it is impossible for it to be.[7]

In the Vietnam War the United States faced an enemy that it did not understand and one that fought to a Maoist script that obstinately refused to yield to the American-edited version. It was in this inability to comprehend the enemy that the final ingredient in American failure in Vietnam lay. The mistaken assumption that it could determine the terms of reference of the war, the lack of any tradition of failure, and a lack of understanding of the enemy were the three major factors that shaped an American failure in a war that the United States could never have won: the issue of victory and defeat was the prerogative of North and South Vietnam, not the United States.

* * *

The war in Vietnam produced a seeming paradox within its result. The North Vietnamese leadership conducted the war according to Maoist principles and brought the war to a close in April 1975 as Maoist concepts dictated, but in the period of the American intervention in southeast Asia the Communists were defeated in all three phases of revolutionary war. The American intervention in 1965 came at a time when Communist forces were operating in regimental strength in the initial phase of conventional warfare, and criticism of the American method of fighting this war often seems to miss the point that the conventional, set-piece battle had to be fought and won between 1965 and 1968, and this battle was won by the Americans. In this period, too, the Americans were responsible for the carrying of the war throughout the Mekong delta and up the river valleys into the Central Highlands. By their actions the Americans carried the war into areas that had not properly been under Saigon's control since 1954 and were responsible for breaking the military effectiveness of the Viet Cong, specifically in the delta, but also, more generally, throughout the country. These were very impressive results, but they were in a sense also irrelevant. The areas were those the Communists could trade if need be, and whatever success the Americans commanded in their endeavors could never compensate for failure in other directions.

What the Americans could never achieve was the pacification of the countryside, and they could never achieve this because it lay beyond their competence. The task of pacification, imposing governmental authority, and weaning the population away from its support of the Communists could only be achieved by the South Vietnamese authorities, and herein problems abounded. The pacification program was wholly inadequate. With a police force that was never set on a war footing and no fewer than 19 different intelligence agencies within the country at one time, South Vietnam was never in a position to attempt to consolidate whatever might have been achieved by field forces in terms of the destruction of Communist counterparts. In the final analysis the war was decided because the South Vietnamese state was unable to sustain a war effort sufficient to ensure its own security, and it was this point that U.S. intervention never changed and in some ways worsened. After 1965 there was a dependency culture on the part of the South Vietnamese state and army which undercut both the military effort of the United States and any attempt to implement genuine social change within South Vietnam that could rally support for Saigon.[8] The latter was a state of affairs that the more perceptive U.S. commanders within South Vietnam came to recognize and as at least one U.S. president acknowledged: if the South Vietnamese state could not or would not provide the basis of its own security, there was nothing that the United States could do to provide security for it.[9]

At different levels within the U.S. military establishment in South Vietnam there was an awareness that the United States had shackled itself to a corpse, but two matters served to prevent rationality asserting itself in terms of an abandonment of South Vietnam or a recasting of policy. The first was the familiar phenomenon of "filter-up, filter-out," which approached the status of art-form in the guise of the infamous credibility gap. The falsification of figures and maps, suppression of evidence, and outright lying that was to characterize so much of the official analysis of the situation within South Vietnam is so well documented as to require no elaboration. But the other factor was no less pernicious: the short tours of duty in South Vietnam served to keep the U.S. military on a learning treadmill, with the result that it never learned. These separate matters came together, the vicious circle of failure was closed, in the question of the importance attached to pacification and its conflict with the U.S. Army's priority, which was attrition. As long as Westmoreland commanded in Vietnam, there was never any prospect of American success because he was wedded to the attritional strategy, which Hanoi sought to turn against itself. It was a point that Westmoreland and the American national leadership never understood until it was too late: it was one that subordinate commands and formations came to appreciate in light of the slow realization that the clearing of successive areas of enemy forces was of no importance if these same areas could not be pacified. Perhaps the best single example of the misdirection and futility of U.S. military policy was provided by the effort expended in covering borders and infiltration routes from the north and the interdiction effort undertaken against forces moving down the Ho Chi Minh Trail. The point that Westmoreland seemingly could never grasp was that the rate of infiltration was dependent not on the level of supply that was available but on the level of insurgency in the south. If the latter could be curbed, whatever was sent from the north would be left in outlying areas, if not to wither and die, then able to operate only with diminishing effectiveness.

The army concept of war, based historically on mass, firepower, and shock action, had been born in the Civil War and raised in two global conflicts. It was a form of warfare that played to American national strengths in terms of manpower and industrial resources, and it sought the realization of strategic objectives through tactical victories that were secured by the application of superior resources. It was a form of warfare that was successful because in the three main wars fought under its terms of reference the U.S. Army was able to force its enemy to fight under conditions that ensured its defeat. But in southeast Asia after 1965 the Communists did not have to conform to any U.S. military initiative, and they could decline battle unless prepared to accept battle—and tactical defeat—in the pursuit of another form of success. This was exactly what Hanoi intended in its attempt to fight a protracted war in which the price to the Americans would become prohibitive in terms of political, financial, and manpower costs. In 1966 and 1967 almost 9 in 10 contacts in the field involving U.S. forces were initiated by the communists. The U.S. military command saw in such contacts evidence of the effectiveness of its policy; in fact, what the contacts revealed was Hanoi's acceptance of battle and losses in order to wear down American will.

The war against the French had served notice to the Vietnamese Communists of the critical importance of domestic French and international opinion in the conduct of war, and in the end the French defeat in Indochina was both political in Paris and military at Dien Bien Phu and along the Street Without Joy. For the Vietnamese communists the two efforts—against national will and on the battlefield—were as one, and the Americans were to find that the North Vietnamese leadership had presented itself with two issues with which to crucify the U.S. effort on the cross of domestic and international opinion.

The first two issues indicated the extent to which the concept of Limited War was flawed. The initial bombing of North Vietnam, Operation Rolling Thunder between March 1965 and November 1968, was implemented as a means of forcing North Vietnam to abandon its war in the south, come to the conference table, and admit defeat. In its original form this effort was very restricted, with the Americans prepared to intensify their attacks if the North Vietnamese leadership persisted in its war. In the lifetime of Rolling Thunder various restrictions were lifted, most obviously in beginning attacks on power facilities in Hanoi and Haiphong (June 1965) and then on communications targets in the same areas (July 1967). In the event, the North Vietnamese declared a willingness to come to the conference table if the bombing was halted, and North Vietnam used the prisoner-of-war issue to place Washington on the horns of a dilemma with regard to domestic opinion: only an American withdrawal would ensure the return of Communist-held U.S. captives. In these two matters Hanoi quite deliberately played the negotiation card as the means to achieve victory by other means, to subject the United States to international condemnation and to undermine the Johnson administration. American national will had been broken by April 1968, when the Johnson administration suspended all operations north of the Nineteenth Parallel, and it was only after this was a fact that Hanoi indicated that it was willing to enter negotiations—seeking to secure at the conference table what it could not win on the battlefield.

The Communist line in developing these two issues illustrated the extent to which Hanoi was very familiar with the needs of media manipulation and was able to tap into widely held prejudices, both international and peculiarly American. Bombing has never enjoyed a good press, and the conduct of the air offensive reinforced moral doubts within the United States that came to the fore with the first television pictures of the deliberate burning of peasant homes in the course of U.S. operations. The initial outrage that greeted these burnings died, but the reality was that such outrage came on top of the fact that there were many Americans who could not understand why an obscure civil war in southeast Asia involved a major U.S. national interest. This basic point would never go away. The basic unanimity that had attended the American involvement in two world wars and the Korean conflict never existed in the case of the Indochina conflict, and dissent hardened as the war took its course and American casualties mounted.

Herein one touches on one of the myths of this war—a "stab-in-the-back" legend of which Ludendorff would have approved—which holds that the American war effort was undermined by failing support at home and a partial media coverage that portrayed the U.S. performance in the worst possible light. There is some truth in this: in the final analysis the American effort in southeast Asia ended because the American public would not support it. There is also some truth in the allegation of a media coverage that was increasingly less helpful to the national effort, but this allegation cannot be separated from the fact that this was the first war with extensive television coverage and as such, any change of attitude could be attributed to its portrayal of events. If the wrong images emerged from the Tet offensive in February 1968, it was not because of the media coverage, but because of the offensive itself, specifically when set against the credibility gap that was all but synonymous with the Johnson administration's policy on Vietnam by 1968. The real point, however, was that the media reflected and did not create a growing public disquiet about the war and its conduct, and the point of significance was that there was an inverse relationship, delayed but unmistakable, between support for the war and U.S. casualties—support in public opinion polls fell as the body bags increased in number. It was not a case of casualties per se, but the awareness that increasingly there seemed no prospect of victory, merely a war lasting into the indefinite future, with the military's answer to any immediate difficulty a demand for more manpower to be made available. Marshall is credited with the observation that the United States could not fight a seven-year war—the quality of impatience that did so much to build the United States could never accept a seemingly indefinite commitment, which is what seven years would represent to an American electorate. One suspects that had he lived beyond 1959, Marshall might have reduced the time allowed for victory, but the fact was that the Vietnam War confirmed the basic point he had made. The U.S. military policy of attrition could not work, if it was ever going to work at all, except over a period of time that politically was not available, and the issue of defeat and victory was resolved on this basic point. The U.S. political and military leadership failed to appreciate it, and the Vietnamese Communists made it central to their policy.

* * *

In the previous chapter it was noted that U.S. presidential elections are supposed to provide choice but usually produce dilemmas. The year 1968 was a presidential election year, and, perhaps predictably, when confronted with a clear choice, the electorate chose wrongly and voted into power a man who was to take crime off the streets and put it into the White House. In the next six years a series of tragedies were to be played out: the personal tragedy of Richard Nixon, a man who did much and could have done much more, but in whom darkness drove out an always inadequate light; the tragedy of the Vietnam War and of southeast Asia, where the unfolding of events revealed that U.S. intervention had merely delayed events; the tragedy of the United States, which was to suffer more casualties after 1968, as it sought to disengage itself from the war, than it did before that time, as it sought to prosecute it; the tragedy of Johnson personally and his vision of the Great Society. Johnson died in 1973, the year that the U.S. military in effect left Vietnam: his Great Society had died by that time.

The war in Vietnam was decided in the year 1968—unless one considers that the U.S. military had already lost their way before then, and all that remained was role-playing with a script long written. The Tet offensive was the greatest victory won by the South Vietnamese and the Americans. The lack of a general uprising was evidence that the Communists had no real basis of support on the part of the population of the south, and the Viet Cong structure in the south was shredded, with the result that thereafter the war was increasingly a struggle between the two states of Vietnam. But Tet was also America's greatest defeat—the point when Johnson's "wise men" realized that the war had become unwinnable, when Walter Kronkite put a nation's hesitations, doubts, and disbelief into words. What remained was for the United States to extricate itself with as much grace as possible and to distance itself from the defeat of its client state. The final defeat was not graceful, and the United States was not able to distance itself from it.

* * *

In terms of perspectives of war and the twentieth century, however, 1968 encompassed much more than the American debacle in Vietnam. By then the revolutionary challenge had been beaten down throughout Latin America, but something else was happening in the field of revolutionary struggle. The Arab–Israeli war of June 1967 had resulted in an overwhelming Israeli victory and an utterly humiliating defeat for Egypt, Jordan, and Syria. In its aftermath there emerged one reality: the

Palestinian Arabs could look only to themselves for redress for the wrongs inflicted upon them by the creation of the state of Israel in 1948–49. After June 1967, in possession of the line of the Suez Canal and of the Jordan and holding the Syrian Heights, Israel was too strongly placed to be attacked directly, and hence the Palestinian Arab cause could only be advanced by action directed against Israeli interests outside Israel and Israeli-occupied territory. In a very real sense, by providing itself with security against military defeat in 1967, Israel ensured for itself war and the internationalization of the Palestinian problem in ways very different from its form over the previous two decades.

The significance of these developments lay in the fact that they came together at a time of change. Those Latin American revolutionaries who survived the debacle of the 1960s were forced to do some thinking for themselves. Their conclusion was obvious: that while there were local factors in the various defeats incurred across the length and breadth of Latin America in the 1960s, the defeats were too emphatic and too consistent for there to be anything other than an underlying general cause. This, they came to realize, lay in their basic strategy—specifically, that the security forces were too well established throughout the rural areas for there to be any chance of raising revolution in the countryside. The conclusion was obvious, not least because the majority of revolutionary rethinking was done in towns where those who had been defeated sought safety: revolutionaries had to turn their attention to the towns, for the simple reason that throughout most of Latin America there was no other place for them to go. To this fact of life there was a rider: at some point in the mid-1960s Latin America became more urban that rural, with more than half of the population concentrated in the towns.

With the evidence of the campaigns waged by the Irgun Zvei Leumi and Stern Gang in Palestine (1944–48), E.O.K.A. in Cyprus, and, most obviously, the Kill-a-Cop-a-Day campaign in Venezuela (1961–63) to serve as examples of urban possibilities, thoughtful revolutionaries drew from demographic and social changes in Latin America the clear lesson that rural insurgency was becoming less relevant, given the increasing importance of the towns. The revolutionaries also began to appreciate exactly what this process of urbanization entailed. In towns were vulnerable targets and an impressionable population, and in the maze of city streets and houses the revolutionaries could hope to find cover, protection, and supply at least the equal of anything they might find in the countryside. The Tupamaros in Uruguay were the first to appreciate this lesson, for obvious reasons: rural guerrilla warfare made absolutely no sense in a country that was 80% urbanized and where half the population of the country lived in the capital city. If revolution was to continue, then it had to be in an urban context. It was this crucial point that was to be picked up by Carlos Marighela in his work, *The Mini-manual of Urban Guerrilla Warfare*. In fact, the premise was wrong: pro-tracted insurgency in the country did have a future, as the F.A.R.C. in Colombia and later the Senero Luminoso in Peru were to prove.[10]

* * *

Marighela's concept of revolution aimed at forcing a government into taking repressive measures that would alienate people, produce a polari-zation of society, and thereby achieve the isolation and defeat of the administration. In a sense the writings of this Brazilian ex-communist relate back to Lenin and the cell organization. In one major sense, how-ever, he went against one of Lenin's basic premises, since he was natu-rally more closely related to the Latin American scene and to the views of Guevara, with whom he is normally contrasted, not compared. Marighela and Guevara agreed about the nature of revolutionary war-fare in South America, but they differed in approach. Both accepted the concept of a revolutionary elite making revolution through military action alone and without waiting for the emergence of Lenin's "revolu-tionary moment." Neither believed extensive political and psychological indoctrination to be relevant in South America. Marighela clearly appre-ciated one point from the whole series of revolutionary reverses in Latin America during the 1960s—that the grip of the security forces on the countryside had to be broken, but that it was too strong at that time for any rural-based insurgency to have any chance of taking root. Marighela also realized the revolutionary potential of the cities in terms of the thousands of marginally employed and unemployed workers, the squalor and degradation of the slums and shanties, the rising levels of expectation and demand, and the phenomenal growth in population, which by the late 1960s saw 45 in every 100 Latin Americans under the age of 15. He saw that industry, wealth and power, and numbers of people were being increasingly concentrated in vulnerable cities at the expense of the countryside and that as long as regimes were able to retain their grip on the towns, they would always be in a position to mobilize counterinsurgent resources for the countryside. Thus Marighela aimed to tie down the security forces in the towns in order to break the grip they had on the countryside. This went in hand-in-hand with demoralizing government forces and revealing to a disenchanted population the gov-ernment's repressive nature. By raids, sabotage, murder, and kidnap-ping, accompanied by astute manipulation of the media, as well as by identification with popular causes, Marighela aimed to overthrow a regime by the polarization and militarization of a society and through the prosecution of complementary urban and rural campaigns. He was killed in November 1969 during a bank raid while trying to put these ideas into practice, but his influence was secured by the publication, shortly before his death, of a pamphlet—*The Minimanual of Urban Guer-rilla Warfare*—which is not simply a theoretical treatise but a practical guide to methods, tactics, and planning. Modern means of communication, both physical and of the spoken and written word, have ensured that *The Minimanual* attracted worldwide readership.

It was widely read in part because the late 1960s saw the communications revolution: mass air travel and transoceanic television came of age in this decade.[11] But at this time, also, Western society was in a state of ferment and intellectual disarray. Everyone wanted to go to San Francisco, and, much more relevantly, Situationists provided the answers, and the Spanish anarchist tradition began to emerge from the shadows of defeat. What tends to be obscured by the events of 1968 is that revolutionary violence in Europe predated the events of Paris in May 1968—the First of May Group carried out its first operation, the kidnapping of a Spanish priest in Italy, in 1966—and certainly the Spanish anarchists, with their *Grupos de Afinidad*, had anticipated the active service unit by decades. But it was onto this scene of ferment and upheaval that this new concept of struggle from Latin American sources emerged, and a second need was there to complement it—the intellectual basis of armed challenge—and this was to be provided by the New Left.

In the emergence of the New Left one can identify three main factors at work in addition to the impact of the Vietnam War, which was in itself both cause and catalyst of change. There was the antagonism of the New Left toward Western society and its values. The late 1960s was a period of considerable discontent with capitalist society, in large part because of its alleged emphasis on materialistic values and its lack of spiritual and moral ethic. In Europe the great material advances that had been recorded since the end of the Second World War had produced a new, young, educated middle-class element that felt alienated from ownership, the means of production, and the prevailing social morality. This latter consideration is in fact the second point: a belief that for all its commitment to change and social welfare, capitalist society remained an instrument of class repression, the dominant social class being both incapable and unwilling to adopt genuinely radical reforms. For the New Left, democracy was for conformists, not radicals—events in 1968 seemed to indicate that democratic society was as repressive and illiberal as any dictatorship. These developments, especially the putting down of the spate of disorders, particularly in West Germany and France, was inextricably linked with the revival of notions of violence and direct action as the only means of bringing about change. This was associated with a revival of anarchism, particular the Spanish variety with its emphasis upon "the propaganda of the deed" that had been in the doldrums since the 1930s. Naturally the failure of constitutional means of change and the use of force by states to ensure social order weakened resistance to the idea of the use of violence as the means of achieving social change. Moreover, there was a more positive aspect: the emergence of the idea of violence as a social cathartic—violence does you good—and the means whereby society might be redeemed. Such ideas had long been a part of certain right-wing philosophies, but they had been discredited since the end of the Second World War. Now, with the writings of such individuals as Franz Fanon, the belief in the correctness of violence—that violence provided the title deeds of a new society—gained new and unexpected currency within the Left.

These elements came together in 1968 because this was the year when the New Left's rhetoric proved self-fulfilling: the radical challenge was broken by states that did not hesitate to use violence to sustain themselves. Thereafter, in the New Left's own phraseology, the states set about "accommodating" radicals with the values that they had so recently opposed, yet there remained an irreducible minority that could not be accommodated within a system that had legitimized the use of counterviolence. Herein the different strands came together. The emergence of armed Palestinian action came with, supported, and was supported by an international freemasonry committed to armed struggle that came into being at exactly this time. It was not coherent, and some of the parties made very strange bedfellows, but despite its seeming incoherence the result was nonetheless potent. The concept of urban guerrilla warfare provided doctrine; the New Left provided the intellectual rationale and discipline of a new phase of revolutionary endeavor; and the events of 1968 provided cause. But things were not to work out quite as intended.

* * *

In the wake of the events of 1968, there was a proliferation of urban guerrilla warfare throughout Western society. North America played host to the Weathermen and Quebec-separatist groups, in Europe there emerged such organizations as the Angry Brigade in Britain, the Red Army Faction in West Germany, and the *Brigate Rosse* in Italy, while Japan produced its share in the form of the *Sekigun Wa* (the Japanese Red Army), which carried out the attack at Lod Airport on behalf of the Palestinian Liberation Organization in May 1972. There were also revolutionary urban groups active in Turkey and, unbelievably, in the Netherlands and in Switzerland. But what was so significant about this wave of urban guerrilla warfare was its failure. It was able to induce crisis in various societies, but only two groups, one of which was not properly an urban guerrilla movement, were able to sustain themselves at any level of effectiveness in the 1970s, and both owed their longevity to origins that had nothing to do with Marighela's concepts of urban revolution. The Catholic Nationalist cause in Northern Ireland and the Palestinian diaspora spawned organizations that were more than able to carry their respective wars to their enemies, yet in a very obvious sense their very success set out the limits of their effectiveness. The Irish Republican Army and successor organizations were able to polarize society, but only along an existing fault line. The Palestinians simply could never bring to bear pressure of the kind that would ever induce Israel into meaningful dialogue and concessions, and their attempt to do so resulted in a series of actions that alienated the very international public opinion that had to be persuaded. Nevertheless, the Palestinians, despite the reaction against such incidents as the Munich Olympics in September 1972, Ma'alot in 1974, and Entebbe in 1976, did establish themselves as a genuine party to the Middle East problem, which, after this time, could never be settled without a Palestinian Arab dimension. The 1970s were to end, however, with the P.L.O. as far from destroying Israel as it was 10 years earlier.

In the 1970s the concept of urban guerrilla warfare foundered upon three inescapable facts of life. The first was inherent within the concept itself, in that Marighela's idea of struggle was not unlike a two-story house without stairs: the movement from the active service unit to mass organization was all but impossible. In the case of the Tupamaros in Uruguay, the attempt resulted in a compromise of security that proved disastrously irreversible once the security forces penetrated the organization. Arguably the transformation of a small organization that owed its survival to secrecy and elusiveness to a popularly based mass movement was what Castro's force had managed to achieve in Cuba and what the Basque *Euzkadi ta Askatazyna* in Spain, the republican factions in Northern Ireland, and the Sandinista insurgents in Nicaragua (1978–79) were to achieve in the 1970s, but in all four cases the basis of support was already in place.

The weakness of the Marighela concept of urban guerrilla warfare, like Guevara's *foco* before it, was that it was mechanistic, and revolution was reduced to mere technique; the 1970s revealed that urban revolutionary struggle could not command assured success with the polarization of society. In both Uruguay (February 1973) and Argentina (March 1976) urban guerrilla forces polarized societies but against themselves, with the result that democratic governments were overthrown by hard-line military dictatorships that proceeded to destroy the revolutionary movements through the use of extreme measures. Given the repression and widespread use of murder and torture by dictatorships, the 1970s represented perhaps the worst single decade in Latin America since independence. To use a comment made about the urban guerrillas in Uruguay at the time, the Tupamaros dug the grave of democracy and fell into it themselves.[12] A similar situation prevailed during the "Years of

Lead" in Italy, where in spring 1978 the kidnap and murder by the *Brigate Rosse* of Aldo Moro provoked a public reaction that enabled the authorities to use draconian security measures to eliminate the revolutionary organization.

The second factor at work against revolutionary struggle during the 1960s was the ebbing of the tide of radicalism after 1968. The events of that year forced a choice. The willingness of authority to use force to sustain itself spelled an end to self-indulgent dissent—according to one commentator, the events of May 1968 constituted "street theater"—and, faced with the Leninist reality that revolution was a profession, the greater part of protest withered and died. Part of the impetus was directed into subpolitical activity in the form of "people politics" and single-issue causes: 22 April 1970 saw the first environmental protests in the United States, which were to give rise to the Greenpeace movement. But by the early 1970s only handfuls of incorruptibles remained faithful to the revolutionary cause, in large measure because the economic and financial crises that settled upon Western society around the turn of the decade ensured a conformity that was the product of rising cost-of-living and unemployment indices.

Third, the reduction of a mass movement to an irreducible militant core was critical in the sense that the very estrangement of this core of society that provided its raison d'être left it with a rationale that made it impossible for it to gain widespread support and sympathy. What was very notable about most of the revolutionary groups that emerged was their incoherence about the type of society that was sought and which justified present violence. Moreover the cult of violence and the fact that many urban revolutionary groups did indeed attract some very disturbed individuals—no new psychopathic cases were admitted to Belfast hospitals between 1969 and 1974—necessarily had circumscribed appeal. To this general point must be added a specific one: in four countries that were affected by urban guerrilla warfare, the peculiarities of domestic arrangements also served to sap revolutionary militancy. The existence of social democrat administrations in West Germany blunted revolutionary appeal, and in Spain the transformation of the Franco dictatorship into a parliamentary democracy, complete with a social democrat government, served to isolate the E.T.A. and to persuade most Basque nationalists to work within the new system. In Italy the refusal of the Communist party to be deflected from its parliamentary path despite the attempt to provoke it into armed militancy was as important in revolutionary failure as it had been in Latin America in the previous decade. Certainly in western Europe in the 1970s the democratic commitment of the main parties of the Left served as a shield against revolutionary violence, while in Canada the ruggedly dismissive treatment afforded the threat posed by the *Front de Libération Québecois* in October 1970 was possible on the part of a prime minister with such impeccable liberal credentials as Pierre Trudeau.

In retrospect, most of the groups that were to emerge in the aftermath of 1968 were to be afforded greater attention than they warranted. For the most part such organizations were to prove short-lived and ineffectual, and their careers were often as bizarre as some of its members. For example, in the case of the original Red Army Faction—more commonly known as the Baader–Meinhof Gang—the distinction between the political and the plainly criminal was seemingly unappreciated by many of its members, not least Andreas Baader, who, with a penchant for fast cars and even faster women, was described as halfway to being a latter-day Robin Hood in that he stole from the rich but had not managed to get round to giving to the poor. In a four-year career, which began in April 1968 before events in Paris, the Baader–Meinhof Gang's main activities were directed to robberies and theft, and only in the last three months of its existence did it undertake a series of bombings that could be described as political. By June 1972 most of its membership had been arrested. But their successors in the Red Army Faction proved much more difficult and indeed provoked a crisis of confidence on the part of the federal authorities, which had been remarkably relaxed in their handling of the Baader–Meinhof Gang. The revived Red Army Faction was involved in the bombing of the West German embassy in Stockholm in April 1975 and in the Entebbe (June–July 1976) and Mogadishu (October 1977) hijackings, but after the latter—the "German Autumn" that in a six-week period saw the abduction and murder of Hans-Martin Schleyer, Mogadishu, and the deaths of Baader, Gudrun Emsslin, and Jan-Carl Raspe in prison—its effectiveness declined. Its attempt to assassinate the U.S. commander in Europe in September 1981 was really its last gasp effort, and by 1983 its second-generation leadership had been all but eliminated. Throughout the 1980s there were to be occasional attacks by left-wing dissident groups, but by that time Bonn was faced with the emergence of neo-Nazi factions, first operational in September 1980, and these were probably given greater public support than anything that the militant groups were able to command during the 1970s. Whatever sympathy the Red Army Faction was able to attract was marginal, though it was not until 1992 that it disbanded itself.

* * *

The period between 1968 and 1974 was one of massive change, and perhaps the most important single development in this period was the collapse of the Bretton Woods system of fixed exchange rates and the international trading system that had been in place since 1949. It was a system that fixed the value of all other currencies against the dollar and had provided the basis of a postwar recovery characterized by stable currencies, industrial growth and rising productivity, low interest rates, and full employment. By 1974 such sureties had passed or were passing from the scene.

In the long term the ending of the Bretton Woods system would seem to have been inevitable, if for no other reason than the fact that it was founded on an American financial and industrial preeminence that was certain to be eroded with the postwar recovery of other economies. But the immediate short-term origins of the collapse of the financial system lay in the fact that between 1965 and 1970, as the Johnson administration sought to finance both the Vietnam War and the Great Society without any increase in taxation, the federal debt rose from $321 billion to $389 billion while inflation rates rose to 7% per annum. Even more seriously, the demands of war and social reform created an import surge that resulted in 1971 in the first deficit on visible trade since 1893 and in the United States having become the world's largest importer of oil, steel, and motor vehicles. The long-term implications of such a development for the world's greatest manufacturing economy—and hitherto the world's largest producer of oil, steel, and motor vehicles—were profound, while its international ramifications were more immediate and dramatic. The end of American self-sufficiency in manufacture and the increasing importance of imports to industrial production meant that by early 1978 the U.S. trade deficit was running at $45 billion a year, whereas in 1972 the sum of trade deficits of all the countries in the world had been $10 billion. But the immediate consequence of the United States' trading deficits at a time of continuing capital export was an international surfeit of dollars. Low interest rates in the United States and the end of gold convertibility in 1971, plus the obvious depreciation of the dollar's real value, meant that there was no real foreign incentive to hold U.S. currency. This was so critical because the Bretton Woods system of fixed exchanges had rested upon American trading surpluses and capital exports. By 1971 an overpriced dollar, with no means to devalue it, had exported the U.S. inflation problem. In an attempt to maintain the system and to help Washington with its short-term problems, foreign governments and banks bought excess dollars at the existing rates of exchange. Between January 1971 and mid-1973 the expansion of the domestic money supply in the eight largest economies after the United States increased by 45%, with the result that by 1973 the U.S. economy was no longer the primary cause of global inflation. But with major industrial commodity prices traded in dollars and doubling between 1972 and 1974, the knock-on effect was becoming obvious by the time that inflation in the eight largest economies averaged 12% per year in late 1973. Thus an unprecedented wave of global inflation was in place before a 350% increase in the price of crude oil was announced by Saudi Arabia in October 1973.

The oil price increase was to initiate a period of financial turbulence throughout the decade as the industrialized countries were forced to deal with renewed inflationary pressures and growing budget deficits, but it was not until 1979, and a series of new increases in the price of oil, that the most serious recession since the Great Depression of the 1930s began to take hold. What made this especially serious for the United States was the fact that during the 1970s productivity fell, and changing industrial patterns began to make their mark on U.S. society. The decline of manufacturing industry in the United States began to make serious inroads into industrial capacity by the 1980s. Another decade was to pass, during which the federal debt doubled and the United States completed the transformation from being the world's largest creditor nation to the largest debtor nation, before the U.S. Navy was to find that before it could go to war it was dependent on suppliers from no fewer than eight foreign states because U.S. industry could no longer supply its needs. Such a state of affairs seems incredible in light of industrial performance in the course of the Second World and Vietnam Wars.

The effects of these changes were varied. Certain economies, such as that of West Germany, by accepting low growth and high interest rates, were able to escape some of the worst of the inflationary pressures. Others, such as that of Japan, accepted inflation as the price of industrial growth and increased productivity, with the result that they were able to ride out the financial storm. Yet, other economies, such as those of Britain and the United States, contrived in differing degrees to get the worst of all eventualities. But generally throughout the 1970s there were unmistakable signs that the trough was finite. The confidence in continued economic growth and growing prosperity that had characterized the 1960s died amid the reality of crippling interest rates, rising unemployment, and falling productivity.

The social consequences were profoundly important. In the United States, the faltering of the economy and changing patterns of production accelerated the emergence of the Rust Belt, which had the effect of maintaining racial segregation while the black share of national wealth fell between 1968 and 1995. In terms of radical endeavor, however, the events of the early 1970s clearly sapped the power and cohesion of the Left, and this at a time when there emerged on the Right very different views of society and the role of the state—views that in effect held that the state was the obstacle to economic growth and rising living standards. In any event, the state, as it had existed since the Second World War, could not survive. The internationalization and deregulation of money markets ensured that individual states did not have the recourse to means of economic and financial management that they had previously commanded. But the real shift in power within Western societies was in terms of perception and in the weakening of institutions of the Left, most obviously the trade unions, which were ever less capable of dealing with the problems caused by unemployment. In a very obvious sense, the success of the Left was synonymous with capitalist expansion in the 1950s and 1960s; the faltering economies in the 1970s undercut the basis of radical and revolutionary endeavor. The urban guerrilla groups in advanced Western counties were the last stand of a past order.

* * *

Western states and societies naturally present themselves for immediate attention in any consideration of the economic and financial changes wrought in the early 1970s, but perhaps the impact of these changes was even more profound for Third World countries. Even before the full effects of oil price increases were felt, Third World countries were increasingly beset by the problems created by the worsening terms of trade. The postwar Green Revolution resulted in an increase in agricultural yields that outstripped population growth at least until the end of the 1970s, with two results. Famine, except as the byproduct of war, was largely eliminated, but agricultural prices remained constant or declined, with obvious implications in terms of purchasing power on the part of states dependent on agriculture for export earnings. For newly independent states, already contending with the problem that the process of decolonialization freed Western states from responsibilities while facilitating their economic domination of former colonies, the consequences were dire. There was no escaping the reality of the proletarianization of the Third World relative to the First World. In terms of stability, the implications of these problems, the reality of capital repatriation by foreign companies, and the fact that many of the newly independent states lacked a genuine cultural identity and consent and were beset by internal policing and border problems, need little in the way of elaboration.

Of course, these are only the present problems; what confronts many Third World states, particularly in Africa, is not simply an intensification of existing problems, but the addition of new ones that might easily overwhelm them—but to what end is far from clear. The continuing desiccation of Africa, the worsening terms of trade, which have afflicted so many primary producers that have been obliged to import Western inflation while their own purchasing power has diminished, and the continued irrelevance of borders that do not relate to realities of relief, natural vegetation, or tribal, ethnic, linguistic, or religious divisions are three of the most obvious problems facing African countries. These are legacies of the past. At the present time, we stand on the brink of three major and obvious crises that will, when they break, present themselves in their most virulent form in the developing countries. Today some four-fifths of humanity has access to about one-fifth of the world's resources. The vast majority of the world's population—which has doubled in the last two generations and has experienced a three-fold increase between 1945 and 1995—has only very limited access or none at all to proper shelter and decent clothing, and a quarter of humanity has no access to clean water. One in five people in developing countries— some 840,000,000 souls—suffers serious hunger, and while 200,000,000 children between the ages of 7 and 11 years are obliged to work for most of the hours of daylight, 3 in 10 of all adults that form the world's employable population lack work and the means to sustain themselves and their dependents. Given continued population growth, in part the result of the continued importance of the family in terms of generating income and security, this situation can only worsen—obviously in terms of pressure on resources, but no less importantly because of changing work patterns. At the present time Kenya devotes 23% of its total state expenditure to education—half of this total on primary education—but in 1989 the total number of children in state secondary education numbered only 30,000. With the population of 27,000,000 in 1993 rising to 35,000,000 in 2000, the fact is that Kenya and other states in the Third World are obliged to devote increased resources for longer periods in order to provide the skilled base for future production, with two obvious riders: such resources are not and will not become generally available, and, at least in relative terms, the human base for future production is ever shrinking.

But lurking beyond the horizon are the food and fuel crises. In October 1994 an article in the *International Herald Tribune* posed the question of whether China could survive beyond the year 2034, by which time it would require the total surplus food requirement of the world. The question was meaningless. The food crisis, given the depletion of the resources of the sea and the fact that in the next decade a quarter of all arable land in the United States will go out of production, is going to explode long before 2034, and in any case the China crisis will present itself in the next decade. Between 1994 and 2004, China must create 250,000,000 new jobs merely to maintain present levels of employment and prosperity. Since it would appear that this could only be achieved by a diversification of light engineering and consumer production, the resultant energy requirement will be equal to the present level of world surplus energy capacity. All other considerations being equal, China's requirements can be met at least in the short term, but seemingly only at the expense of a major increase in energy prices at a time when alternative food sources must be developed, and none need reminding of the disastrous consequences of the 1974 and 1978 oil price increases for the countries of the Third World.

In light of these developing crises in food, fuel, and employment, it seems unlikely that Western-style democracy will have little if anything to offer the greater part of humanity in years to come, and this leaves aside the fact that what we in the West understand to be the basis of liberal democracy—the rule of law, consent, compromise, the concept of opposition, and the denial of the right of any individual issue to justify systemic resistance—are not well founded in Third World countries. Indeed, even in the Western world such values are under an attack unprecedented in the last 50 years. Yet the real point is that the Western capitalist system, which has imposed itself upon the world, since the time of Locke and Smith has been based upon a double premise in terms of the stability of individual countries—economic expansion and an acceptance of labor dislocation as the short-term cost inherent in long-term growth and advancing prosperity. We have been assured that "technology makes possible the limitless accumulation of wealth" and that

liberal principles in economics—the "free market"—has spread, and have succeeded in producing unprecedented levels of material prosperity, both in industrially developed countries and in countries that had been, at the close of World War II, part of the impoverished Third World.[13]

One remains less than convinced—not merely on account of the deprivation in such countries as Bangladesh, where per capita income totals £3 per week and two-thirds of all children suffer from malnourishment, but because both elements of the double premise that have underpinned the capitalist system would seem to be dead. Leaving aside the fact that we have no guarantee that the trough is not finite, that at the end of such a process as the limitless accumulation of wealth one would not be forced back on the definitive reality of food resources as the basis of real wealth, the real social problem that is likely to emerge is the reality of permanent labor dislocation. The impact of the Information Revolution has been to reduce the wealth-producing base within society in real terms, while the pattern of education and social development of the last 50 years means that those who fall outside this base are unlikely ever to regain a position within it, and that the greater part of society will remain outside it. The long-term implications of an ever greater concentration of wealth in relatively fewer hands and the existence of political expectation created in a previous age can hardly be missed. One suspects that even as a new generation emerges with lower levels of expectation in the first couple of decades of the present century the greatest source of tension in Western society will be the clash of interests of a shrinking class of producers and the demands of a growing class of consumers, most members of the latter certainly lacking the means and perhaps even the inclination to join the ranks of the former.

It is possible, therefore, to see in present developments a basis of common action on the part of the disadvantaged, the disinherited, both within Western society and in various parts of the Third World. The emergence of a permanent underclass that consists of individuals stranded at the bottom of the qualifications league and therefore wholly unappealing to any potential employer has already resulted in depressed city centers, a rise in drug-related criminal violence in these same areas, and a mass refusal to participate in the political system—a deliberate self-disenfranchisement on the part of an alienated part of society that has equipped itself with its own *mores* and culture.

Western Europe has yet to experience anything like the Eighteenth Street phenomenon in the United States, but the point would seem to be that the state has been weakened over the last two decades, in ways that extend beyond a failing police control over deprived inner-city areas. The real weakening of the state exists in the erosion of power, authority, and will—specifically, in terms of the use of power in an anticipatory manner. Moreover, anticipatory demands are increasing and, because of the impact of television and the Information Revolution, the time available to meet such demands has lessened. In Western society we may be witness to the weak politics of increasing poverty and elsewhere enfeebled authoritarianism may well become the norm, the latter being accompanied in many parts of the world by the spin-off from the many conflicts that have erupted over the last decade. A permanent low-grade militarization of society in many Third World countries and the development of the politics of grievance in advanced Western societies may well be the constants of political life in future. Arguably, already in the west we have seen both. The rise of the militias in the United States and the emergence of what has been dubbed subpolitical activity—protest and the rise of the politics of grievance—would seem to be permanent, irreducible features of national life, and armed militancy may well follow in their wake. Most certainly militancy has underpinned religious fundamentalism—whether Christian, Hindu, Islamic, or Jewish—in the last decade in response to the stresses of modern society, most obviously in dealing with nonbelievers.[14]

In terms of many Third World countries, indeed even some of the countries of eastern Europe, such problems may seem self-indulgent luxury. Most certainly there would seem to be more immediate, direct problems, not least because in various parts of the world the breakdown of consensus and reassertion of traditional loyalties and identities held in check by some form of *ancien régime* has been accompanied by a savagery and ferocity that suggests a new barbarism. In various parts of Africa a relapse into tribalism has been accompanied by a reprimitivization of warfare in terms of weaponry and practice, while in Bosnia–Herzegovina the relapse into barbarism witnessed the crucifixion and quartering of Serbian children by Moslem militias and the burning alive of whole Serb communities by armed Croatian groups—atrocities that were repaid in kind by the Serbs when opportunity permitted. Moreover, in Rwanda in 1994 the massacre of perhaps as many as 700,000 Tutsis by Hutu militias proved to be the basis not of inaction on the part of the international community but, contemptibly, the withdrawal of peace-keeping forces in August 1994, while the international community's final involvement in Bosnia–Herzegovina was both surprising in its tardiness and disgraceful in terms of lack of impartiality. Nonetheless the very indifference exhibited in these two cases may mean that the outside world will not be able to ignore such crises in the future. Two points, however, need be made. It has been estimated that in 1992 there were more than 60 wars—separatist, secessionist, civil, or of some such pedigree—being fought around the world, and the international community can hardly hope to deal with all of these, not least because so many threaten to be "complex emergencies"—the U.N. term for wars with "added" dimensions such as famine, flood, or drought. The extent of the demands on the international community that such future crises may bring can be glimpsed by reference to the fact that in 1991 the United Nations was involved in five operations that involved 10,000 personnel. This number had increased to 12 by 1993, involving 47,000 troops, 2,000 military observers, 4,400 civilian police (where there had been only 35 in 1987), and 10,000 civilian personnel. By mid-1994 the United Nations had some 17 commitments involving 85,000 personnel drawn from no fewer than 70 different countries. What this meant in terms of cost bordered on the disastrous. As late as 1988, the cost of U.N. operations was $233,000,000. This was to rise to $1.4 billion in 1992, to $2.9 billion in 1993, and to $3.2 billion in 1994. The obvious political and financial problems that followed in the wake of these increases need no elaboration, either with reference to what happened at the time or what is likely to happen in the future.

* * *

But if this period between 1968 and 1975 was characterized by great changes in terms of the state and society, warfare was undergoing immense change. At the time the significance of these changes was largely obscured by more immediate and dramatic developments. The most obvious of these was the humbling of the United States in southeast

Asia. There was also the emergence of the Soviet Union as a genuine superpower, and the start of a new direct relationship with the United States that reflected this fact. In 1971 the United Nations admitted Communist China at the expense of Taiwan. In February 1972 there was Nixon's historic opening to Communist China and after 1969 the start of West German *Ostpolitik* and the attempt by Bonn to normalize relations with the countries of eastern Europe. But in terms of warfare this period was to mark a watershed in Western military thinking, for a reason that is not immediately obvious. At the present time much of Western military thought concerns itself with Maneuver Warfare, and its immediate origins lay in this period. The mechanistic interpretation of history suggests that Maneuver Warfare was the product of a post-Vietnam "lessons-to-be-learnt" process and of the new technology that was then becoming available, but in reality it was much more. Maneuver warfare was the product of an intellectual process plus the other factors, but the roots of this intellectual effort lay primarily in the events of the late 1960s and early 1970s and were not concerned with Vietnam, lessons learned and unlearned.

This period was the time when the Soviet Union achieved strategic parity with the United States and the two superpowers moved into a situation of mutually assured destruction. This reality of strategic parity was crucially important. It provided the basis of détente, and the ABM Treaty signed in Moscow in May 1972 for the first time limited the number of nuclear weapons held by the two superpowers. The significance of this treaty was twofold. It was to form the basis of subsequent arms control negotiations between the superpowers. It was also the first treaty in history whereby the parties accepted, as the basis of their common security, the principle of not attempting to defend their territories and societies against attack.[15] But there was one important by-product of strategic equality. Soviet attention had begun to turn to conventional forces and to the question of how a war in Europe would be fought. The point was, of course, that even before this occurred, in terms of numbers of trained men, tanks, artillery pieces, and aircraft, the Soviet Union and its associates possessed a margin of conventional superiority over NATO forces in the European theater of operations.

The critical point, however, was that in concentrating on the state of conventional forces, the Soviet Union stole a march on a NATO distracted by European reluctance to embrace Flexible Response and the growing U.S. commitment in southeast Asia. In securing this advantage, the Soviet military set about two tasks in the late 1960s—namely, the reconsideration of doctrine and the improvement of conventional capability. On the first score Soviet doctrine had languished after the Second World War initially because of Stalinist repressiveness and cult of personality and later because of Khrushchev's overwhelming concern with strategic nuclear weapons. But with the 1960s the Soviet military, conditioned by the experience of the Great Patriotic War, returned to *P.U. 36: Soviet Field Regulations* and Deep Battle concepts as the basis of its doctrine for fighting and winning a conventional war. There was to be, however, one very great difference in the situation that confronted the Soviet military from the one that had existed in the latter stages of the Second World War. By the late 1960s, the Soviets had the means to realize all aspects of Deep Battle, including those that had proved elusive in the last year of the Great Patriotic War. The contraction of armies, the extent of motorization within the Soviet army, and the development of airborne forces offered the Soviet military the means to develop a fully mechanized, properly supplied field army capable of striking in depth across the NATO area.

The results that were achieved by the Soviets in terms of capacity of conventional forces in the decade between 1965 and 1975 were singularly impressive: the firepower of divisions doubled, and the lift capacity increased by a factor of six. The development of airborne forces enabled the Soviets to reach for the air-mechanization concept that had proved so elusive in 1944–45, and the operational mobile group emerged by the 1980s in the form of complete armies. The development of Soviet forces, specifically Group of Soviet Forces Germany, at the very time when the Soviet Union attained strategic equality with the United States, was very striking, not least because it was accompanied by a remarkably open discussion in the Soviet military press on doctrinal and tactical issues.

It was precisely at this time, from the early 1970s, that there was taking place in Western military establishments one profoundly important change. By this time a new generation had emerged that had been born after the Second World War and was not tied to fixed Cold War attitudes, and the first attempts to look seriously and objectively at what had happened on the Eastern Front in the Second World War were being made. There had been certain individuals before this time who had attempted to do this, but for the most part their influence had been restricted: dispassionate examination of the Soviet enemy was not a very high priority for the NATO military until Flexible Response suddenly made it very important to know what the potential enemy would seek to do on the battlefield.

The change in Western attitude produced some very uneven results, and clearly by the early 1970s much remained to be done in terms of the Western military's understanding the Eastern Front and the Soviet conduct of operations. But at this time the openness of the Soviet military debate dovetailed with the fact that the basic means whereby such understanding could be acquired were in place. Moreover, as it with-

drew from southeast Asia, the U.S. military's attention naturally re-
focused on the European theater of operations, where, it realized, it
faced something that was unprecedented in the American military experience of the previous 100 years.

* * *

From the time of Grant, the United States waged industrialized warfare. The American way of war was the prosecution of war by industrial
means. Strategic objectives were achieved through a combination of
tactical victories, which were registered by the concentration of superior
material and manpower and winning the individual battle basically
through attrition. The American way of war was not marked by subtlety,
but it proved highly effective, because it was based on the reality of
American demographic and industrial superiority over any and all enemies. In the early 1970s the U.S. military had to face the fact that a war
in Europe against the Soviet Union and its Warsaw Pact allies would
have to be waged on the basis of inferiority. Moreover, in such a war
there was the very real prospect in the initial phase of hostilities of defeat
that would prove irreversible.

Perhaps predictably, the U.S. military refused to face this fact. The
mental habits of decades proved resistant to new realities, and unfortunately one war fought in the early 1970s served to disguise the potential
seriousness of the problem that the U.S. military faced on the Inner-
German border. In 1973 the U.S. Army created its Training and Doctrine
Command (TRADOC), and with this organization the military should
have acquired the means to begin the process of critical self-analysis, but
in this same year, in October, there was fought yet another Arab–Israeli
war. All too predictably, the mainstream U.S. military, as represented by
TRADOC, learned the wrong lesson—the lesson it wanted to learn—
from this war.

The October 1973 War was a very unusual one. It resulted in an
overwhelming Israeli military victory, but it proved to be politically
drawn, with perhaps the balance of advantage lying with the Arabs. The
war destroyed the myth of Israeli invincibility despite its military outcome. Its abiding image was the Egyptian army attacking across the
Suez Canal and establishing itself on Israeli defensive positions in the
Sinai. No number of subsequent Israeli victories could ever quite eliminate that first and recurring impression of the war: the despised Arabs
attacking a superior enemy and doing battle with it for nearly three
weeks. That the Arab armies were brought to within measurable distance of total defeat by war's end was not important when set against
perception and the force of diplomatic events set in train by a conflict
won in its initial stage by Arab states.

The October 1973 War was initiated by Egypt and Syria with a twofold intention: to inflict a series of defeats on Israel by virtue of surprise offensives and thereafter to engage in defensive battles of attrition and provoke superpower intervention that would ensure the return to the Arabs of lands that they knew they could not recover by force of arms. Confronted by an enemy superior in the air and in technique, the Arab leadership knew that any attempt to fight a mobile, armored battle could only result in defeat. Accordingly, Egypt and Syria determined upon a limited war, fought not for the destruction of the state of Israel but the return of their lost territories and a solution to the Palestinian problem. In the south the Egyptian intention was to secure positions on the east bank of the Suez Canal from which a defensive battle could be fought, not to try to advance deep into the Sinai. In the north the Syrian intention was to clear the Syrian Heights that had been lost in the 1967 war. By taking the initiative, the Arab leadership planned that Israel would be forced to conform to Arab will and would be checked in a battle in which Israeli advantages would be offset by massed firepower and numbers. By virtue of the limited and defensive victories that were to be won, the Arab leadership anticipated outside intervention to impose a cease-fire and to broker an arrangement whereby the wider Arab objectives might to realized. In order to encourage such intervention, the Egyptian leadership was to enlist Saudi help in the form of the oil weapon. In the event, the oil weapon was to be used by the Arabs not as the means of consolidating success, but to try to avert final defeat.

By very narrow margins the basic Arab intention miscarried. In the north this failure became clear very quickly. The Syrians began their offensive on 6 October with two armored and three mechanized divisions on a 30-mile front, the armor being held in the second echelon. Opposed by two Israeli armored brigades with about 150 tanks, the Syrian attacks were naturally channeled into killing zones that had been set out and prepared by the Israelis. In the first two days the Syrian divisions in effect destroyed the two Israeli brigades on the Syrian Heights but were themselves all but destroyed—one mechanized division lost 200 tanks—by the time the first Israeli armored reinforcements arrived on the battlefield. By 7 October the logic of the situation on this front was inescapable: having failed to defeat the Israelis on the Syrian Heights when attacking under conditions of maximum numerical advantage, the defeat of the Syrians was certain. On 8 October they were forced to ask the Iraqis for assistance, and by the following day the Israelis had pushed the Syrians more or less back to the original starting line. Over the next four days the Israelis conducted a series of local attacks, and what remained of the Syrian forces were able to conduct an orderly withdrawal into the Sasa Line, which the Israelis, having secured positions from which Damascus could be menaced, declined to attack. Thereafter a series of division-size Arab counterattacks on 15, 16, and 19 October were all defeated by the latter with relative ease before the Israelis cleared the Mount Hermon position on 22 October, in the very last hours before a cease-fire came into effect. Overall, the Syrians lost about 1,400 tanks and APCs—that is, the equivalent of the whole of their original attack force of five divisions. The Israelis lost about 250 tanks, of which 150 were recovered by virtue of possession of the battlefield.

In the south the fact that the Arab intention miscarried took longer to manifest itself and indeed was largely disguised by the very real success that the Egyptian armies commanded in the opening days of the war. On the first day the Egyptian Second and Third Armies, at a cost of 208 dead, crossed the Suez Canal, and over the next two days they beat off no fewer than 23 improvised Israeli counterattacks, none smaller than battalion-size. Though the Egyptians were not able to clear the last Israeli positions in the Bar Lev Line on the Canal until 13 October and, critically, were not able to advance into the Sinai to the depth of the main lateral road parallel to the Canal, which would have given them control of Israeli deployment and reserve positions, their success in this phase of the war provided the basis of the subsequent Arab claim on victory. In these opening days the Egyptian army drew a line under the humiliations of 1956 and 1967, and it did so as a result of four factors. These were the speed and effectiveness of the crossing of the Canal and movement into the Sinai; the advantage it enjoyed by virtue of surprise, which enabled it to deal with an enemy that had to fight as it could as opposed to as it would; its use of massed firepower to break Israeli armored counterattacks; and its ability to counter Israeli air supremacy with a massed, integrated air defense system. The latter was crucial. After the 1967 debacle and mindful that Israeli air supremacy could not be challenged by Arab air forces, the Egyptian plan involved the fighting a defensive battle below the cover provided by concentrated SAM batteries and antiaircraft artillery.

The key to Egyptian tactical success in the initial phase of the war was the combination of the Israelis being taken by surprise and the massed firepower deployed by the Egyptian armies, the Israelis losing an estimated 400 tanks in the Sinai in the first six days of the war. On the ground the Egyptians used a combination of conventional firepower, precision munitions in the form of antitank guided weapons, specifically the Miliutka/AT-3 Sagger, and the RPG-7 to counter Israeli armor. In the event it seems that the major agent of Israeli losses was not the Sagger, as was assumed in the immediate aftermath of the war, but the RPG-7. It appears that the AT-3 claimed between 30 and 40 of the 840 Israeli tanks lost during the war but was primarily responsible for breaking up Israeli armored formations and left separated, individual tanks vulnerable to the more numerous RPG-7.[16] In the air the Egyptians used SAM-2 Guideline and SAM-3 Goa to harass Israeli aircraft at high and medium altitudes and SAM-6 Gainful, shoulder-fired missiles, the ZSU 23-4 and ZSU 57-2, and artillery to meet low-level air attack. The Israeli air force had encountered SAM defenses in summer 1970 in the final part of the War of Attrition that had been fought over the Suez Canal, and the Americans had encountered an integrated missile defense system over North Vietnam, but 1973 was the first occasion on which such defenses had been marshaled on a battlefield. Initially the Israeli air force had no answer to the problems that an integrated air defense system presented and was unable to support ground forces. The fact that it began to attack strategic targets in Syria on 8 October was partial acknowledgment of its having been neutralized tactically in the first two days of the war. By the 8th, however, it had begun to equip itself with chaff and decoy flares, and by the following week the Americans had delivered advanced ECM equipment, the AGM-62 Walleye and Shrike ARMs. Thus supplied, the Israeli air force reappeared over the battlefield in its anointed role. Between 18 and 22 October it flew 1,419 sorties over the Sinai Front and destroyed 43 SAM batteries, but the decision of the war had been reached in what had been, more or less, its absence.[17]

With the defeat of its counterattacks on the Suez Canal, the Israeli ground forces had been obliged to assume the defensive in order to reorganize and await the outcome of the battle in the north, and the outcome of that battle forced the Egyptian hand. The Israeli victory on the Syrian Heights prompted a Syrian request for an Egyptian offensive in the Sinai that would relieve the mounting pressure being exerted by the Israelis, and on 11 October, and in the face of opposition on the part of his senior military commanders, President Sadat, with little alternative if he was to keep Egypt's credibility, ordered such an offensive. In order to carry out this offensive, the Egyptian armored reserve, held on the west bank of the Canal, was committed to the Sinai. With this action, the Egyptian high command in effect stripped itself of the force covering the two main armies in the Sinai and left the west bank without effective defense.

The full enormity of the decision is difficult to appreciate, even after all this time, but what it involved was that an army that had been in action for a week, with all that that entailed in depleted ammunition stocks and manpower exhaustion, was to undertake an offensive against an enemy of proven superiority in mobile warfare. Moreover, this enemy had time to reorganize and concentrate its formations in defensive positions and had an air force that would be able to intervene in the battle because the Egyptian effort would involve moving beyond the range of its antiaircraft cover. When these considerations are tied to two other factors—that the Egyptians emptied their reserves in order to make this effort and that the two Egyptian armies in the Sinai had failed properly to bind together their shared boundary—Sadat's decision to undertake an offensive in support of Egypt's Syrian ally could only end disastrously.

After initial probing attacks on the 13 October, the main Egyptian effort was made on 14 October: by the end of the day the effort had been crushed and the Egyptian forces were in retreat, with the Israeli army having claimed to have destroyed 264 Egyptian tanks for the loss of six of its own. While the latter appears to have been understated, there was no denying that the Israelis won an overwhelming victory on 13 and 14 October, and at this stage the military logic that had unfolded on the Syrian Heights by 7 October now applied in the Sinai. By the 15th the Egyptian formations in the Sinai were on the defensive and faced a superior enemy with a choice of how and in what form to take the war to the west bank of the Canal.

Taking any war into Egypt proper had been part of prewar Israeli planning; indeed, it had been the basis of Israeli success in the War of Attrition. There was never any real question within the Israeli high command that any future war with Egypt would be fought on the west bank and not in the Sinai. As early as 11 October, with the situation on the Syrian Heights stabilized, Israeli military attention had begun to turn to the possibility of an assault across the Canal, and by this time the Americans, as a result of SR-71 Blackbird reconnaissance missions, had informed the Israelis that the Egyptian armies in the Sinai had failed to bind their common flanks together. The result was obvious: the Israelis were able to make their effort at the weakest point of the Egyptian position in the Sinai and against a largely unpatrolled west bank. The first Israeli crossings of the Canal were conducted during the night of 15–16 October, and by 18 October the Israelis had established themselves in strength on the west bank. With their subsequent operations on the ground eliminating the remaining SAM batteries,[18] the Israelis were able to begin the task of rolling up Egyptian positions, the main Israeli effort being made southward toward the Gulf of Suez against the Third Army. In spite of increasingly strong American pressure to desist, the Israelis continued their operations until 24 October, by which time the Israeli thumb was all but pressing upon the Third Army windpipe.

* * *

The 1973 war proved to be a watershed in the Arab–Israeli dispute. It forced the United States to intervene in the Middle East, for obvious reasons. The threat to its oil supplies and the realization that nothing was to be gained by allowing Israel to smash its neighbors had destroyed the premise that had governed U.S. policy since 1967—to ensure against war by creating an imbalance of force in the area. In 1973 the United States found that there was an Arab interest that extended beyond the supply of oil, and the sequel was interesting: within five years of this war, the United States was the dominant external influence in the Middle East, and the Soviet Union had been marginalized. For the Israelis the experience of war—specifically the experience of defeat—was traumatic, and the alleged failure of the Labour government in its conduct of the nation's affairs was a major factor in the electoral reverses of early 1974. The retention of power in 1974 was to be the last Labour victory for more than a decade, and within three years the hard-line Likud coalition was to come to power.

For the Arabs, the results were mixed. Superpower intervention resulted in a series of disengagement treaties and arrangements that allowed the Suez Canal to be reopened in June 1975, and herein a basic divergence between Egypt and the rest of the Arab world became apparent. Sadat had only turned to the military option in 1973 because of a failure to secure a solution to the Arab–Israeli problem by other means, but the lesson of the 1973 war was clear for Sadat: if the Arabs could not win a war in which they held major initial advantages, then they were never going to be able to realize their objectives by force of arms. Peace and diplomatic means seemed to offer better prospects than war, especially when they yielded parts of Sinai to a nation that desperately needed peace in order to attend to its massive domestic problems. Without oil reserves of any note, Egypt was caught after 1973 between Egyptian national and Arab interests. But the very credible Egyptian performance in the 1973, war was critically important in that it allowed the Egyptian leadership to seek peace on the basis of equality, without having the burden of humiliating, abject defeat to undermine its every effort and to seek concessions from a position of abject military weakness. In November 1977 Sadat went to Israel and stated the Egyptian national and Arab cases: the Camp David agreement was to follow in September 1978. The basic problem was, however, that the Egyptians could not persuade other Arabs to follow their lead, and whatever arrangements Egypt and Israel made between themselves, four basic problems remained unaddressed. These were the legitimate security interests of all parties, not just one or two, in the dispute between Israel and its neighbors; the Palestinian question and the critical fact that Camp David left unresolved the future of the Gaza Strip and West Bank; the difficulties presented by Israel's determination to retain the Syrian Heights; and the special difficulty presented by Jerusalem. Camp David left unanswered many more questions than it resolved, and in one very obvious sense opened another problem. The elimination of the southern threat left the Likud government in Israel free to turn its malignant attention to the Lebanon, which after 1975 was plagued by a civil war exacerbated by the Palestinian presence in the country.

* * *

For the Americans, and to a lesser extent for the European NATO members, the October 1973 War provided the wrong lessons because it seemed to confirm the critical importance of material factors in Israeli military success. The battles on the Syrian Heights and the destruction of the Egyptian armored attack into the Sinai in the second week of the 1973 War represented Israeli successes that seemed to underwrite both the general concept of Flexible Response and the specific idea of preparing killing zones in which Soviet armor would be destroyed by massed defensive firepower. Moreover, there was no escaping the fact that even if the Israelis had been able to break the Syrian offensive with what had been available at the outset of the war, what the United States had made available in its course—advanced ECM equipment, smart bombs, TOW missiles, and intelligence—had proved crucially important in shaping events and determining their outcome. In a very obvious sense, therefore, the lesson that could be read from the 1973 War was comforting and reassuring as far as the U.S. military was concerned. Moreover, the conclusion that the counter to Soviet massed armored offensives lay in increased fighting effectiveness achieved by major reequipment of NATO forces coincided with lessons that were being drawn from the Vietnam War and the arrival on the scene of new weapons systems that could result in the gains in fighting effectiveness that were needed. In a very real sense, and the irony appears to have eluded TRADOC before 1977, its answer to the basic problem that it faced in the European theater of operations after 1973—how to wage war on the basis of inferiority— was to embrace a form of warfare that stressed attrition and continued to depend upon industrial supremacy as the basis of the American way of warfare.

In effect, the TRADOC response to the problem it faced was "more and better of the same," but in fact warfare stood on the brink of profound change. For some 30 years the basis of conventional military power had been armor, and Soviet development over the previous few years had been concentrated on qualitative improvement, with the massed armored formation the basis of maneuver and attrition. In fact, technology had placed to hand what could be at one and the same time both a supplement and an alternative to mass and the Holy Grail of quantitative superiority. The realization of this development, and the implications that were to follow from it, were to initiate enormous changes in the conduct of conventional warfare over the next generation.

NOTES

1. Much of the above has been culled from Nicholas Humphrey, "Four Minutes to Midnight," *The Listener*, 29 October 1981.

2. Speech in January 1997 at the Henry L. Stimson Center, Washington, D.C., as reported in the *International Herald Tribune*, 23 January 1997.

3. Carl von Clausewitz, *On War*. Book VI, *Defense*. Edited and translated by Michael Howard and Peter Paret, with commentary by Bernard Brodie (Princeton, NJ: Princeton University Press, 1976). Chapter 26, "Arming the People".

4. Brigadier-General Samuel B. Griffith II (translator), *Mao Tse-tung on Guerilla Warfare*. Part III, "Yu Chi Chan (Guerilla Warfare)". Chapter 1, "What Is Guerilla Warfare?" (Baltimore, MD: Nautical and Aviation Company of America, 1992), pp. 71–72.

5. Carl von Clausewitz, *On War*. Book I, *The Nature of War*, edited by Anatol Rapoport (London: Penguin, 1968).

6. Jean Lartéguy, *Yellow Fever*, translated by Xan Fielding (London: Hutchinson, 1965), p. 62.

7. Clausewitz, *On War*. Book I, *The Nature of War*, edited by Anatol Rapoport.

8. Neil Sheenan, *A Bright Shining Lie: John Paul Vann and America in Vietnam* (New York: Random House, 1988), p. 628. Sheenan brings out the profoundly disruptive effect of the American presence in Vietnam in terms of denuding the countryside, a destructive inflation, and crime-related activities.

9. Robert S. McNamara, *In Retrospect: The Tragedy and Lessons of Vietnam* (New York: Random House, 1995), p. 61.

10. It needs be noted, however, that from the time of its beginning operations in 1980, (to give it its full title), "The Communist Party of Peru by the Shining Path of Jose Carlos Mariategui and Marxism, Leninism, Maoism and the Thoughts of Chairman Gonzalo" was active in both rural and urban areas, adopting a Maoist formula for the countryside and terrorism and Bolshevik-type subversion for the urban areas, that in Guatemala the insurgency movement, the U.R.N.G., was obliged to turn to the countryside after an unavailing struggle in the towns that lasted a full 12 years, and that the subsequent campaign lasted a murderous 24 years, after which the struggle assumed a political as opposed to military character.

11. In 1958 for the first time more people crossed the North Atlantic by air than by sea, while this decade saw television "come of age," the seminal events being the Murrow–McCarthy broadcast in 1954 and, in Britain, the coronation in 1953. By the end of the 1950s 90% of all households in the United States possessed a television set, but in terms of communications mobility the impact of television was mainly concentrated in the 1960s, with the first intercontinental public broadcast in 1963 and the transmission of the opening ceremony of the Tokyo Olympics in October 1964. The first world-wide program, with presentations from 19 countries on five continents and broadcast to 39 countries simultaneously, was on 25 June 1967.

12. As, indeed, did the *Senero Luminoso* in Peru. In a campaign that has curious parallels first with what had happened in Cuba between 1956 and 1958 and ultimately with what happened in Argentina and Uruguay in the course of the 1980s, the *Senero Luminoso* proved very effective in attracting widespread middle-

class support when confronted with a corrupt and incompetent government and military. In April 1992, however, President Alberto Fujimori introduced "new democracy"—that is, he suspended the constitution, congress, and most civil rights, and he initiated a major campaign of repression. The capture of Chairman Abimael Guzman—that is, Gonzalo—and part of the Central Committee in September 1992, the detention of much of the original leadership, and the dissipation of popular sympathy for the *Senero Luminoso* thereafter broke the power of the organization, though the fragmentation of the revolution movement means that insurgency remains endemic in Peru, as the events of December 1996 indicated.

13. Francis Fukuyama, *The End of History and the Last Man* (New York: Free Press, 1992), pp. xiii–xiv.

14. Written originally in 1996 and, with desperate irony, deleted from the original on the morning of 11 September 2001. Restored 12 October 2001.

15. The treaty gave both superpowers the right to build two ABM complexes, one around the capital and one around an ICBM concentration. In practice both superpowers only built one: the U.S. system, at Grand Forks in North Dakota, became operational on 1 October 1975. With the whole ABM endeavor deemed "the most expensive sieve in history," it was closed on the following day.

16. Anthony H. Cordesman and Abraham R. Wagner, *The Lessons of Modern War*. Vol. I, *The Arab–Israeli Conflicts, 1973–1989* (Boulder, CO: Westview Press, 1990), p. 64.

17. Reliable figures for air losses are elusive. The Israelis admitted the loss of 115 aircraft and 50 pilots during the war, though the American estimate was that the Israeli air force lost about 200 aircraft; unofficially, it seems that Israeli pilot losses amounted to 160. Cordesman and Wagner, *The Lessons of Modern War*, states that in the first two days of the 1973 War the Egyptians destroyed 14 aircraft, and 30 aircraft in the first four days. Cordesman gives the overall total of losses as 102, with 42 destroyed by surface-to-air missiles. Brassey's *Defence Yearbook* (London: Centre for Defence Studies, King's College, 1976), p. 108, gives Israeli losses to antiaircraft artillery and surface-to-air missiles as 96 aircraft and in air-to-air combat 6 aircraft.

18. The overall total of SAM batteries eliminated by the Israeli air force in 1973 is given as 32 destroyed and 11 damaged on the Sinai Front and 3 destroyed and 8 damaged in the north: Israeli ground operations are credited with the destruction of 11 Egyptian and one Syrian batteries. The Arab order of battle indicates that Egypt deployed 150 batteries and Syria 65, perhaps as many as two-thirds of which were SA-2 Gainful and SA-3 Goa. The number destroyed or damaged more or less accords with front-line strength. The main Israeli air effort against Syrian SAM batteries was conducted on and after the 18 October and against Egyptian batteries on the northern sector of the Canal on and after 13 October. The elimination of Egyptian SAM batteries by Israeli ground forces came in the center and was directed against a system that was already beginning to unravel—see Cordesman and Wagner, *The Lessons of Modern War*, pp. 74–85.

5

Doctrine as the "Danger on the Utmost Edge of Hazard"

Between 1945 and 1975 there was much in the way of research and development of weapons systems, and many new systems entered various national inventories, but for the most part these various developments represented qualitative improvements over existing weaponry. The North Vietnamese T-54/55 tanks that completed the conquest of the south in 1975 clearly derived from the Second World War. The majority of U.S. carriers that served in the Gulf of Tonkin may have been modernized in the 1950s and 1960s and thereafter represented massive qualitative improvement over their previous form off the Japanese home islands, but they remained ships that first entered service during the Second World War. Only in terms of aircraft and missiles was there development of the kind that represented quantum change in the conduct of war—witness such systems as the P.1127 VTOL Harrier, which was designed between 1957 and 1959, and the AIM-54/AAM-N-11 Phoenix air-to-air missile, which began life in 1960 and which, in prototype form in 1965, destroyed a target aircraft at a launch range of 127 miles. Such systems did represent something that was new, but the elements of novelty that were apparent in southeast Asia in the 1960s primarily concerned jet aircraft and the helicopter, the Vietnamese war being the first in which both were used on an extensive scale. The Korean War had seen their employment, but the intervening decade between this conflict and the Vietnam War had seen developments that had transformed both. When the U.S. Navy's F-4B Phantom fighter was tested in 1961, it was found to be superior to all existing fighters in U.S.

service by very wide margins in virtually every aspect of performance; by the second half of the 1950s improvements of engines, couplings, and rotors, and streamlining had produced the power, lift, speed, and mechanical reliability enabled the helicopter to perform a number of different tactical roles over the battlefield. The increased importance of aircraft and helicopters in the conduct of operations was made evident in the course of the Vietnam War. In a way that was unique at the time, this war was synonymous with the aircraft and the helicopter.

* * *

TRADOC was formed under the command of General William E. Depuy in 1973—the year that saw the completion of the withdrawal of U.S. combat formations from southeast Asia and the October War in the Middle East. In evaluating these conflicts it was perhaps inevitable that TRADOC's studies should have concerned themselves with three aspects of operations in South Vietnam. First, as early as 1966, the First Cavalry Division, complete with its equipment and supplies, was able to undertake sustained operations over several provinces over a four-month period, while, second, in 1968 the same formation, in the course of Operation Liberty Canyon and at one day's notice, was redeployed over a distance of 570 miles in two weeks. It was able to assign its leading brigades to other divisions before being reformed with the arrival of divisional headquarters.[1] Such mobility was unprecedented, and it is small wonder that in the aftermath of the Vietnam War American military attention should have turned to air mobility to "square the circle" within the European theater of operations. Third, the Vietnam War brought home to the U.S. military the practicality of the concentration of firepower by air. The combination of command helicopters, fighter-bomber and AH-1G Huey Cobra strikes, scout helicopters for the marking of B-52 missions, and the use of such aircraft as the AC-130H and KC-130 Hercules and the Chinook in the support role enabled the Americans to concentrate overwhelming firepower in the course of operations. There was a disastrous reverse side to this capability: the use of massed firepower devastated the countryside and cost the Americans much in terms of potential support among an uprooted Vietnamese peasantry, which was forced to flee to crime-racked slums, but in terms of the conventional battle, the potential importance of concentrated and properly coordinated airborne firepower was evident, especially when tied to the development of such weapons as TOW missiles. Thus at the very time when the Soviets sought to enhance conventional capability with the improvement of firepower, mobility, and supply of massed armored formations, the Vietnam War opened American eyes to another combination of fire and movement in the form of air mobility.[2]

The implications of air mobility were to point U.S. military attention in three different directions. The concept of air mobility pointed to the need for new forms of tactical organization, specifically for smaller but more agile, powerfully equipped units and formations than presently arranged. Air mobility undoubtedly proved valuable in southeast Asia, but the concept of air mobility in the NATO theater of operations necessarily involved having to fight and win the battle for air supremacy against an enemy with formidable offensive and defensive capabilities. The concept of concentrating firepower by deployment of air assets necessarily demanded formidable intelligence and command and control capabilities. These were problems that the U.S. military had to address at the time when TRADOC began to consider how the future battle would be fought, but outside developments, and especially the apparent lessons of the October 1973 war, served to push TRADOC down the "more-of-the-same" path. The concentration of attention on material factors as critical to the increase of fighting effectiveness served to deflect American military attention from the basic questions of organization and doctrine that had to be addressed. In part this was because at this time there were development and procurement programs in hand that made the idea of fighting and winning an attritional battle against massed armored formations on the basis of overwhelming qualitative rather than numerical advantage a realistic possibility.

* * *

The programs in hand in late 1973 in the United States embraced an awesome array of weaponry at every level of operations, including deterrence, and they involved all three services. The navy, because of the block obsolescence of so many of its ships and the emergence of a genuine blue-water enemy, was perhaps the service most affected. At the strategic level MIRV had been unveiled in December 1967 and was tested in August 1968; it provided the Nixon administration with a belief in a continuing and insurmountable U.S. technical superiority that enabled it to conclude the ABM Treaty. The B-1 Lance bomber, though beset by doubts about costs that were likely to prove prohibitive, was less than a year from its maiden flight, while in May 1973 much-improved engines redeemed the fortunes of the much-troubled F-111 all-weather attack bomber and allowed the new F-111-F to replace the older B-52 bombers with the Strategic Air Command. In late 1971 the *Ohio*-class submarine, and the program that ultimately resulted in the D-5 missile, had been adopted by the Nixon administration. On the ground, 1973 saw the ordering of the prototypes that were to result in the M1A1 Abrams tank and the M2 Bradley armored personnel carrier and the testing of the missile of what was to yield the MIM-104 Patriot HIMAD system. In the air, and in addition to the E-3A AWACS program, which represented the world's most costly military aircraft to date, a new generation of fighters, strike aircraft, and helicopters was in the process of coming on line, while the experience of the bombing campaigns against North Vietnam in 1972 and in the October 1973 War pushed the United States into the search for stealth technology in the form of reduced Radar Cross Sections of aircraft. The development contract for such an aircraft was placed in November 1978, and the prototype F-117 Nighthawk flew for the first time in June 1981. The missile programs in hand in the United States by the end of 1973 were all but bewildering in their diversity and implications though the most contentious, the cruise missile program, had only been initiated in 1972 as a derivative of the program that was to result in the SLAM antiship AGM-84E Harpoon, which entered service in 1977. At this time there was no appreciation of the problems that this program, specifically its land- and sea-based versions, were to entail for SALT II and the European members of NATO—the AGM-109 Tomahawk II MRASM was tested in 1974. In terms of air-to-air missiles, the Phoenix had entered service in 1970 and complemented the constantly updated AIM-7 Sparrow and AIM-9 Sidewinder. Air-to-surface weaponry was smartly represented by the laser-guided Paveway and the AGM-62 Walleye electro-optical bomb, both of which had entered service in 1965–66 with mixed results, but which, between 1971 and 1974, were updated and subjected to major improvement and increases in size. The AGM-88 HARM, the successor to the AGM-45 Shrike and AGM-75 Standard, and the Hellfire antitank missile were under development in 1973. The A-10 Thunderbolt, designed for the close support role, had undergone trials in autumn 1972 and was scheduled for delivery in 1974; after the abandonment of the AH-56 Cheyenne gunship program in 1972, the specifications for new Advanced Attack and Utility Tactical Transport helicopters had been issued and competition narrowed to two designs in each category by mid-1973.

The sum of these various programs, when allied to parallel developments in communications, ECM, and surveillance equipment, potentially represented major changes in the conduct of battle. The most conspicuous changes were those affecting aircraft—specifically the fighters: the F-14 Tomcat first flew in December 1970 and the F-15 Eagle in July 1972, while the F-16 Fighting Falcon was to make its maiden flight in January 1974. The significance of the F-15 Eagle and F-16 Falcon lay in the fact that, given the development of the F-100 engine, they were the first aircraft to possess thrust-to-weight ratios of more than one, and both incorporated fly-by-wire and electro-optical "heads-up display" technology. They were to the Phantom what that aircraft had been to all other aircraft when it had entered service. The new aircraft could outmaneuver any other fighter in service with ease, while HUD allowed a pilot to engage an enemy without switching attention between the sky and instrument panel. Fly-by-wire technology allowed aircraft to be deliberately designed or loaded to be unstable but handle correctly and conferred a tolerance to damage that was denied aircraft with conventional hydraulic control systems. Subsequent advances in microminiaturization of computer software produced aircraft capable of flying themselves. When the F-15A entered service in November 1974, it was equipped with 60,000 avionic software codes, but by 1990 its successor, the F-15E, carried 40 times as many. The qualitative advantage thus conferred on this new generation of fighters can be gauged by the claim that the Tomcat, equipped with multiple target track-while-scan and look-down/shoot-down capability, could track a maximum of 22 targets and engage six simultaneously. The U.S. Navy's calculation was that the new aircraft would be able to deal with minimum odds of 4:1 in combat with Soviet land-based fighters, and the corollary needed little in the way of elaboration: with the new fighters coming into service, the Americans possessed confidence in their ability to fight and win the battle for air supremacy in the NATO theater of operations. But two matters were of immediate importance. In 1973 the United Sates was a few years from the deployment of the new aircraft that would enable it to fight and win the air battle with the Warsaw Pact, and between 1973 and 1976 the long-term implications of developments in aircraft and weaponry did not impinge overmuch on the deliberations of TRADOC, an organization overwhelmingly concerned with more immediate issues.

* * *

At the time when it was formed, TRADOC was part not of an army that had been defeated but of something that was worse: a defeated army that had never been beaten in the field. The end of the Vietnam War found the U.S. Army exhibiting all the symptoms of defeat; its relationship with the government was characterized by mutual incomprehension, and its relationship with society was almost one of mutual antipathy. It contained within its ranks warrant and noncommissioned officers who had refused to lead patrols in Vietnam, and junior officers who had proved either unable or unwilling to impose their authority on subordinates. It was an army demoralized by its failure, by the nature of the war it had fought, and by the indifference of society to its ordeal.

In such a situation it was small wonder that TRADOC's and the U.S. Army's first concern was training rather than doctrine. At the same time, the U.S. Army was involved in weeding out the junior, warrant, and noncommissioned officer ranks in one basic structural reorganization. Prior to the Vietnam War, the U.S. Army had been organized on the "hollow-divisions" principle—formations that existed only in skeletal form but were fleshed out by draftees. With the end of the draft, the U.S.

Army, as a fully professional force, was obliged to constitute its field
force differently. After 1978, instead of organizing complete regular
divisions, it adopted a system whereby part of every division existed in
cadre form for reserve and National Guard units, with the majority of
the noncombat arms, combat support, and combat service support specifically drawn from reserve forces. In this way the U.S. military establishment ensured that for practical purposes it could not be committed to
any major endeavor without calling up reserves and thus could only be
committed to operations with full congressional support. For the U.S.
military establishment the failure of the Johnson administration to have
secured such support was the real lesson to be drawn from the Vietnam
War.

But if in the aftermath of Vietnam the U.S. Army and TRADOC were
primarily concerned with basics of organization and training, the
question of how to fight presented itself in with immediate urgency.
TRADOC's reaction was to form the story of AirLand Battle, but this
story is beset with two basic problems of narration and interpretation.
In tracing the evolution of U.S. doctrine between 1973 and 1986, there is
the problem of deciding whether the 1982 field manual was a halfway
house on the journey to the 1986 edition, or whether the 1986 field
manual was merely a postscript to the 1982 version. At the same time the
basis of this evolution is difficult to discern. There is an interpretation of
this process that is frankly determinist and recounts the shift to operational concepts of war primarily in terms of the Vietnam experience and
the nature of the weapons systems that were becoming available in the
course of the 1970s. Conversely, there is an interpretation that provides
an account of this same process in personal terms, citing the Maneuver
Warfare school and such people as Edward Luttwark, but, more specifically, seeing certain individuals such as John Boyd, Steven Canby,
William Lind, Norman Polmar, and Pierre Sprey, who together were the
leading members of the reform caucus, as the critical factor in the
change. Quite clearly the shift in U.S. doctrinal thinking was an intellectual process and therefore the emergence of AirLand Battle cannot be
explained solely or primarily in material terms. AirLand Battle, because
it embraced an operational concept of warfare never previously acknowledged in U.S. military doctrine, cannot be explained by reference
to the Vietnam experience and a recognition of the worth of weapons
systems then becoming available. The intellectual and the material complemented one another, but there were other factors at work that are
difficult to incorporate into an account of these proceedings. For example, the debut of AirLand Battle in the form of FM100-5 1982 could not be
separated from interservice and bureaucratic struggles within the U.S.
Department of Defense, for the simple reason that the paper raised

crucial questions of funding and definition of the relationship between army and air force.

Such matters were two presidents away when, in 1976, TRADOC produced its first FM100-5 and the concept of Active Defense. This concept sought to interpret the NATO strategy of Flexible Response by ensuring battlefield success through the conduct of the defensive battle in depth by the employment of massed firepower and mobile formations. Active Defense conformed to mainstream U.S. military thought— in effect, it sought to deal with the requirements of battle at the tactical level by the use of firepower. In so doing, Active Defense invited active opposition, and for good reason: if it sought to overcome strategic inferiority by inflicting a series of tactical defeats upon an enemy, it ran the very real danger of ensuring that the defense would win every battle except the last one. The concept of Active Defense was attritional, and the danger inherent in seeking to fight attritional battles against a superior enemy had an obvious historical example in the Army of Northern Virginia in the 1864–65 campaign. This was a danger that Active Defense did not address, yet this was the very real prospect that NATO faced and precisely the point that the critics of Active Defense, the Maneuver Warfare school, recognized. It formed perhaps the most important single premise of the assault on the ideas underlying FM100-5 1976 over the next two years.[3]

The course of events as TRADOC moved from FM100-5 1976 to FM100-5 1982 proved as tortuous as some of the arguments of Active Defense's detractors, but in a sense the basic argument of the latter never changed, and it was the point to which their opponents always had to return not least because another set of factors increasingly impinged upon American calculations. The second half of the 1970s saw NATO forced to face two difficulties presented by Warsaw Pact development. First, from the time that NATO first flirted with Flexible Response, the Soviet military faced a situation that was unprecedented. Because of its emphasis upon conventional forces, Flexible Response presented the possibility that the one clear advantage that the Warsaw Pact had enjoyed over NATO would be eroded. Thus the Soviet military in the latter part of the 1960s was forced to consider something that had previously been taken for granted: how to overrun western Europe in the course of a conventional campaign. From 1964 onwards, therefore, this consideration produced three related developments as the Soviet military turned its attention to the future battle: the massive strengthening of the firepower and logistical capability of existing divisions, the raising of more airborne divisions, and the development of the Operational Maneuver Group concept. What the Soviet military sought was to implement qualitative improvements that would ensure the continued viability of the

Deep Battle concept by increased firepower, improvement of logistical arrangements that would ensure a greater tempo of operations, and the ability to strike in strength and in depth across the NATO area.

The second development, after this strengthening of the lead formations, was the reinforcement of the formations in the western military districts of the homeland. This inevitably raised Soviet conventional capability still further and had, by the latter half of the 1970s, at the time when the Active Defense battle was joined, created an additional problem for NATO. In its previous calculations and planning NATO had assumed that its formations would be able to break an offensive by Group of Soviet Forces Germany. Its problem was that NATO formations would be very severely mauled in the process. The realization that the formations in the Soviet second strategic echelon, with their improved capabilities, would be able to move to the battlefield and maintain the offensive against gravely weakened NATO forces was to recognize that defeat in conventional battle would be inevitable. But herein the arguments within the U.S. military produced an attempt to square the circle that elicited only amazement on the part of the United States' allies. Recognition that in effect the real threat to NATO's integrity was presented by the formations moving from the western military districts gave rise to an American determination to seal off the battle area from these forces and thus prevent their intervention by the offensive use of air power. The European NATO military, faced with real difficulties in dealing with the first-echelon forces and a major Soviet air capability, was less than impressed by the prospect of using air power to deal with the second-echelon formations. There was little if any point in preventing the second-echelon formations getting to the battlefield if there was no guarantee of being able to destroy the first, and lurking behind this concern was a certain skepticism about American claims, given the state of the U.S. Army at this time.

This, however, was but one of three major sources of tension within the Active Defense argument that affected the U.S. military, both internally and in its dealings with its allies. The second was to emerge over time, as TRADOC moved from Active Defense to embrace AirLand Battle, and it did so because of the very nature of the answer that the AirLand Battle concept gave to the problem of fighting a defensive battle on the basis of tactical inferiority. That answer was the dispersal of force—an idea that contradicted every known military wisdom. The third source of tension was a well-nigh incomprehensible misuse of language on the part of Active Defense's detractors, which was a source of considerable confusion as the military on both sides of the North Atlantic sought to try to understand the intricacies and subtleties of the AirLand Battle argument, bedeviled as it was by the Maneuver Warfare school's highly selective use and misuse of terms and historical arguments.

This latter problem was very real. Those who were to mount the assault on Active Defense were to adopt the title Maneuver Warfare for their alternative, and in so doing they made clear their distance from concepts of warfare that were based upon attrition. But this choice of title was unfortunate and indeed erroneous, not least because attrition and maneuver are not opposites. The reverse side of the coin marked attritional battle is the battle of annihilation, and that of maneuver is positional. Given the fact that no war has ever been fought without maneuver, the u e of the term Maneuver Warfare was something of a disservice to the cause of general understanding, and the term itself became ever more meaningless with the subsequent attempts by successive chairmen of the Joint Chiefs of Staff drawn from the army to impose the "Maneuvrist Approach to Warfare"—a corporate credo sanctified as an all-encompassing truth—on the navy and the air force. What the opponents of Active Defense really meant with their alternative was a means of restoring decisiveness to warfare and to do so by the concentration of firepower against enemy "critical vulnerabilities." But whatever the title and the basic tenets of its credo, the AirLand Battle concept was doubly ill-advised in the adoption of the term Maneuver Warfare because it implied stress upon movement, whereas its main argument in effect was to seek decision through the combination of firepower and mobility. As it was, the emphasis upon maneuver in its own title lent itself to such observations as

firepower can rarely substitute satisfactorily for manoeuvre. Manoeuvre used to secure a position of advantage has an enduring effect, which compels the enemy to respond by acting on our terms. The effect of firepower is, however, not sustainable indefinitely and may not provoke a reaction that can be exploited,[4]

which would seem to be wholly beside the point: firepower might not win battles and campaigns, but maneuver never has and never will. The weakness of this assertion is that it fails to recognize the critical interdependence of firepower and movement by depicting the two parts as conflicting rather than complementary.

The very term Maneuver Warfare created problems of understanding, partly because customary use of the word "maneuver" implies the movement of formations, whereas under the new definition it primarily concerned the concentration of firepower. Problems of comprehension concerned themselves with the idea of dispersal of force in the face of a superior enemy, but opponents of Active Defense were to be vindicated in argument because the idea of tactical dispersal was only a part of a concept of operational concentration directed against will and cohesion as much as physical strength.

Perhaps somewhat strangely, the basis of these ideas lay in contemporary Soviet doctrine—a state of affairs that passed unacknowledged in FM100-5 1982. NATO's adoption of Flexible Response forced upon alliance members the study of Soviet doctrine and organization, and it was in the early 1970s that the writings of such people as Svechin, Triandafillov, and Tukhachevskii slowly began to percolate through Western military consciousness. The fact that such concepts as Deep Battle and the operational level of war had no meaning in the U.S. military vocabulary pointed to the extent to which much of the idea of Maneuver Warfare was lifted from Soviet military literature and experience.

The awareness of how the Soviet army would attempt to conduct an offensive into western Europe was critical because within the idea of fighting in depth across the battlefield with formations *en echelon* there were weaknesses, as there must be in any military plan or concept of operations. The Soviet concept of Deep Battle at this time was a Schlieffen Plan, complete with a synchronization of its parts that risked breakdown and failure because of the checking of one of its interdependent parts. The Maneuver Warfare school's relevance lay in its appreciation that an ability to check the enemy at one point of the latter's effort across the depth of his offensive either through the destruction of forces or through the denial of prescribed axes of advance provided the basis for his operational defeat.

Maneuver Warfare as a concept encompassed a number of ideas, but the notion of the defeat of an offensive through the checking of capability and intention formed its central part. Other ideas, and the various technological changes then in the process of working their way into military inventories, both reinforced this basic tenet and provided the means of realization. Inevitably, given the fact that repudiation of attrition as the means of ensuring victory was central to the Maneuver Warfare school thesis, the notion of checking the capability and intention of an enemy was synonymous with paralysis and the destruction of the enemy's will to fight. Central to this was the notion, embodied in Boyd's OODA Loop concept, of beating the enemy in terms of speed of decision and thereby imposing one's own will on the battle and ensuring the concentration of firepower at different points across the depth of the enemy deployment, the enemy being forced to react defensively and without the time to be effective. Herein the emphasis of this new American thinking was primarily on the deep strike by aircraft and by highly mobile formations, thereby avoiding the potentially costly close-quarter battle, though the reality that close contact could not be entirely avoided was acknowledged.[5] With the use of concentrated firepower and such formations, the Maneuver Warfare school sought to engage and defeat the enemy operationally and, in a cause-and-effect context, secure or ensure retention of the initiative and to disrupt the enemy's plans and cohesion and hence his operations in depth. In this manner it sought to embrace concepts that would enable the very strengths of a Soviet doctrine based upon maneuver, momentum, depth, and successive operations by formations staggered *en echelon* to be turned upon themselves. The Maneuver Warfare school's concept of disruption as the key to victory was the counterpoint to the Soviet concept of operational shock as the basis of strategic success.

* * *

As noted elsewhere, the adjective "revolutionary" is much over-used with reference to military change. Lind, perhaps the most celebrated member of this school, wrote in 1985 that Maneuver Warfare was not new, but it is very difficult to resist the notion that the concept of Maneuver Warfare most certainly was new—indeed, revolutionary. The Maneuver Warfare school In the United States was not alone in developing its ideas—Marshal Ogarkov in the Soviet Union was arguing along very similar lines and to much more radical conclusions at this very same time—but the sum of its ideas, when finally assembled in FM100-5 1986, most definitely represented a radical departure from received military wisdom, not least in its abandonment of the linear concept of battle and the adoption of the principle of concentration of firepower across the depth of the enemy deployment. This was something different and broke with the practice of two world wars but represented an impossible aim: to have fought AirLand Battle at that time would have demanded an intelligence base that did not exist and communications on a scale that simply were not available.

Arguably the most important of these elements needed to provide Maneuver Warfare with credibility concerned command and intelligence: the ability to read the battle over time and distance and to be able to respond to developments more rapidly than the enemy were in many ways the crucial considerations that would spell the difference between victory and defeat. Under the definitions supplied in the 1982 manual, the depth of battle for a corps involved surveillance sufficient to provide 96 hours' notice of the approach of enemy formations, and in theater terms the NATO area of interest extended to a depth of some 600 miles. This was one area where the Maneuver Warfare alternative was weak. The proposed use of the TR-1 for strategic reconnaissance and targeting was some way in the future and in any event encountered major funding problems, while the means of detailed tactical surveillance (the JSTARS program) was only initiated in May 1982, the first E-8A flight taking place in December 1988. In 1991 the E-8A was able to read the battle to a depth of 155 miles, but even at that stage, more than eight years after the publication of FM100-5 1982, the E-8A was some six years off entering service. In one sense the situation was not quite so dire as might appear, not even in the period 1976–82, because of the availability of other forms of surveillance then coming to hand, but in reality American confidence in being able to read the battlefield was misplaced. The basis of American belief was in the constraints that were believed to place themselves upon Soviet deployment. Given the distances involved and such considerations as the life-expectancy of engines and tracks of armored vehicles, the intelligence calculation was that the movement of formations from the western military districts of the Soviet Union to the central European battlefield could take place only by rail, and between the Carpathians and the Baltic strategic movement was in effect restricted to just three major double-track lines. The monitoring of three lines was within American capability in the second part of the 1970s, and the ability to strike these lines had been demonstrated between 6 April and 30 June 1972 in the course of Linebacker I, when Phantoms using smart bombs destroyed no fewer than 106 bridges in North Vietnam, including the Paul Doumer bridge on 10–11 May and the Thanh Hoa bridge on 13 May.[6] But the fact was that Soviet armor was designed and built to move on roads or across country over hundreds of miles, not to use a rail system that was vulnerable, dependent upon available rolling stock, and not necessarily quicker in the deployment of forces than the road system. Between the Carpathians and the Baltic there were three major road systems and six minor rail lines (capable of handling half a motor rifle division per day) across which Soviet forces in the western military districts could have moved without any significant loss of combat effectiveness. In light of the diversity of routes and in terms of real-time intelligence and command and control arrangements, at this time NATO's ability effectively to seal off the battle zone from Soviet reinforcements from the western military districts was highly doubtful.

Even more seriously, the mobility and firepower that were needed to fight and win the battle at the tactical and operational levels were not available in the period between 1976 and 1982. The production order for the UH-60 Black Hawk helicopter was issued in 1977, and deliveries began in 1980, but the production order for the AH-64 Apache was not issued until 1982, and deliveries did not begin until January 1984. With the example of the October 1973 War to serve as evidence of the importance of PGM, the concept of Maneuver Warfare rested in large measure upon small, highly mobile units able to disperse firepower effectively, in direct contradiction to the historical trend of concentration. The *sine qua non* of Maneuver Warfare was air mobile units, specifically the Cheyenne or Apache attack helicopter, but these systems and the capability made possible by network systems were not in place in this period of AirLand Battle's gestation. Equally, at this stage the Maneuver Warfare school's argument with respect to devolved command and initiative was a tacit acknowledgment of their absence; indeed, the 1982 manual's claims about the U.S. Army's history and capabilities were little more than feeble homilies with little or no historical justification.

Perhaps inevitably, argument involved "sound bytes as instant wisdom," and the Maneuver Warfare thesis had four, which, enshrined in FM100-5 1982, are synonymous with the very name AirLand Battle: initiative, depth, agility, and synchronization. These, however, were tied to the idea of devolved command—"mission-command" or "mission-orientated command," or, to borrow its German original, *Auftragstaktik*—which was one of the key elements of Maneuver Warfare. This implied a level of understanding, competence, and initiative that the 1982 field manual, with its repeated assertion of their importance, unconsciously acknowledged did not exist—nor could they exist. An army that throughout its existence had been subjected to the "orders-command" system [*Befehlstaktik*] could not assume the levels of competence, notably with respect to anticipation of superior intent on the part of subordinate commanders, that Maneuver Warfare entailed, given its need to guard against a collapse of command and control systems under the attack of an enemy's electronic countermeasures.

If the U.S. Army was to secure the levels of initiative and competence that Maneuver Warfare demanded, many years needed to pass in order to allow it to equip itself with an understanding of the concept of the operational level of war. Richard E. Simpkin's *Race to the Swift: Thoughts on Twenty-First Century Warfare*, published in 1985, complete with its somewhat esoteric five criteria,[7] and *Deep Battle, The Brainchild of Marshal Tukhachevskii*, published in 1987, provided the basis of understanding of the concept of the operation level of war, but arguably the real basis of a historical understanding of the concept did not exist before 1991 and the publication of David Glantz's authoritative *Soviet Military Operational Art: In Pursuit of Deep Battle*. By the same token, many years needed to pass to allow a new generation of junior officers, nurtured on the concept, to enter the service. The wooden performance of army units during the course of the Grenada venture in October 1983 against an "enemy" that offered resistance that ranged between the negligible and the nonexistent was clear evidence of what remained to be done on this particular score some 14 months after the publication of FM100-5 1982. But if the U.S. military needed time to take up the challenge presented by the concept of mission-command, another set of events was unfolding that was to both reinforce and make possible the system of devolved command. Other than its increasing capacity to irritate, the telephone barely changed in the 100 years after its invention in 1876: likewise, the computer changed relatively little between the turn of the century and 1970, though it had moved from mechanical to electro-mechanical systems. But by the 1970s, and in part under the impact of a space race, which had resulted in satellites displacing even such aircraft as the SR-71 Blackbird in the strategic reconnaissance role, integrated circuitry had resulted in 1971 in the development of the microprocessor. The development of the Intel 8086 microprocessor in 1978 effectively marked the point where the reduced cost of computing power meant that computer technology ceased to remain the closed preserve of major institutions with only very limited relevance to subordinates. If the concept of networks and the impact of fiber optics remained perhaps a decade into the future, at least some of the military implications of these developments were recognized, though very obviously these remain somewhat debatable. The assumption that the new technology would "empower" lower levels of authority does not sit easily alongside the historical reality that communications developments since the telegraph was patented in 1837 have served to strengthen superior authority by enabling it to exercise ever closer supervision of subordinates. Armies are hierarchical in organization and practice, and they have never been able to institutionalize a means of encouraging innovation and free-thinking on the part of subordinates, lest these become challenges to established authority. Certainly film of proceedings within the British Defence Ministry, showing junior minister, permanent under-secretary, and chief of the Defense Staff discussing the funding of a platoon, hardly represents evidence of assured *Auftragstaktik* as the product of the Information Revolution.[8]

* * *

The Maneuver Warfare school embodied paradox: virtually every single argument, tenet, and imperative was hopelessly flawed, hence the basic soundness of its whole. Its validity lay in its anticipation of means that were not available at the time it joined battle with the Active Defense establishment and in its recognition that new concepts of warfare were needed to overcome conventional materiel inferiority. Its success was ensured by the latter, as TRADOC's movement away from Active Defense after 1976 acknowledged. But if Maneuver Warfare and AirLand Battle were primarily the products of various military and technological factors, three other ingredients were critical to their development and timing. The first of these was the fact that the decades that followed the Vietnam War were ones of turmoil and upheaval within the U.S. military establishment, and in such a context the Maneuver Warfare school was able to mark out its ground in a way that was perhaps unprecedented. The place that civilian academics and retired service personnel had played in the development of defense ideas in the United States had been assured for many years, but much of the driving force behind Maneuver Warfare derived from Congress, most notably Senator Gary Hart, and the whole process had been initiated jointly by Lind and Senator Robert Taft in 1976. But this was an unusual period. Both the Carter and Reagan administrations encouraged the Maneuver Warfare school without understanding either its arguments or the implications of its ideas. The Carter administration, dealing with the weakness of the U.S. strategic position in the aftermath of the Vietnam War, and the Reagan administration, on the basis of its overweening confidence in American power, both encouraged the search for radical innovation. During this period the idea of fighting and winning limited wars became common currency within the U.S. military establishment, and the U.S. Army became increasingly insistent upon its ability, and its right to be allowed, to fight such wars on its own terms and, by virtue of "overwhelming force," to win such conflicts.

* * *

The second ingredient crucial to the development and timing of Maneuver Warfare ideas was the person of Lieutenant-General Donn Starry, after July 1977 the second commander of TRADOC. Somewhat skeptical of Active Defense doctrine before he took up the appointment of Commander of U.S. Land Forces in Europe, his time in West Germany served to convince Starry that the Active Defense concept had passed its sell-by date. The emergence of AirLand Battle doctrine in his extended time at TRADOC was in large part the result of his personal move to embrace most of Maneuver Warfare's concepts, and since there was no open repudiation of FM100-5 1976 and Active Defense, he was able to take the bulk of army opinion with him as he did so. Starry's time at TRADOC was thus marked by gradual shifts to the Central Battle corps-concept in 1978, to the corps-plus-air-force idea of the Integrated Battle in 1979, where for the first time the concept of operational shock in depth was grasped, and critically, under the influence of SACEUR's "follow-on forces attack" concept, to the Extended Battlefield in 1980. These developments occurred even as the argument between rival schools passed its peak, and in this process the articulation of the Carter Doctrine in the State of the Union address on 23 January 1980 and the formation of the Rapid Deployment Task Force in March 1980 were of major importance. The Carter Doctrine was formulated at a time when U.S. power seemed to be in retreat in the wake of Soviet success in upholding its Ethiopian client in its war with Somalia (February–March 1978), the Iranian revolution (16 January 1979), the seizure of the U.S. embassy in Tehran (4 November 1979), and the Soviet invasion of Afghanistan (26 December

1979). It committed the United States to a five-year program of moderni-zation of its armed forces. The creation of the Rapid Deployment Task Force, the precursor of Central Command, was designed to provide the United States with the means to respond to crises around the world. In effect, however, the combination of the Carter Doctrine and the new command organization marked out the Gulf and Middle East as vital to U.S. national security. But by creating an organization with army and Marine Corps formations, the Carter administration presented the armed forces with the twin demands that they synchronize their various capabilities and be able to operate if necessary under conditions of major inferiority. Thus the U.S. Army was obliged to accommodate the de-mands of the Carter Doctrine, and the U.S. Navy and U.S. Air Force were drawn into the process at the very time that the doctrinal net was being thrown ever wider by the Maneuver Warfare school and by Starry's shift toward endorsement of its main arguments.

The third and last of the factors that shaped the development and timing of Maneuver Warfare and AirLand Battle was provided in the form of the Reagan administration and a 15% increase in defense spend-ing. The implications of this development were to take different forms, not least for the U.S. Navy, which, having decided upon the "600-ship Navy," had to produce the rationale for such a force, hence "The Mari-time Strategy" paper of August–September 1982. What was at issue was procurement programs and service status, and specifically which of the services was to gather the lion's share of what was to hand. The AirLand Battle concept was the army's attempt to ensure its own priority ahead of the air force, and publication of FM100-5 in 1982 all but wrecked the very delicate consultation that was then being undertaken by the army and air force with regard to *AirLand Battle 2000*. To assert that the air force was less than enthusiastic about FM100-5 1982 would be to understate the situation with a vengeance: the air force did not regard its prime purpose in life to be at the beck and call of the army. FM100-5 1982 left the air force bitterly resentful and implacably opposed to a concept of warfare that effectively denied it any role other than close support. The air force resisted acceptance of commitments under the terms of FM100-5 until 1984 and the "31 Initiatives" agreement with the army, and one of the most notable features of FM100-5 1986 was the balance between land and air that was so conspicuously lacking in the 1982 edition. What was also conspicuous about the two papers was that the 1986 paper lacked the frenetic breathlessness and sense of incompleteness of the 1982 ver-sion: the 1982 document is a proselytizing screed, whereas the 1986 document is the authorized version of an established church. As it was, AirLand Battle, in the form of FM100-5, was published on 20 August 1982 after the West Point conference of the previous month.[9] Sometimes regarded as the point at which old ideas were laid to rest, this meeting of the congressional Reform Group and defense intellectuals was really more important for the new ideas being officially unveiled and endorsed, the U.S. Air Force notwithstanding.

* * *

The conference came in a month that witnessed two wars. In the South Atlantic the Argentinian occupation of the Falkland Islands was ended in a highly unusual campaign, which was cruelly if not inaccurately described as a fight between two bald men about a comb: a nation that had turned its back on aircraft carriers and commitments outside the NATO area was able to improvise an operation across 8,000 miles of ocean and fight and win a campaign in which surface warships, with minimal air support, were able to overcome land-based aircraft operating at the limit of endurance. In the Middle East another round of the Arab–Israeli conflict began with the Israeli invasion of Lebanon, which had been engulfed by civil war since April 1975. Both wars saw the employment of high-technology weapons and were linked by the fact that the last missile fired at a British warship in the South Atlantic was a Gabriel, supplied to Argentina by an Israeli aircraft, courtesy of refueling facilities in Libya. But if in this war the narrowness of the margin of British victory could be measured by the number of British warships struck by bombs that failed to explode, the war in southern Lebanon was to be much more significant in terms of its implications for warfare.

* * *

The episode that went under the name Operation Peace for Galilee, and which ensured everything but, was profoundly significant in terms of both warfare and the Arab–Israeli dispute. Freed after March 1979 from any immediate commitment on its southern border as a result of the treaty with Egypt,[10] the Israeli offensive into southern Lebanon in June 1982 introduced Israel to two new experiences. For the first time in its existence Israel embarked upon a military operation against a neighbor that opened deep divisions within Israeli society, this being an act of calculated aggression that many Israelis found wholly unacceptable. Moreover, for the first time in its existence Israel encountered military failure. In the short term it was successful, but whatever military success was commanded counted for little alongside the reality that Israel embraced a long-term commitment in southern Lebanon that it could not escape. In much of this area Israeli forces were welcomed by the indigenous population, weary of war and resentful of the Palestinian presence in their country. But Israel's behavior turned this population against it and saddled it with a commitment to support Christian Falangist forces that, in the final analysis, were unable to sustain themselves without its backing. The Israeli idea of securing its northern border by proxy, which had begun in March 1978 with its incursion into Lebanon and the establishment of a *cordon sanitaire* in the border area, finally miscarried. In fact, the attempt in Lebanon to reassert a Christian supremacy that had long died provoked the inevitable reaction among the various peoples of southern Lebanon that Israel had to win to its side, and in so doing the Israelis rescued defeat from the very real victory that had been won in the first three days of this operation.

What was no less significant was that in the process the Israeli state lost the moral initiative. The massacres at the Sabra and Shatilla refugee camps in southern Beirut by Falangist militia operating in an area controlled by Israeli forces (16–18 September 1982) and the Israeli bombardment and blockade of the Moslem areas of the city, with the denial of food, medical supplies, electricity, and water, cost Israel its claims on the moral high ground, both in this specific conflict but more generally in the context of the Arab–Israeli dispute as a whole. Before this time, Israeli terrorism had been selective and for the most part discreet, whereas Palestinian terrorism most definitely was neither: Israeli behavior in southern Lebanon in 1982 meant that the various denunciatory labels thereafter attached themselves to both sides with equal impartiality.

In terms of warfare, Operation Peace for Galilee was significant because of the manner in which it was fought, specifically on two separate counts. First, given the initial intention to destroy Palestinian forces in southern Lebanon, Northern Command allocated a total of seven divisions, "force-packaged" a corps equivalent on three separate axes of advance, along the coastal plain, via Beaufort Castle into the area between the Litani and Zaharani rivers, and up the Beqaa valley. Given the nature of the terrain and the wretchedness of the roads in these areas, each formation was specially strengthened with engineers, but with a plan that involved a series of divergent attacks across a linear front and with fully mechanized formations, the Israelis adopted a form of attack and all-arms formation that was very similar to that to which the Soviet army had begun to move in the 1970s. The need to integrate armor and infantry and to have the whole properly supported by artillery and services was the prime lesson of the October 1973 War, and in practical terms this meant a mechanized infantry able to put down general suppressive fire. With the Merkava tank making its operational debut in this conflict, the Israelis invested their separate efforts with considerable defensive power and relied upon mobility and the support afforded primarily by Cobra and Defender helicopters for firepower. This is not to suggest, however, that either the Israelis were not without their problems or that their arrangements were innovative. The U.S. military assessment of the Israeli performance was that the 1982 campaign revealed very little advance relative to the October 1973 War, while the Israeli effort in southern Lebanon was beset by logistical problems and over-concentration of helicopters in the assault role.

In the first two days of Operation Peace for Galilee the Israelis were able to sweep aside hopelessly outgunned and outclassed Palestinian forces and almost reached the line of the Awali river; within another 24 hours they had advanced on Damour and through the Shouf to secure Beit el Dine, some 10 miles south of the main Beirut–Damascus road. But on the unsecured right flank Syrian forces remained, and despite an initial Israeli intention not to seek battle with these forces, fire was exchanged in the Beqaa on the first day, and the Israelis had prepared an alternative plan, Operation Big Pines, that involved an offensive against both the Palestinian and Syrian forces in Lebanon. On the second day of the campaign the Israelis again encountered Syrian resistance, this time around Jezzine, and they strengthened their forces in the eastern sector. On the third day Israeli formations clashed with and defeated Syrian forces in front of the Bessri and around Jezzine and pushed up the Beqaa valley to within 10 miles of the main Syrian defensive positions around Rashaiya. Herein the second factor of significance in terms of the manner in which this conflict was fought was summoned.

The unprecedented scale and extent of the Israeli offensive throughout southern Lebanon compromised the Syrian position. Having intervened in March 1976, ostensibly to end the civil war but in effect to save the Christians from being defeated by the Lebanese Moslems and their PLO allies, in June 1982 Syria could not stand aside while the Palestinians were defeated and its own military position within Lebanon compromised. But its strengthening of its forces in the Beqaa and the Ante-Lebanon led the Israelis to implement their second alternative, which opened on 9 June. Over the previous days the Israelis had conducted extensive electronic surveillance of Syrian positions and installations, both in Syria itself and in eastern Lebanon, and on the fourth day of this campaign they began a series of operations designed to force the Syrian air force to give battle. In this the Israelis were successful, and a minimum of 22 Syrian fighters that were put into the air were destroyed in a single action by an Israeli air force that, having used drones to read Syrian radar signatures, used four E-2C Hawkeye AWACS/ESM and four Boeing E-3 ECM/ELINT aircraft to jam Syrian radar and communications and to direct Israeli fighters to the battle. In addition, the E-2C, which can track 200 aircraft simultaneously and fly an F-14 and fire its missiles, were able to direct the attention of Israel ECM fighter-bombers and strike aircraft, which were equipped with jam-resistant secured voice and data links, against the Syrian missile batteries in the Beqaa, the Israelis using AGM-45 Shrikes against the missile radars and ordinary bombs against the missiles and their launchers. With 198 aircraft committed in two strikes, the Israelis, in addition to winning the air battle, were able in one three-hour period on 9 June to destroy 17 of 19 SAM-6 Gainful batteries, plus a number of obsolescent SAM-2 Guideline and SAM-3 Goa batteries. The two surviving Gainful batteries were destroyed the next day. No Israeli aircraft were lost in the course of these operations.

Operation Peace for Galilee was to continue, despite a number of cease-fires, until 3 September 1982, with a peace-keeping force drawn from France, Italy, and the United States deployed in Beirut in the last 10 days of August to ensure the orderly and safe withdrawal of Palestinian and Syrian forces trapped in the city. West and southwest Beirut were subjected to siege after 26 June, by which stage the Israelis had overrun the whole of southern Lebanon, dominated the Beirut–Damascus road, and controlled the whole of the southern part of the Beqaa valley. In the process the Israelis mauled various Syrian formations, destroying an estimated 400 tanks, while losing about 40 of their own in the course of the whole operation. Militarily the campaign was as one-sided as all the previous conflicts between Israel and its neighbors had been, and its outcome was the result of a general Israeli possession of the initiative and superior technique. The events of 9 June clearly possessed singular significance.

The first use of electronic countermeasures in war occurred in February 1904 in the very first days of the first war that saw the employment of wireless: Russian radio operators at Port Arthur jammed transmissions by Japanese warships off the base. In the First World War the French use of jamming from the Eiffel Tower is well known, but in the opening weeks of hostilities, when both mobility and time were at a premium, all the major combatants employed jamming and eavesdropped on enemies that were obliged to transmit in clear. In the Second World War the naval wars in both the North Atlantic and the Pacific, the German bombing campaign against Britain, and the Allied strategic bombing campaign against Germany all witnessed technological, radio and intelligence struggles that were of major importance in deciding the course of events. The Vietnam and 1973 wars brought home the critical importance of defensive ECM. But the sequence of events on 9 June 1982 clearly represented something that was very significant. It was not that the Israelis were able to win air supremacy, since there can be little doubt that the Israeli air force held supremacy before that date and would have won any campaign against the Syrian air force, but that the Israeli air force was able to command air space by virtue of its ability to paralyze its enemy and prevent its offering battle effectively. Those Syrian aircraft that did challenge Israeli supremacy on 9 June 1982 were denied effectiveness on account of the Israeli ability to destroy Syrian command and control facilities through electronic countermeasures, and the extent of

Israeli effectiveness was proven not just in the ease with which Syrian aircraft were destroyed in the air on this particular day, but in the fact that the Israeli air force was able to beat down every subsequent Syrian attempt to challenge Israeli air supremacy with equal ease. In the course of Operation Peace for Galilee Israeli fighters, primarily using third-generation AIM-9L Sidewinder, shot down a total of 85 Syrian fighters while suffering the loss of 3 aircraft.[11] Israeli superiority in the realm of electronic warfare meant that Syrian aircraft that sought to give battle were blinded and singly, successively, and collectively destroyed.

* * *

The circumstances of the 9 June effort, plus the Israeli air strike that had destroyed the nuclear power station then nearing completion at Osirak outside Baghdad one year previously (Operation Babylon), pointed to a future possibility that was not lost upon the U.S. Air Force; indeed, it had anticipated it and hence its chagrin at the way in which the AirLand Battle episode unfolded after October 1981. The concept of supremacy had been at the heart of air power certainly since 1916, but it had proved elusive and was won only at considerable cost and through protracted attritional campaigns during two world wars. Israeli success in the June 1967 War was very different—so different as to be both unique and unrepeatable, since it was a war that brought the premissile era to a close—but 1982 again was very different. In a very meaningful sense it brought the ideas of Douhet, specifically the concept of commanding the skies through the exercise of air power, appreciably closer to realization. Inevitably the subsequent public argument was dominated by a simple sound bite—control of the electro-magnetic spectrum—that belied the complexity of what was involved. But by this time, 1981–82, the reality was that with the new generation of fighters and missiles in place, the U.S. Air Force had equipped itself with a means to win a battle for air supremacy that possibly was unnecessary. The 1994 TRADOC prediction that command and control supremacy was essential before air supremacy could be won[12] was belated acknowledgment of the obvious, as far as the air force was concerned: the events of June 1982 showed that command and control supremacy provided the route to control of the air.

* * *

One is tempted to conclude that the real difference between FM100-5 1982 and 1986 is that the latter is more measured and has the assurance conferred by acceptance. Certainly there are points of difference—most notably the recognition in FM100-5 1986 that the battle in depth, given Soviet capability, would involve rear area operations as well as those at forward point of contact and along an enemy axis of deployment that the

1982 manual had stressed. FM100-5 1986 certainly marked the end of the journey from Active Defense; it also marked the end of this process in another sense: the congressional decision in 1985 not to fund follow-on programs that were under consideration as part of *AirLand Battle 2000*, which was to provide for the period 1995–2005, indicated that the impetus of the Reagan administration was spent, at least in terms of a defense budget cornucopia. But in another sense the linking of the two manuals is misleading, for a reason that is not immediately obvious. One can see the Gulf campaign of 1991 in terms of FM100-5 1986 but not so directly of FM100-5 1982. The difference is not to be explained simply by reference to the weapons and surveillance systems that moved onto center stage in the intervening years.

Discerning threads of continuity and change beset any attempt to interpret the 1991 campaign. The latter was barely over when the first claims set out the view that the campaign was not AirLand Battle, and if an air force pedigree invited the obvious comment of what could one expect from a pig except a grunt, one fact was inescapable: the claim was quite correct. The essence of AirLand Battle, as defined in successive field manuals, was the use of air and naval assets in support of ground forces to fight and win tactical battles linked operationally; however much the latter might try to evade the issue, the fact was that in this conflict the primary task of destruction fell upon air power, without reference to the conduct of a land campaign. But this, in itself, describes rather than explains, and in seeking to explain the 1991 campaign by reference to FM100-5 1982 and 1986, two matters critical to an understanding of the elements of continuity and change would seem to be relevant.

The first matter relates to what appears to be a shift between field manuals in dealing with maneuver and concentration. In the 1982 manual the concept of maneuver concerned both formations and firepower, with the emphasis placed upon the destruction of enemy forces as the means of disruption and paralysis. In the 1986 manual the concept of maneuver concerned both firepower and formations, with the emphasis placed upon separation and destruction of enemy forces as the means of disruption and paralysis. The difference between the two manuals is not explicit, yet the qualitative leap in military imagination between the two concepts is to be found, for those inclined to look, in Soviet concepts and practice of Deep Battle. The Soviet way of war sought to separate enemy front-line formations from rear support in the certain knowledge that if an armored mass could be concentrated between those elements of the enemy that had to be shielded and those that had to be supplied, the defeat of both would follow—the extent of that defeat and depth of penetration being largely dependent upon the size of force and its speed of operations. In the Second World War the operational shock thus imparted to an enemy defensive system was primarily inflicted by armored movement into the enemy rear areas—a concept that would seem to have been adopted in FM100-5 1982. By the 1970s, however, enhanced conventional capability meant that the Soviets had moved to deep strike by ground forces supported by airborne and air forces. FM100-5 1986 followed and developed that move, with the emphasis seemingly placed upon disruption induced less by the forward movement of ground forces than by concentrated firepower. The points of difference between the 1982 and 1986 manuals are elusive and beset by the problems of the reading of the record backward and wrongly attributing matters that came after 1986 to the period between the two manuals. But the critical point would seem to be that in a process that was evolutionary and that continued after 1986, in the 1982 manual the elements of ground, air mobile, and air forces were weighted in favor of ground formations moving across the battlefield to the point of contact, whereas in the 1986 manual the ground element complemented the others—specifically firepower. What cannot be doubted is that between them the two manuals represented a move from manpower and formations to firepower, though recognition of this change was not forthcoming—not even in 1991—except on the part of the U.S. Air Force.

The second matter that would seem to be relevant in any consideration of the 1991 campaign relative to the 1982 and 1986 field manuals concerns the definition of attrition. It may be argued that annihilation represents instant attrition, but on the evidence of the 1991 campaign it may be that attrition can at present be inflicted on a scale and at a speed that renders it all but indistinguishable from annihilation. Major wars, because of their protracted nature, have necessarily involved attrition, but if the 1991 campaign heralded the restoration of decisiveness to warfare, it may well be that the distinction between attrition and annihilation will be rendered ever less meaningful. By extension, an examination of the 1991 campaign would present the question of whether or not the Coalition effort represented the realization of the elusive "decisive battle."

The idea of the *Vernichtungsschlacht*, or the single battle of annihilation, was so discredited in the course of the twentieth century that the suggestion that the technological developments of the last two decades may have restored such battles to the military repertoire would seem to border on the absurd. Certainly the suggestion is flawed in one respect. The concept of the "decisive battle" historically has concerned itself with a narrowly military phenomenon—namely, the destruction of enemy field formations. But the idea of a defeat that did not embrace state, society, and military would seem to be wholly unrealistic: the nature of the state, given twentieth-century history, renders the idea of a victory with only a military dimension—over a field army—quixotic. But, perversely, any consideration of the 1991 campaign must provoke two thoughts: that the decrease in the size of armies since the 1960s and the difficulties of reconstitution must expose an army to the danger of defeat in a single battle, and that in 1991 what was nominally the fifth-largest military establishment in the world was effectively destroyed in a single campaign. Arguably, such a defeat as the one sustained by the Iraqi military in 1991, a comprehensive defeat incurred within a single campaign, was something that had not occurred since 1940, and the parallels between the two events are quite close. Both France in 1940 and Iraq in 1991 shared a lack of strategic depth despite considerable area, massive inferiority in the air, less-than-adequate understanding of the balance between the offense and defense as it existed at the times in question, and communications systems that were simply overwhelmed. They were trapped by experience of outdated forms of warfare that actually contributed to defeat. The defeat of France in 1940, however, is very much the exception in warfare in the twentieth century: 1940 excepted, in two world wars the *Vernichtungsschlacht* was incapable of realization. Without dignifying Iraq with such status, its defeat in 1991 would seem to mark the point in time when the element of decisiveness was restored to war by virtue of the fact that such a battle had once more emerged as a practical and practicable option in the conduct of operations. The one crucial point would seem to be that on the evidence of the 1991 campaign a *Vernichtungsschlacht* can now be fought and won by air power alone.

* * *

Stating the matter delicately, Maneuver Warfare and AirLand Battle aroused a certain skepticism on the part of America's allies: at best somewhat futuristic, FM100-5 1982 most obviously left a great deal to chance, given its dependence on highly advanced technology, not all of which was in place in 1982. AirLand Battle was a statement of belief on the part of the U.S. military and demanded an act of faith on the part of America's partners, but in this respect the whole of the seven years before AirLand Battle's adoption had involved an act of faith on their part. The aftermath of the Vietnam War, the uncertainties and irresolution of the Carter years, and the first chaotic year or so of the Reagan administration were years of endurance, and if AirLand Battle seemed to some of these allies to border on the fantastical, it was a model of both simplicity and sanity compared to some aspects of the handling of strategic nuclear issues in this period.

* * *

The gestation period of AirLand Battle coincided with a major deterioration of Soviet–U.S. relations; indeed, it has been suggested that by 1975 détente was dead, though very few people realized it at the time. Undoubtedly the relationship between the two superpowers was a major factor in the complexity of nuclear issues in the 1970s, but the real difficulties that arose stemmed, ironically, from the stability that had been brought about by virtue of the fact that the Soviet Union achieved strategic parity with the United States. That it was able to do so was the result of the massive investment in strategic systems undertaken by the Soviet Union after the 1962 Cuban crisis and something that was certainly unusual, perhaps unprecedented, in history: the decision by a great power—in this case the United States—to limit itself voluntarily in order to allow a potential enemy to achieve parity. As a result of the massive increase of its nuclear arsenal during the 1960s, the United States, possessing enough weapons to destroy all life on this planet several times over, recognized the reality that merely adding to its number of nuclear weapons would not somehow enhance its security. It was, by the standards of the time and of nations, a rather strange decision, but undoubtedly one that was both brave and correct: the realities of mutually assured destruction and invulnerable retaliatory capacity pointed to the fact that there was no point in further building up nuclear systems. But an acceptance of equality with another power was something that the American public mentality found very difficult to accept, and it was subjected to much ill-considered abuse.

The reality of strategic parity was crucially important in that it provided the basis of détente and of the first attempts to limit the number of nuclear weapons held by the two superpowers—the SALT I Treaty was signed in Moscow in May 1972. But there was one important byproduct of strategic equality, and that was that the Nixon administration, in embracing the concept of "sufficiency" for the U.S. nuclear arsenal, believed that the United States still retained and should seek to preserve qualitative advantage over the Soviet Union in strategic weapons. The decision to procure the *Ohio*-class submarines and the D-5 Trident missile stemmed from this determination to retain a technological lead. But the real point was that SALT I was agreed by two states with very little shared interest other than a desire to limit ABM systems and divided by the asymmetry of their nuclear arsenals and the weapons systems then being developed.

This asymmetry meant that when the second SALT negotiations began, questions of equivalence inevitably concentrated upon dissimilarities, with the result that weapons presented themselves in different classifications—specifically strategic, intermediate, and short-range. The immediate difficulties that this presented worried the European NATO powers, which were already somewhat concerned about the implications of Flexible Response and not sure of the distinction between different types of nuclear missiles, all of which could strike at their homelands. Inevitably, there was unease on the part of these powers at the prospect of the superpowers dividing the negotiations into separate packages that would separate strategic and theater issues. But what was also at work at this time and was equally alarming to the European powers was the consequence of the certainty of ever greater accuracy of weapons systems, and the two—separation and certainty together—had one very odd effect. While they did not prevent a SALT II agreement eventually being signed on 18 June 1979, they served to redirect attention to what had been discredited in the 1950s, the idea of Limited Nuclear War and escalation up a nuclear ladder.

There was, however, an ironic twist. The viability of the deterrent after 1962 had rested upon the secure second strike vested in the Polaris–Poseidon submarine force and was directed against civilian society, in large measure because sea-launched missiles lacked the accuracy to strike against military targets. Increased accuracy of weapons systems meant that a precision counterstrike could be contemplated, and with it the full-scale exchange directed against military targets: with the commissioning of the first Trident system, all the systems in the American nuclear arsenal had first-strike capability. This future reality led to the adoption in 1980 of P.D. 59 and the concept of countervailing strategy within the context of protracted and large-scale, but not all-out, nuclear war. If the Carter administration's idea was that the United States should seek to retain effective options at different levels of war, the distinctions were largely lost upon allies such as West Germany and most certainly fell foul of one basic reality: the elements of detachment and deliberate calculation were very unlikely to impose themselves at the forefront of the decision-making process in the event of nuclear weapons having already been used. But what compounded this unreality was the notion that the accuracy of systems would allow strikes against command and control facilities within the Soviet Union, the nadir of this line of lack of reasoning coming in the form of the proposal for attacks on key Soviet political and military installations that were justified on the basis of Just War criteria with the claims that such attacks would be moral, most certainly in comparison with the policy of countervalue targeting and its deliberate selection of cities as the targets of a retaliatory strike.[13] How warheads were to distinguish between a Communist party command system within a city and civilian society was not exactly clear, and such wondrous logic could have been dismissed by affording it the silent contempt it deserved, but for the fact that with the installation of the Reagan administration it seemed that the hesitations of the 1970s, and the stability born of parity, had been set aside in favor of individuals who genuinely did believe that a future war could and should involve the use of nuclear weapons and that a nuclear war could be won. In a very obvious sense the whole idea of U.S. armed forces being "freed" to win a war to which they were committed came full circle with the inauguration of an administration that seemingly repudiated the entire détente and SALT processes and was apparently unconcerned by the prospect of global nuclear war.

* * *

The Reagan years were years of paradox: in virtually every field of activity, not excluding the conduct of the nation's defense and its wars, the predominant characteristic was the disparity between policy and reality, between cause and effect. Perhaps the most serious, at least in its long-term implications, was manifested in social policy and its consequences. The Reagan administration was fervent in its assault upon the concept of the state as it had evolved since the time of Roosevelt, yet the resultant social problems were treated as wholly unrelated; indeed, they were the product of the disastrously corrosive effects of liberal policies of previous administrations. But the most obvious manifestations of the disparity between policy and reality were presented in the conduct of foreign policy, specifically with regard to dealings with the Soviet Union. In his first administration, between 1981 and 1985, Reagan dealt with as many General Secretaries of the CPSU as there had been between 1917 and 1980. More accurately, between 1981 and 1985 Reagan refused to deal with as many General Secretaries as there had been between 1917 and 1980, and herein lay a paradox typical of the Reagan administration: despite personnel changes, there was a consistency and continuity in Soviet policy that stood in awful contrast to the lack of coherence, cohesion, and vision in Washington that was the direct result of Reagan's administrative ineptitude and lack of any real leadership qualities. Yet after November 1985, while there was a certain element of continuity in the Reagan administration, change, innovation, and the initiative were all but Soviet prerogatives, and the man of the hour was Mikhail Gorbachev.

Certainly the relationship between the two superpowers in the period from 1981 to 1985 was worse than at any time since the death of Stalin in 1953, yet within another four years there had emerged the basis of cooperation that was unprecedented. In this process the president who had sought to abolish nuclear weapons, who had, in November 1981, made his "zero-option" proposal, who made the "build-down" proposal but nevertheless rejected the "Walk in the Woods" suggestion in 1982, who deliberately violated the SALT II agreement with the B-52/ALCM program, who launched the strategic defense initiative and scuttled the Reykjavik summit in October 1986, ultimately committed the United States to the START process and to the "double-zero global option" embodied in the INF treaty of 8 December 1987. In this process, too, and very perversely, it was to be the Reaganite program that emerged triumphant, yet even in its success there was inconsistency and paradox. The policy of confrontation with the Soviet Union and deliberately seeking to destroy the latter by the intensification of programs that would impose impossible financial demands upon the latter could have provoked only one reaction on the part of the Soviet Union if the Reagan rhetoric that attributed to the Soviet leadership the meanest behavior was accurate. If the Soviet Union was as consistent or persistent in its pursuit of a wholly amoral program as was alleged, then it followed that it would have used any means to ensure that it was not destroyed in the competition that Reagan imposed upon it.

There were elements in the Soviet leadership that were prepared to meet the U.S. challenge. Ogarkov coined the phrase "the revolution in military affairs" as part of an answer that would have resulted in the deliberate reduction of consumer production in order to ensure the militarization of industry and society. There were some who appeared willing to make use of a seeming "window of opportunity" to ensure the survival of the Soviet system.

Leaving aside the question of the wisdom or otherwise of embarking upon a race to destruction with a hostile leadership thus described, the fact that the Soviet leadership desisted from such a course of action, admittedly in part because it never fully understood the extent of Soviet weakness, would suggest that the Reagan rhetoric was somewhat flawed. In any event, the Reagan administration never understood the process that it set in train, still less the result. The collapse of the Soviet empire in eastern Europe and the demise of the Soviet Union itself was seen as the triumph of American values, but left unaddressed was the fact that in the 12 years of the Reagan and Bush administrations the U.S. national debt quadrupled and that in the Reagan years the United States went from the greatest creditor to the greatest debtor state in the world and for a brief period seemed to have left Japan as the real winner of the Cold War. Moreover, the assumption that underpinned so much of whatever little thinking Reagan ever did, the trinity of economic liberalization, democracy, and stability, was never more than a chimera. The experience of Latin America provided example enough that capitalism and democracy need not go hand in hand, and it never seemed to have occurred to the Washington of Reagan and Bush, with its insistence that the Soviet Union accelerate the process of economic change, that the maintenance of an intact, united, strong Russian state could provide the basis of future stability and peace. The collapse of the Soviet empire and the fragmentation of the Soviet Union had much the same result as the process of decolonialization in Africa: historically, both the Soviet and the Western imperialist systems had the effect of holding in check very powerful ethnic, cultural, or tribal hatreds, which virulently reasserted themselves when these systems passed into history. The comparison between the Soviet and Chinese systems in how they sought and implemented reform in their respective crises in the 1980s, and the very different results of their endeavors, is salutary, though the real test of the latter, notwithstanding the Tiananmen Square massacre of 2 June 1989, admittedly still lies in the future.

* * *

Somehow it seems very appropriate that the military test of the Reagan administration was provided during the Bush presidency—specifically the 1991 Gulf campaign. Maneuver Warfare, and specifically AirLand Battle, was not really the product of the Reagan years, even though FM100-5 1982 was not formally adopted until 20 months into the Reagan presidency. As such, the record of the Reagan administration and AirLand Battle invite examination on three counts: a consideration of the Reagan administration's conduct of war, an evaluation of the phenomenon of AirLand Battle relative to the context of reform, and an assessment of the 1991 campaign in the Middle East in light of the terms of reference supplied by the Maneuver Warfare school and the 1982 and 1986 manuals.

* * *

There was, in the lifetime of the Reagan administration, a frequency of American use of military force and a certain unevenness of performance and results. The low points of the Reagan years were the suicide bombing of the Marine compound in Beirut on 23 October 1983, which resulted in the deaths of 241 servicemen, and the destruction of an Iranian civilian airliner over the Persian Gulf on 3 July 1988 by the U.S. cruiser *Vincennes*, with the loss of all 290 persons aboard. The loss of two carrier aircraft on 4 December 1983 over the Beqaa valley to Syrian SAMs and the crippling of the frigate *Stark* by an Iraqi Mirage F-1 on 4 May 1987 were other low points; indeed, with respect to the December 1983 episode having to rely on Jessie Jackson, of all people, to ask the Syrians if the United States could have its airmen back was perhaps the nadir of this administration's military fortunes.

But in the Alice-in-Wonderland atmosphere that prevailed throughout and beyond the lifetime of the Reagan presidency, the administration was able to walk away from debacles that would have inflicted probably irreversible damage upon any other presidency since 1945. Certainly the ability of this administration to evade responsibility for its failures stands in ironic contrast to the Bush administration's failure to reap the credit of success. But if the Middle East provided these two administrations with very different challenges and results, the Reagan presidency's political immunity from the consequence of failure was the product of three factors. First, the effectiveness of the Reagan administration, both in terms of what passed for policy and evading resultant responsibility, lay in one fundamental societal change for which Reagan, by virtue of his previous career, was prepared: the trivialization of issues on behalf of a media that had moved from the news conference, the photograph, and serious written journalism to simplistic reporting, invariably related in terms of personality and more often than not violence-orientated. The sheer banality of news coverage on American television and a docile press curbed by the Republican Party in the aftermath of the Watergate scandal ensured that the Reagan administration was afforded an indulgence denied all presidents since Kennedy. But no less important in these Teflon years was the simple fact that Reagan gave the American public a confidence that had been lacking over the previous generation of defeat and upheaval—an electorate and presidency that wanted to believe in the national greatness of the United States flattered, deceived, and believed one another. Thus the major military disasters of the Reagan years were dismissed as being of no account, troubles on which the nation turned its collective back and which were in any event balanced against apparent success in other ventures.

Second, for an administration that demanded enemies to oppose, be they foreign or domestic, three presented themselves in addition to the two—the Soviet Union and Castro's Cuba—that were permanent fixtures: the Sandinista regime of Nicaragua, the Gaddafi administration of Libya, and Ayatollah Khomeini's Iran. Of these, Libya proved the most public and least difficult, Gaddafi's posturing and exclusion zones notwithstanding. Three major American operations were conducted, one against a battery on 24 March 1986, the raids on Tripoli and Benghazi on 15 April 1986, and the shooting down of two Libyan Mig-21s by F-14 Tomcats on 4 January 1989 in the very last days of the Reagan administration. The only notable features of these episodes were the fact that a Soviet destroyer was sunk in the course of the attack on Tripoli—something that both the Americans and Soviets took care to try to conceal—and that this raid was conducted within a month of the French, who denied the United States use of national air space in the conduct of this attack, having destroyed three-quarters of the Libyan air force in a series of raids (Operation Sparrowhawk) staged from Chad. With regard to Iran, the U.S. attacks on Iranian oil gunboats and installations in 1988 amounted to a de facto support for Baghdad, despite the unprovoked Iraqi attack on the *Stark*, the fact that Iraqi aggression had been responsible for the Iran–Iraq war (1980–88), and that the Iraqis had begun attacks on cities and oil installations and had used chemical agents both against Iranian troops on the battlefield and against the Kurdish population of northern Iraq. But Iran's diplomatic isolation and powerlessness, the extent of the U.S. public's hostility toward that country after the events of 1979–81, and the strength of the American national position in light of the increasingly obvious weakening of the Soviet Union meant that the destruction of the Iranian Airbus went unchallenged domestically and internationally.

The Nicaragua of the Sandinista revolution, however, provided a more difficult and protracted problem, and the Reagan administration's handling of a problem largely of its own making was to prove the issue that marked its unraveling in the form of the Irangate scandal. In the event, the Reagan administration was to be successful in that in February–March 1989 the Managua regime conceded the principle of free elections and, somewhat surprisingly, accepted its own defeat in February 1990. Even in success, however, the Reagan administration's policy begged a number of very pertinent questions, not least why the United States should have pursued so aggressive a policy toward the Sandinistas after having succored and sustained the corrupt and murderous Samoza regime for over 30 years. It is somewhat difficult to resist the notion that after the successful overthrow of the Samoza dictatorship in July 1979, U.S. policy toward Nicaragua repeated the disastrous mistakes that had been perpetrated after 1959 with respect to Cuba, but perversely with a very different result. Certainly the parallels between the two revolutions were close, and arguably both represent the only successful Marighellian insurgency efforts in that repressive incumbent regimes were defeated—and forced into luxurious exile in the United States—as a result of combined urban and rural campaigns that were based upon widespread public endorsement. No less certainly, both regimes were pushed toward the Soviet camp as a result of overt American hostility. But if the Reagan administration indeed did embrace a dubious morality over Nicaragua, bestowed upon its regime an importance it never merited, and turned a potentially popular movement into an enemy, its success had a curious parallel in the dramatic change that occurred between 1960 and 1990 in the governance of Latin America. In 1960 dictatorship—specifically military dictatorship—provided the dominant form of government in Latin America. By 1990 dictatorships had become increasingly uncommon, and hand-in-hand with this change went a factor that ensured that the social stability that had existed in the 1960s as a result of the straight choice between the status quo and Cuban–Soviet revolution remained intact: however imperfect the form and practice of democratic institutions in many Latin American countries in the 1980s, their very existence undercut revolutionary imperatives.

The third factor at work in insulating the Reagan administration from the consequences of its worst errors of judgment was specific circumstances that worked to its advantage at the times of greatest vulnerability. The decision to conduct Operation Urgent Fury, the invasion of Grenada on 25 October, was taken on the same day as the Beirut bombing and was intended as a distraction. In this respect it was successful. At the cost of 59 American dead and 152 wounded in an operation that resulted in the award of more medals than the number of military personnel involved in the operation, the threat presented to American national security by an island of some 120 square miles and a population of 95,000 people was eliminated, and what could have been a crisis of confidence in the Reagan administration passed, with the result that the administration very literally walked away from the Beirut debacle. The withdrawal of the multinational peace-keeping force in February–March 1984 as the Lebanon slid ever deeper into civil war closed the door on this particular episode for the United States. But while the power of image and a masterly manipulation of information on the part of the Reagan administration were crucially important in its being able to distance itself from unwanted responsibilities, the magnitude of events—specifically the shaping of the upheaval in eastern Europe that was to result in the collapse of the Soviet empire and the demise of the Soviet Union—were much more important. The importance of the superpower relationship and the changes that took place in the years of the second Reagan administration rightly took precedence over all other considerations and set the Grenada and Libyan episodes in proper perspective.

* * *

But if the START process, the Soviet withdrawal from Afghanistan beginning in 1989, and the convulsions that first gripped and then overwhelmed the Soviet system after 1988 dominated the second half of the 1980s and provided the lasting legacy of the Reagan administration, the 1991 campaign was nevertheless the test of its commitment to defense and of the Maneuver Warfare school and AirLand Battle. And here one faces an immediate difficulty: the years that have elapsed since this campaign have been noted for a proliferation of accounts of this conflict and an outpouring of doctrinal screeds, most of them relating to the "Maneuvrist Approach to Warfare," whatever that phrase might mean, if anything. What is not clear, however, is the historical basis of much of what today passes for doctrine and whether or not what has been written about the 1991 campaign really does represent an accurate record and assessment. Put very simply, one can legitimately question whether on the basis of the evidence provided by the Gulf campaign current doctrine represents the product or the negation of history.

* * *

In the opening chapter certain conclusions about the 1991 campaign were suggested for the purposes of argument and with varying degrees of conviction, but their recounting provides the starting line for a detailed consideration of this conflict. The conclusions that were suggested were that this campaign witnessed the arrival of the 24-hour battle, an unprecedented reach inland of direct naval firepower, and the first occasion in history when ground elements operated in support of air and naval power. These same conclusions suggested that the 1991 campaign was the first in which space provided a dimension of war and in which air power was the primary agency of destruction, and was illustrative of a trend to use it either primarily or alone in the conduct of war. It was stated that this conflict was perhaps the first occasion when the fight for air supremacy was synonymous with the use of air power and when a state of reasonable size and depth was subjected to attack across its entire area in an initial offensive operation. It was suggested that the campaign witnessed the comprehensive defeat of a nation, which was quite separate from the defeat and destruction of its armed forces, that the Iraqi state could have been defeated without its armed forces having been subjected to attack, and that this campaign witnessed the conclusive defeat of a state without the necessity of having to complete the wholesale destruction of its industrial infrastructure, society, and armed forces. Finally, it was stated that this campaign can be argued to mark the point in time when the power of decision of war was restored. To these could have been added another conclusion: that this conflict was the first in which there was real-time coverage by the media.

Any careful consideration of the 1991 campaign relative to FM100-5 1982 and 1986 raises two issues: the question of how far the planning and conduct of the campaign fulfilled basic AirLand Battle dictates and the relationship between the air and ground offensives. On the first there are certain aspects of both the planning and conduct of operations that prompt the question of the extent to which AirLand Battle doctrine had been understood within the U.S. Army. Most clearly, the confusion that surrounded the army's planning of the ground offensive, particularly the detail of its initial planning efforts, provides the basis of skepticism about the military's grasp on Maneuver Warfare theory.

One month into the Kuwait crisis, by early September 1990, CENTCOM (Central Command) had no plan of campaign or even the basis of a plan. CENTCOM's previous concerns with Iran and the Soviet Union, and then the immediacy of problems in receiving forces in theater and the preparation of defensive plans, meant that a deliberate consideration of the form of an offensive plan of campaign was a relatively low priority for Schwarzkopf and his senior planners during the first weeks of Desert Shield. In this situation the Army Chief of Staff offered CENTCOM the services of four graduates from the School of Advanced Military Studies, these officers supposedly being steeped in the concept of Maneuver Warfare. Gathered in Saudi Arabia by 18 September, another week was to pass before these officers were issued with a directive that specified that a plan of campaign should be prepared on the basis of a one-corps equivalent being available. The directive stipulated that the strongest Iraqi defenses should be avoided, that Iraqi forces were to be driven from Kuwait, and that the Republican Guard, defined as the Iraqi "operational center of gravity," should be destroyed in the process.

The first SAMS proposal was presented on 6 October and took the form of three options: a direct attack and alternative left flanking attacks. According to the U.S. Army's official history, the flanking alternatives were discounted by the SAMS personnel because of insufficient forces, the distances involved, and the lift that would be required. There were also doubts about being able to supply a deep advance and a fear of exposing supply lines to counterattack. The SAMS preference, therefore, was for an offensive with the equivalent of a mechanized corps along an axis some 60 miles to the east of the Wadi Al-Batin directed to the Basra–Kuwait City highway in the area of Randhatain, with provision for an advance to the Iraq–Kuwait border if necessary. This attack was to be supported on its right flank by a marine division and a helicopter assault with one division that was to secure the highway junction at Al Jahrah; one French and two Egyptian divisions were to support the left flank by efforts astride the Wadi Al-Batin. The equivalent of one Saudi division was to conduct an offensive into Kuwait along the coastal strip, while feint amphibious landings were to be staged for the purposes of distraction. The overall plan, dubbed the "one-corps concept," acknowledged an overall Iraqi numerical advantage but envisaged a local 3:1 advantage before the offensive began and anticipated a 6:1 advantage at the point of penetration, it being calculated that air operations would have inflicted 50% losses on Iraqi armor before ground operations commenced.[14]

The SAMS reasoning was accepted by Schwarzkopf, who had sketched out a similar plan to Chairman of the Joint Chiefs of Staff Powell in mid-August, and the outline proposal was presented successively to Powell and to Bush, Secretary Cheney, and senior administration officials on 10 and 11 October, at the same time as the air plan was presented. The "one-corps concept" received a somewhat incredulous reception from civilian authorities, their main criticism concentrating on the proposal to attack into the mass of the Iraqi army while declining the open flank. With CENTCOM's representative indicating that Schwarzkopf entertained serious reservations about the plan that was being proposed, it was left to Bush to ask what was required to launch the flanking attack and to Cheney, in effect, to veto the direct attack into Kuwait.

A little more than two months after the Iraqi invasion of Kuwait, therefore, CENTCOM had no real idea of the form that a ground offensive to liberate Kuwait would take, and over the next 10 days three different options appeared from three different sources. From the Secretary's office there emerged a plan that would have involved an offensive across the whole of southern and western Iraq, while from Powell's staff there was proposed a more modest plan which was, in the event, very close to the one that was finally implemented: its essential characteristic was the concentration of a second corps for a flanking attack that was to be conducted with "overwhelming force" and which was to rely upon sheer strength to overwhelm enemy formations. But from the SAMS graduates, directed by Schwarzkopf to prepare a plan of attack with two corps, came the even more modest proposal for a massed attack along an axis some 60 miles to the west of the Wadi Al-Batin directed to the Euphrates, and to a head-on clash with the bulk of the Republican Guard. This plan was put to, and accepted by, Schwarzkopf on 21 October and was then put to Powell on the following day. Knowing that this plan was wholly unacceptable to Cheney, Powell argued in favor of his own staff's plan, and for a second time Schwarzkopf abandoned his own proposal. With the principle of the plan thus determined, flesh was added, with the result that by 14 November, by which time Bush had announced the deployment of VII Corps to Saudi Arabia, Schwarzkopf was able to brief his commanders on the basis of a plan of campaign that envisaged feint amphibious landings to tie down Iraqi formations along the coast, a direct attack into Kuwait by Marine and Arab forces in the coastal strip, and the main offensive by XVIII and VII Corps through the desert. Perhaps somewhat surprisingly in light of his later declaration of the influence of Hannibal and the battle of Cannae in the preparation of the plan of campaign, at this briefing one of Schwarzkopf's comments bears consideration:

We need to destroy—not attack, not damage, not surround. . . . I want to pin them with their backs against the sea, then go in and wipe them out.[15]

The comment invites the observation that with such rhetoric Schwarzkopf provided inadvertent evidence of his mastery of the principles of war and ignorance of both history and operational art.

The planning process and final plan of campaign would seem to present certain difficulties of understanding, not least how it was that the initiative for the flanking attack came from Bush and Cheney, and not from the military. What is perhaps the most surprising aspect of a consistent military antipathy toward the flanking attack was the SAMS' embrace of "the arithmetic of the battlefield" and the concept of the head-on battle à la FM100-5 1976. The SAMS graduates saw no reason to sweep through the desert because the area was not occupied by enemy formations. Such a reason would seem to be the best possible justification for such an offensive, since it has long been known that the most intelligent way of fighting is to attack where the enemy is not. Leaving this point aside, the SAMS proposals would barely seem to meet any

Maneuver Warfare criteria or, indeed, even the terms of reference supplied by higher command. The first proposal would not have resulted in the destruction of the enemy's "operational center of gravity," since most Guard formations were beyond the final stop line; the second proposal, with its direct clash with these formations, envisaged the very type of action that the Maneuver Warfare idea sought to avoid. Moreover, despite the fact that air forces may well regard the process as straightforward destruction, the requirement to write down Iraqi armor by half before the start of a ground offensive was an open embrace of attritional warfare, which FM100-5 1982 and 1986 were supposed to have buried. Additionally, if it is difficult to see how the force ratio calculations of early October represented anything other than a FM100-5 1976 heritage, the December 1990 calculations on the part of CENTCOM provoke two thoughts. These estimates suggested force correlation by axes of 1.4:1 for the main attack and for Egyptian and Syrian forces, of 1.3:1 for the supporting effort, and, very interestingly, 0.75:1 for the Marines and the secondary offensive. The figures for the final actions indicated a 2.2:1 advantage for the main effort and a 2.7:1 advantage for the supporting attacks.[16] That these figures could be set down as the basis of planning would suggest that the number count, so beloved by U.S. commanders in Vietnam 20 years earlier, was alive and well. Furthermore, selection of geographical objectives—in the case of SAMS the ridge, the Al Jahrah junction and the border, and for Schwarzkopf the sea—hardly smack of the essence of the battle of annihilation. In fact, they represent a reversal of operational priorities. A geographical point, as Svechin argued more than 60 years earlier, is essentially irrelevant in a battle of annihilation unless the enemy has been first dispersed and rendered ineffective, since a geographical objective represents the end, not the means, of achieving encirclement and annihilation.[17] The definition of a geographical objective represented the main flaw in the plan of campaign that was to become increasingly obvious in and after February 1991; there was no provision for cutting off and annihilating the Iraqi "operational center of gravity" concentrated in front of Basra.

But if the planning process and final plan of campaign present difficulties of interpretation relative to FM100-5 1976, 1982, and 1986, then three different aspects of the conduct of operations in February 1991 present problems of understanding. The first of these three concerns the handling of "The Great Wheel," specifically the assertion that for the divisions of VII Corps

alignment was important to avoid piecemeal engagement once contact with the Republican Guard was made. If the rotation went according to plan, all five divisions would turn shoulder to shoulder and slam simultaneously into the Guard in a collision of unprecedented violence and shock effect.[18]

This is indeed how the offensive was conducted and events unfolded, but for the fact that the greater part of the Guard escaped.

It is somewhat difficult to understand how such a plan and the conduct of VII Corps' offensive in February 1991 accorded with Maneuver Warfare concepts, not least because such a deployment and movement would seem to give a whole old meaning to the idea of synchronization. AirLand Battle envisaged a fragmented battlefield, a deliberately fragmented, noncohesive, and nonlinear battlefield without flanks or front, but not a chaotic battlefield. Moreover, synchronization was one of effort across depth, not of movement of forces as if on parade. AirLand Battle never envisaged direct attack and most definitely never envisaged simultaneous direct attack that most clearly would rely for success upon "unprecedented violence and shock effect." Such a formula belonged to the 1976 field manual, complete with the historical concept of "maneuver to fire," not the 1982 and 1986 versions. Moreover, the element of deliberation in the conduct of this offensive compounded this aspect of divergence between theory and practice and arguably was the major factor in ensuring that the military objectives of the Coalition formations proved elusive.

It was not until the afternoon of 26 February that VII Corps' divisions were brought into line and the full weight of the flanking offensive was developed, and by that time, and for reasons that partly lay outside the bailiwick of Third Army,[19] its opportunity to complete the destruction of the Guard had passed. But the Third Army had not helped its own cause in one vital respect, this being the second of the three aspects of the conduct of operations in February 1991 that present problems of understanding. On the night of 24–25 February 1991, all the divisions of VII Corps were halted for the hours of darkness; on the following night the First Armored Division was halted, and on the night of 26–27 February three divisions were halted. Such inactivity would hardly seem to be consistent not merely with the intensity of operations dictated by AirLand Battle criteria but with the fact that one of the greatest single advantages of Coalition forces over Iraqi formations was night-fighting equipment and technique. As it was, the reasoning that dictated the halting of operations at night as somewhat tenuous, not least the 12 hours lost by the First Armored Division because of its unwillingness to move at night against Iraqi positions, and five T-55 tanks, whereabouts unknown, in and around Al-Busayyah. These positions were overrun in a matters of minutes in what the official U.S. Army described as "little more than a skirmish" on the morning of 26 February after a bombardment throughout the night and a wholly disproportionate set-piece attack.[20]

The conduct of this offensive, particularly an obsession with alignment, symmetry, and "geometric cohesion,"[21] provokes obvious and unfavorable comparisons, not least with Soviet "Deep Battle" concepts and practice. The willingness of both German and Soviet armor at different times in the Second World War to fight with open flanks stands in very sharp contrast to VII Corps' planning and conduct of operations. Moreover, the order given at 1730 hrs on 25 February for the three divisions that made up the main strike element of the formation to begin to turn to the east and into the main strength of the Republican Guard[22] would seem to be wholly inconsistent with the basic military concepts of seeking enemy flanks and rear and conducting battles of encirclement. The Third Army and VII Corps do appear to have shared a common fixation with the thickest part of the fence. Herein one may surmise that, in the pages of Norman Dixon's celebrated *On the Psychology of Military Incompetence*,[23] besetting the planning and conduct of this campaign was the tendency of generals, when confronted with the unknown, to embrace what they know, that with which they are familiar. The commander of VII Corps, Lieutenant-General Frederick Franks, Jr., has indicated that he sought "a firm fist rather than a spread-out group of fingers" in the mounting of this offensive, and what is very striking about the conduct of operations is the extent of supervision and control from higher headquarters, to the extent that Schwarzkopf sought to control events and decisions at three levels below his own command.[24] Both would seem to be the negation of AirLand Battle concepts and the negation of initiative. Indeed such criticism has been official, albeit from a not impartial and disinterested source:

It was clear to many that there was more to Maneuver Warfare than the ability to execute a carefully planned, centrally-directed, methodical maneuver—synchronization. The absence of a total understanding of Maneuver Warfare was dramatically demonstrated when the Army VII Corps defended its inability to close the Basrah road due to their (sic) having to slow down to synchronize their forces. Bill Lind would say that synchronization is the very essence of the 1939–1940 French-style methodical battle—the diametrical opposite of Maneuver Warfare.[25]

Herein this consideration of the events of February 1991 touches upon the third of the three aspects of the conduct of operations that present problems of understanding and of reconciling with Maneuver Warfare criteria: operational aim. According to Schwarzkopf's account, the Department of Defense's report to Congress and the army's 1993 version of FM100-5, the operational aim of destroying the Republican Guard was to be achieved via the battle of encirclement and annihilation.[26] But according to the U.S. Army's own official history there was never any intention of advancing into the Guard's rear area,[27] and, too easy to miss, Schwarzkopf's briefing of 14 November recorded that the aim was not to surround.[28] It was to block the western escape route up the Euphrates valley and to wheel VII Corps into the mass of the Iraqi forces in Kuwait. This definition of intent is confirmed by Operational Order 91-001 and by the air force version of events, which indicates that the latter was supposed to block the routes between Kuwait and Basra and from Basra up the Tigris, which would have ensured that Iraqi forces would have been trapped and crushed by VII Corps.[29]

There would seem to be some discrepancy between the various official accounts of Third Army's intentions, but what does seem to have been the case is that before the ground offensive began, the Coalition high command never fully considered the possibility of a general Iraqi retreat through and beyond Basra, and it did not realize that a retreat up the Tigris valley was in progress until the evening of 27 February. The balance of possibilities suggests that at least part of the Republican Guard must have begun to withdraw to positions beyond Basra from the theater of operations on 26 February.[30] What this has to imply is that by the time that VII Corps was able to deploy its main strike formations in line abreast in readiness for an attack into what it imagined was the mass of Iraqi forces, any real chance of annihilating the enemy has passed. Certainly it would appear that it was on 26 February that CENTCOM realized for the first time that Iraqi formations might attempt to withdraw up the Tigris valley, but Schwarzkopf's release of the First Cavalry Division from the reserve to VII Corps, and the order to this formation to move 250 km in a day and to be on the extreme left flank by the afternoon of 27 February, would seem to indicate an acknowledgment, perhaps inadvertent, that the main effort by VII Corps was misdirected. In the event, the congestion facing First Cavalry Division as it tried to move across the lines of communication of three divisions ensured that it was not able to begin offensive operations on the afternoon of 27 February, as ordered. Without this formation, the VII Corps effort, which therefore had to fall short of Basra, gives the appearance on the map of a tide that pushed Iraqi forces through the only escape route open to them—perhaps a case of the Falaise Gap revisited. The least that can be said about this channeling of Iraqi formations in the one direction whence lay their salvation is that it seems to provide a completely new dimension to the concept of synchronization.

The release and deployment of First Cavalry Division to the most distant and congested of sectors, with the result that it saw no action between 24 and 28 February, can be legitimately questioned, most obviously on account of a very viable alternative—namely, its commitment through the breach opened to the east of the Wadi Al-Batin by Egyptian forces. Given the much shorter distances involved, the First Cavalry Division could have been brought into a position either on or even inside the left flank of Republican Guard formations as these faced the mass of VII Corps and, perhaps, closer to Basra than these formations. But leaving aside this possibility other than to note that the First Cavalry Division was used in the only way that could ensure that it would not contribute to the battle, it would seem that the circle could have been squared in any of three quite separate ways: if air power could have destroyed or blocked the escape routes to and from Basra; if XVIII Corps had been used in the offensive role on the left flank of VII Corps rather than holding positions in the Euphrates valley, where the majority of its formations could never make a meaningful contribution in blocking the escape of Iraqi forces;[31] if Schwarzkopf had ordered VII Corps to open its offensive on 20 February, when he publicly claimed that Iraqi formations were "on the verge of collapse," rather than having delayed ordering VII Corps forward until after the attack by First Marine Expeditionary Force had begun.

In effect, the success of the secondary offensive provoked an Iraqi withdrawal before VII Corps was committed to battle, with the result that VII Corps was always at least one step behind the requirements of entrapment.[32] The speed and success of First M.E.F. was the last thing that was needed. What was required of the secondary effort was a holding action that prevented the enemy from disengaging from this battle. Yet the fact that the Guard was able to organize and carry out an orderly withdrawal in the face of overwhelming enemy supremacy points to three self-evident facts: that Iraqi command and control systems were still functioning efficiently even at this stage of proceedings; that the destruction of the communications infrastructure in and behind Basra had proved to be beyond the capabilities of Coalition air power; that the U.S. command system proved inflexible in the last two days of the campaign, specifically in its inability to reorder fire support control lines and formation boundaries and thereby permit Apache attacks on the routes and units behind Basra. Certainly the cause was not helped by the concentration of ground controllers with VII Corps rather than with the most advanced elements. But with the relevant daily Air Tasking Orders allocating only minimal attention to these routes and three days old by the time they came to be implemented and thus unable to respond to the changing situation on the ground, the whole question of whether air power could have blocked the northern escape route seems spurious but for one inescapable fact.

In August 1990 the original air plan had been opposed, and rightly, by the army on the grounds that even the most successful air offensive could not guarantee the withdrawal of Iraqi military formations from Kuwait. Yet by February 1991 the assumption on the part of senior army personnel appears to have been that the air offensive could prevent it. The two are not mutually exclusive, but by the same token they are dubiously compatible; the apparent switch from believing that air power could not ensure the departure of Iraqi forces to the assumption that it could ensure that they stayed should not obscure the real point. If the Guard formations were able to escape, and the majority of its divisions did with about half their combat capability still intact, then they were able to do so because the Coalition plan of campaign did not recognize that encirclement, being physical, could not be achieved by an interdiction effort but by ground forces alone. The various "other" failings in the conduct of operations were not the main cause or causes of the failure to achieve the destruction of the Iraqi "operational center of gravity," but they compounded the basic error of failing to recognize "that to trap (the Guard) would be the best way to destroy it."[33] Here was a failure that can be traced to the basic inconsistency of aim—namely, to clear Kuwait of Iraqi forces but at the same time to destroy Republican Guard formations, which could best be achieved if the enemy was trapped inside Kuwait. Faced with four possibilities, Schwarzkopf appears to have embraced the only combination of options that could have guaranteed that victory slipped through his fingers.

* * *

The 1991 campaign represented triumph without victory,[34] in large measure because neither Bush nor Powell understood the difference between a war and a campaign. The result was that over the next five years the United States was forced to try to reaffirm whatever success had been commanded in 1991, and to ever-decreasing effect. Yet flawed though this success was, the 1991 campaign was nevertheless massively significant in terms of the conduct of war, and the military achievement in routing Iraqi formations in Kuwait and southern Iraq cannot be gainsaid. The fifth largest military establishment in the world was comprehensively defeated in the field in six weeks and at a cost to the Coalition of less than one aircraft and six dead a day. The Balkan wars, the 1940 campaign, the Balkans campaign in 1941, and various Arab–Israeli wars stand comparison to the 1991 campaign in terms of speed and relative scale of victory, but in terms of the combination of speed, scale, and economy the 1991 campaign most obviously represented something that was very different from the experience of war in the twentieth century. It points clearly in the direction of a restoration of the element of decisiveness in the conduct of war, and specifically to the fact that the decisive battle of annihilation has been returned to the military vocabulary. Much has recently been made of "the modern trinity," a concept that is Clausewitzian in inspiration even as it seeks to oust his ideas. This trinity is defined as doctrine, combat power, and morale, yet it misses the point: this "modern trinity" concerns itself with combat or fighting, not with war, and the real "modern trinity," an operational trinity, is to be found in the combination of scale, area, and time. The restoration of the element of decisiveness in the conduct of a single campaign, perhaps even a single battle, has been rendered possible because of the reduced size of armies and the ability to conduct operations across ever greater area and with unprecedented intensity and effectiveness, hence with ever greater compression of time. The change in the conduct of war that the events of 1991 may be said to mark is to be found in variations of these three elements in relation to one another.

The element of military decisiveness in the 1991 campaign was primarily the result of the Iraqi military being denied the capacity both to absorb punishment and to reconstitute formations: the speed at which cumulative and irreversible damage was inflicted in the course of this campaign represented the element of novelty in the conduct of war. The critical factor in producing such a state of affairs was the increased capability of air power, but the problem presented by such claims and by the argument of the effectiveness of air power with respect to a reincarnated *Vernichtungsschlacht* is self-evident. In the course of the 1991 campaign, air power did not achieve the results that were claimed on its behalf and was not able to record success in any of its stated operational tasks. If this was the case, then it would seem to be impossible to use this campaign to justify any claim regarding the effectiveness of air power. This seeming paradox thus raises the obvious question of what air power achieved and failed to achieve in the 1991 campaign, with all the overtones of interservice fratricide thus entailed.

* * *

In many ways it is the negative aspects of air power in the 1991 campaign that command attention: it is easier to deal with what air power did not do than with what it achieved. It is one of those unfortunate aspects of air power that it always seem to have to defend its record, specifically its failings, in a way that armies and navies somehow seem to avoid, and more often than not the defense of its record has proved a rancorous affair.[35] In no small part, however, this has been a self-inflicted wound, one that reflects the strident certainties of its proponents, and in this respect the air offensive in the 1991 campaign labored under the problems imposed upon it by the Instant Thunder claims of August 1990. As set down in the briefings of 10 and 17 August, Instant Thunder was to be a six-day campaign designed to incapacitate the Iraqi leadership and destroy key military installations. It stopped short of claiming that the bombing campaign would bring about an Iraqi military withdrawal from Kuwait, though the inference was clear; it did set out the claim that the crippling of Iraqi strategic capability could be achieved by 150 strike aircraft in six days—a claim curiously similar to Chennault's 1942 insistence that 80 bombers and 150 fighters based in China could bring about the defeat of Japan. The *ex post facto* rationalization of a 1991 inability to deliver on the promise—that air power was not allowed to operate in the manner and to the end that had been predicted—represents nothing other than disingenuous, special pleading. If the air planners could not work the 150 aircraft/six days formula within the 39 days of the air offensive and the maximum total of 2,700 aircraft that were involved in this campaign, then lack of opportunity can hardly be entered as a plea of mitigation, not least because the number of strike aircraft directed against strategic targets never fell below 200 on any day in the first five weeks of the air campaign. The second counterargument, the increase in the planning phase of the number of strategic targets that were to be attacked, in turn raises the question of the basis of the original claims. If more than 500 targets made their way into the plan of campaign for the strategic air offensive, then one is left to wonder about the basis of the original claim that the destruction of 84 targets in six days would result in the defeat of the Iraqi state.

The logic of these two points cannot be disputed; perversely, however, whether the points are valid is another matter. Any consideration of the strategic air offensive conducted in January–February 1991 suggests some basis for the air force argument because, on the basis of official figures,[36] it would seem that less than one-sixth of all sorties classified as strategic were directed against what would be understood to be, in historical terms, strategic targets, as represented in italics in Table 5.1.

Table 5.1.   Strategic Targets: Level of Effort

Strategic target	Sorties	As percentage	Definition
Air defenses	436	2.39	*Strategic Integrated Air Defence System*
Airfields	3,047	16.67	aircraft, shelters
C3	601	3.29	*command, control & communication facilities*
Communications	712	3.90	*railroads, bridges, etc.*
Electrical industry	215	1.18	*power distribution system*
Military support	2,756	15.08	production and storage
National Command	429	2.35	*main government institutions*
Naval facilities	247	1.35	warships, bases
NBC facilities	902	4.94	production and storage
Oil facilities	518	2.83	*refineries/storage depots*
Republican Guard	5,646	30.89	military formations
Short-range ballistic missiles	2,767	15.14	SCUD production and storage, not the "hunt"
Total	**18,276**	—	

The definition of certain targets under this strategic label is somewhat dubious: certainly centers of military production do come within the definition of strategic targets, but in this case of somewhat doubtful relevance, while the inclusion of naval and air base facilities is rather questionable. But the overall point would seem to be that the balance of the strategic air offensive does seem to vindicate, at least in part, air force assertions that it was not allowed to conduct the offensive of its choice. The greater part of the strategic air offensive was not directed against strategic targets, and what was registered against strategic targets, such as command and control assets, was correspondingly impressive, given the modest scale of attack to which they were subjected. Given such distractions as the SCUD and other efforts, and irritating as it is to admit it, the fact may well be that air force claims were correct, or at least reasonable. But what is no less interesting is the fact that these figures add an extra dimension to the failure to seek the encirclement of the Republican Guard formations. The air operations against the Iraqi "operational center of gravity" have been included in the strategic targets list, and, given the fact that at the "two-corps concept" briefing of 21 October Schwarzkopf stated as his objective the physical destruction of Republican Guard formations, which were defined to be "a strategic center of gravity in the KTO,"[37] the fact that these formations escaped destruction and were never subjected to an attempted encirclement becomes ever more curious. The escape of an "operational center of gravity" is perhaps understandable, but not to attempt the encirclement of "a strategic center of gravity" but to leave the task of ensuring that it did not escape to a strategic air effort that was much smaller in scale than the tactical air effort would seem to be inexplicable. It seems very strange, for example, that half of the anti-Silkworm strikes flown during the campaign should have been staged during the four days of the ground offensive when the need to strike at Republican Guard formations was never greater, and the effort appears doubly strange in light of the fact that no Silkworms were fired before the ground offensive began.[38]

Leaving this point aside, air power, specifically the strategic air campaign, was not able to accomplish "the progressive and systematic collapse of Saddam Hussein's entire war machine" and regime, and it failed to bring about the collapse of the Iraqi military command and control systems; the orderly withdrawal of the greater part of the Republican Guard, and the Hussein regime's subsequent ability to put down two internal rebellions by shifting formations between widely separated parts of Iraq, clearly pointed to this second failure. In addition, the prewar belief that Coalition air power would not be able to prevent Iraqi movement but would prevent maneuver was belied by events, as the Iraqi redeployment of six armored brigades from four divisions of the Jihad Corps to face the threat emerging on the flank on 24–25 February and the escape of the greater part of the Republican Guard formations showed only too clearly. In addition, Coalition aircraft failed to account for a single mobile SCUD and, almost as a comment on the post-1991 concept of "dominant battlefield knowledge," failed to make any real impression upon Iraqi NBC capability, for the very simple reason that the extent of Iraqi facilities was largely unknown until U.N. inspection teams were inside Iraq after the end of hostilities. Before, the campaign planners had known of only two Iraqi nuclear facilities whereas subsequent investigation revealed the existence of 21, 16 of which were major installations. Even if the rebellions that gripped Iraq after the cease-fire revealed the extent to which the dictatorship's ability to control its people had been compromised by the air offensive, the fact was that the massive redundancy that had been built into the Iraqi state system mostly during the war with Iran—a capacity estimated to be three times requirement—allowed it to survive the strategic air campaign[39] even as its commercial counterpart was shut down, in no case more obviously than with the electric grid system. By use of back-up systems and an extensive repair effort, the Iraqi state was able to sustain itself despite the strategic air offensive shutting down some 55% of the grid system in the first 10 days of hostilities and reducing overall Iraqi production by something approaching 90% of capacity in the course of the campaign.

Moreover, Coalition air power failed to register the 50% attrition of Iraqi forces before the onset of the ground offensive, as was required under the terms of the plan of campaign and which the air planners claimed would be achieved in 17 days, and failed to isolate both the Iraqi high command from its armed forces and the theater of operations from Iraq proper. But leaving aside the adverse impact of weather and the fact that tactical strikes against Iraqi forces in Kuwait did not reach planning levels until three weeks into the campaign, the first of these two failures does seem to be somewhat ungenerous in light of the fact that U.S. estimates suggest that 39% of Iraqi armor, 32% of armored personnel carriers, and 47% of guns were destroyed by air attack before the start of operations by ground forces. Moreover it is ungenerous in light of the fact that the 50% figure initially represented not an air force claim but an army requirement, and it cannot be denied that part of the reason for the failure to register the desired result was because of the diversion of resources to the SCUD effort. But of the 46 Iraqi divisions in Kuwait and southern Iraq in the course of this campaign, 17 incurred the loss of 75% or more and another 10 losses of 50% or more of their armor and artillery. For Coalition ground forces, this, particularly the neutralizing of Iraqi artillery and thereby reducing the threat of chemical attack, represented success. The effectiveness of air power in dealing with dug-in armor was unprecedented, and certain Iraqi formations were devastated by air attack. There are recorded examples of one division that had lost only a tenth of its artillery before the ground campaign opened but which had but a tenth left within a day as the weight of air attack (and, it must be noted, long-range artillery) was concentrated upon it, and one Iraqi division very literally ceased to exist and was reduced to double figures in terms of manpower. Ironically, in the case of the latter it was not the accuracy and lethal nature of air attack, but the protracted, attritional nature of the tactical air offensive that was so important—day after day of conventional attack with dumb bombs broke what little resolve was at Iraqi disposal as the division "voted with its feet." In addition, it needs be noted that air attack made major inroads into Iraqi supply capacity, to the extent that convoys had to be broken down and vehicles as often as not sent singly to front-line units. But the fact remains that no Iraqi formation was defeated for want of supplies or armor in the course of this campaign, and the intention to delay the flow of information between the Iraqi high command and its forces in order to impose a 12-hour cycle and thus enable Coalition forces to operate within the Iraqi decision-making loop was of no real strategic, operational, and tactical account, given the fact that the air offensive lasted 38 days. Only in the last two or three days of the campaign could any delay in the Iraqi decision-making process have been significant, and at that stage VII Corps' formations were too distant to take advantage of any communications superiority gained as a result of the air effort. Moreover, this same dichotomy between the timing of what was achieved and what was needed for success had its parallel in the attack on Iraqi lines of communication. The Coalition air offensive accounted for three in four of all bridges linking the Kuwait theater of operations and Iraq proper and slashed the rate of supply reaching Iraqi divisions at the front, but this was of no real account in the absence of a ground offensive.

What was needed to complement the interdiction campaign was a concurrent ground offensive that would have imposed massive demands upon Iraqi lines of supply, and had the air and ground efforts been synchronized, Iraqi lines of communications would in all likelihood have collapsed. But in the absence of a ground offensive the interdiction campaign was all but certain to fall short of its objectives because the Iraqi system carried sufficient redundancy to allow formations to survive and continue to function to the extent that they were able to attempt to withdraw in the final days of the campaign. The air offensive against both the Iraqi command systems and logistical support made little sense, in part because of its length and in part because it was directed against a static enemy with minimal communications and logistical needs; only when Iraqi divisions were engaged or in movement could the interdiction effort have registered significant results. As it is, the argument that the interdiction effort was successful in denying Iraqi formations the ability to fight a protracted campaign is undoubtedly correct, but given the fact that it was never the Coalition's intention to allow the Iraqis the opportunity to fight a protracted campaign, this argument does seem somewhat curious, if not downright mendacious.

Yet, paradoxically, the air campaign was successful, and it provided the basis of whatever military success was commanded by the anti-Iraqi Coalition. Air power did inflict massive strategic damage—though perhaps the attack by two F-111-Fs using GBU-15 precision bombs on the Al Ahmadi refineries on 27 January after the deliberate Iraqi discharge of oil into the sea was perhaps its most important single and certainly unusual contribution and represented the first use of strategic bombing in order to prevent destruction—and it did so without inflicting disproportionate civilian casualties in the process. Iraqi sources indicate 2,300 civilian dead in the course of a 43-day onslaught—a total that is remarkably light given the scale of the air offensive and its predilection with urban centers. Moreover, air power provided the confidence in victory on the part of Coalition forces: its senior commanders and planners believed by the first dawn of the campaign that the issue had been decided within the first 10 to 15 minutes of the first bombings. Coalition air power was responsible for the securing of air supremacy and, crucially important, thus all but invested the ground forces with immunity from attack and prevented detection during the redeployment phase. Air power played a crucial role in defeating the one Iraqi offensive of the war at Ra's Al Khafji (29–31 January).[40]

In the campaign as a whole, the air offensive inflicted such losses on Iraqi divisions—specifically the Iraqi army's heavy divisions, which lost about three-quarters of their armor—that they were rendered incapable of conducting any offensive operations and indeed were barely capable of defending themselves by the end of hostilities. Air power could not register a comprehensive or total military victory, and air power could not have forced an Iraqi evacuation of Kuwait. Victory remained to be completed when the ground offensive began, and the fact that some Iraqi formations and units escaped virtually unscathed from the air offensive was evidence of this fact. One Iraqi armored unit reportedly lost two of its 39 T-72s in the five weeks of the air offensive, and the remainder in six minutes when it encountered the Second Armored Cavalry Regiment.[41] But victory was assured, and indeed had been won, because the Iraqi forces in Kuwait and southern Iraq had already been defeated by the time the ground offensive opened. The extreme land-power argument, to the effect that in four days ground forces achieved what air power had failed to do in 39 days, is even more facetious than its air power equivalent. The basis of Coalition—primarily American—success lay in the possession of supremacy, of which the most immediately important element was air supremacy. The reality of air power as the basis of military victory provided the critical aspect of U.S. conduct of operations in 1991, and the reality of supremacy in terms of resources and capability provided the basis of the U.S. conduct of war throughout the twentieth century. But in any consideration of the 1991 campaign, the questions that present themselves for attention are whether the doctrinal solutions that provided the operational basis of the victory that was won do indeed represent "the future of warfare," and the financial and industrial basis of that future, and, immediate and short-term, the identity and cause of whatever failures and weaknesses attended the planning and conduct of the air offensive against Iraq.

* * *

With reference to this latter question, one has noted that a month into the Kuwait crisis, by early September 1990, CENTCOM had no plan of campaign or even the basis of a plan; if one is to assess the air campaign, then it is altogether proper that its most important contribution, and one often passed over, is recognized. The air force plan, in the form of Warden and the Five Circles Concept, provided the basis of an offensive plan of campaign, did so within a matter of days at a time when the United States lacked any other offensive option, and provided the basis of subsequent planning. It is important to recognize, as these pages hopefully have made clear, that the original plan was flawed, and perhaps the best means of understanding what was originally proposed by Warden and what was ultimately attempted was provided by the air force commander through analogy: the original was to the final product as the larva is to the butterfly.

With this single comment Horner, the commander of the Coalition air forces, explained one relationship that was largely obscured, both at the time and subsequently, by various institutional and personal rivalries and antipathies. The original air power package most certainly did not command immediate and uncritical support, and it needs be noted that the most persistent and virulent opposition to Warden and the plan for an independent air offensive paradoxically emerged from within the air force itself: by an ironic twist it was the army leadership that picked up the main ideas that were presented by Warden. This latter support was not uncritical, but it and the air plan proved mutually supporting: the air plan provided the basis for offensive action when no other option existed: the military ensured that the strategic air offensive idea gradually shifted from being the main element of the plan to being one of its parts. But the real points of criticism of the air plan, both in its original form and as implemented, primarily concern themselves with one matter: the plan embraced Western concepts that were wholly misplaced in terms of the enemy. The Five Circles Concept is based upon Western concepts of government and society, and the direct relationship between institutional authority and power. Any coincidence between such matters and the Iraqi system was coincidental. There was within Iraq a formal state structure, but the real point was that there was a party structure that backed the state administrative structure, and there was a secret policy system that contained within itself no fewer than seven separate secret police organizations. In addition, of course, the Revolutionary Guard presented an alternative system to the army. The Revolutionary Guard had two organizations, the Guard per se and the Special Republican Guard, and behind all this was a regional and tribal power structure that ultimately was reduced to a kinship system, and it was these that represented the real power system by which Saddam Hussein maintained his personal authority throughout Iraq.

It is possible to argue that no amount of bombing could ever have resulted in the destruction of the Hussein regime because Western air power simply never had any real understanding of the problem—the nature and organization of the Iraqi system—that it faced. This is an argument that is very difficult to resist, but it is complicated by two other considerations. The first, simply, is that the political leadership of the Coalition—that is, the White House—never defined whether the overthrow of the Hussein regime represented a war aim. The basic problem, which never seems to have been recognized by the Bush administration, was the Weimar syndrome—the difficulty inherent in seeking the defeat of an enemy system that would in turn discredit a successor regime obliged to take responsibility for a national defeat that was not of its own making. The Bush administration refused to have as much as a single contact with any Iraqi exile political organization throughout the duration of the crisis, from August 1990 to March 1991, and it failed to grasp one basic fact that, admittedly, Warden himself recognized only belatedly. The Republican Guard, not the army with its massed ranks of unwilling, resentful conscripts, had to be the real "military" center of gravity, and the air effort against rank-and-file divisions was not simply effort wasted but doubly disastrous. In the very last days of the campaign, Warden recognized this with the proposal, dismissed without any serious consideration in Washington, that all bombing of army formations be halted, that all the offensive air capacity be directed in an improvised effort against Republican Guard formations, and that coalition airlift capacity be used to ferry Iraqi military formations to Baghdad in order to ensure that these would destroy the Hussein system. The clear point, too easy to miss, is that the Warden concepts, for all their weaknesses and shortcomings, did address the basic problem that was faced—the Hussein regime—rather than the effect—the Iraqi occupation of Kuwait. Bush and Powell addressed neither. The expression of hope that Saddam Hussein would be overthrown, a direct encouragement without picking up the obligation of assistance, resulted in the regime being able to survive and suppress the uprisings in the south, more than 200,000 people being killed in the process.

The second consideration is the lack of definition of aim that transcended the campaign, both in the air and on the ground, which found expression in two forms. First, there was the unilateral declaration by Washington of the end of the campaign, and, second, there was the fact that Schwarzkopf was given no instructions from Weasington with reference to the terms to be exacted in the conclusion of the final armistice arrangements, and the Iraqi representatives were not obliged to sign any document. It is difficult to believe that such omission represents anything other than dereliction of duty, abdication of responsibility, on the part of the authorities in Washington, and it prompts the answer of nobody to the question of who was in charge in Washington. The basic point, however, is simple enough, and made elsewhere: the power and effectiveness available to the United States should have pointed in the direction of ever more detailed definition of the political terms of reference governing the use of force, not less.

* * *

The security of the U.S. achievement in the course of the 1991 campaign is most obviously and immediately beset by problems of cost and limited industrial capacity in the most advanced sector of the economy. In the course of the 1991 campaign, precision munitions accounted for 7,400 of the 84,200 tons of munitions expended by U.S. aircraft and warships, but as late as August 1994 U.S. industry had been unable to replace the full range of precision munitions that had been used in January and February 1991. Perhaps even more seriously, most of the U.S. aircraft involved in the suppression of Iraqi defense systems in 1991 are no longer in production and, given the ever-lengthening lead-times involved in procurement programs, cannot be replaced in the foreseeable future. With the cost of nonreturnable cruise missiles, which are incapable of attacking hardened targets, estimated to have been about $1,500,000 each or some 20 times the cost of a smart bomb, the F-117A Nighthawk, costing about $42,000,000 apiece, the F-22, scheduled to cost perhaps $80,000,000 each, and the original 15 B-2 Spirit stealth bombers, at $2,959,000,000 each costing more than a guided-missile cruiser or air group for a carrier,[42] new technology places certain very interesting question marks against future procurement programs and raises a host of divisive interservice issues. With U.S. stealth technology basically limited to one major producer and the obvious difficulty in foreseeing the circumstances under which such aircraft as the B-2 Spirit could possibly represent the difference between success and failure in war, the weapons systems available at the present time border on the very limits of procurement ability, even for such a country as the United States. Cost has served to destroy the notion that stealth will do away with the need to fight the conventional battle for air supremacy because no nation could equip itself with a stealth-only air force. The problem such cost entails is even more acute for anything other than a superpower. The price-tag of the cruise missile equivalent of the total 1991 expenditure of all precision munitions has been calculated at $17,760,000,000, or the equivalent of six months' defense budget for such countries as Britain, France, and Germany, and this sum was one-third greater than the total British defense procurement expenditure for FY1990–1991.[43] American military and intelligence expenditure on satellites and communications at the present time is greater than the entire British defense budget. In light of the costs that are involved in Maneuver Warfare and the doctrinal changes that have been initiated in recent years, one wonders, somewhat cynically, if the present cycle of espousal of a new doctrine and orthodoxy is not merely a part of a phenomenon that has repeated itself throughout this century, most often at times of reduced military expenditure, and with ever less conviction. In the twentieth century technology has driven doctrinal change and fostered claims to be able to affect the nature and conduct of war. At different times during the last century mechanization, aircraft, and atomic weapons have held out various promises—to win wars, to prevent war, to be able to do ever more with ever less—and these most recent developments may indeed conform to this established, well-known pattern, with one important difference. The manner in which the concept of Maneuver Warfare has been taken in hand by lesser powers prompts the thought that at the present time technological and doctrinal change provide the means of trying to disguise the fact that a lesser power might not be able to fight at all—that, in the case of Britain, with an army in the process of being reduced to little more than 100,000 men, the concept is being paraded to conceal the reality that the king does not have any clothes to wear.

But questions of costs, and specifically the cost of reconnaissance and communications, raise two quite separate issues—namely, their importance in the conduct of the 1991 campaign and their wider impact upon the conduct of war. The first can be considered quickly. The 1991 effort was notable for the fact that in the first 90 days of Desert Shield the United States put more communications capacity into Saudi Arabia than it had put into NATO in more than 40 years,[44] and it was forced to resort to commercial facilities, secured with difficulty and at considerable cost in terms of time, in order to endow itself with the strategic capacity of 200,000,000 bytes a second that was able to provide for approximately 90% of intertheater requirements. But given that such capacity was marginal to U.S. requirements, the viability of AirLand Battle against mobile Soviet formations in the European theater of operations is obviously open to question, as indeed is the vulnerability of the systems on which the Americans were dependent. With regard to intelligence, the 1991 campaign clearly pointed to the shift in importance from the agent to the analyst—a trend identifiable over several decades—but the campaign also pointed to the fact that the old problem of securing real-time intelligence had not been overcome by modern technology. Ironically, the U.S. strategic intelligence capability in 1991 was probably less than it had been in 1945, most certainly in the Pacific. The problems of evaluation and dissemination remained as difficult and as slow as ever, and, of course, intelligence could not provide the United States with timely warning of the Iraqi intention of occupying Kuwait. In 1990 CENTCOM, which initiated a watch condition as early as 25 April because of Iraq's increasingly strident attitude, worked on the premise of receiving 30 days' warning of any aggression in the Gulf area, and what this was to mean was that, given the date of the Iraqi invasion, it would have needed indicators, and to have recognized them as such, by 3 July. It was not until 12 July that CENTCOM really began to be concerned by the situation in the Gulf, and it was not until 19 July that indicators that pointed to Iraqi aggression were noted. But after an initial war warning was rejected by Washington on 25 July, the final DIA/CENTCOM assessment on 28 July was that Iraqi military action was unlikely and that a diplomatic solution to Iraq's dispute with Kuwait would be found. Thus there was no way in which the United States, even if it had divined Iraqi intentions, could have discerned the Baghdad regime's designs and acted in such a way and at a time to have deflected Iraqi aggression against Kuwait, in part because of considerations of timing and in part because any U.S. attempt to deter Baghdad before 1 August 1990 would have lacked any credibility.

But the wider question of the conduct of war is more difficult, in large measure because it brings to the table the much more important question of the nature of war. The complexity of these questions can be illustrated simply by reference to one event in the campaign: the bombing of the Al Firdos command bunker in Baghdad on the night of 12–13 February 1991.[45] The 1991 campaign may have been notable for the fact that problems of securing real-time intelligence remained despite new technology, but new technology provided real-time coverage. Perhaps the most important single fact that emerged from the 1991 campaign was that in one instance the plan of campaign was altered and in another the campaign itself was curtailed directly as a result of fear of public reaction following live television coverage of events on the ground. The second of these points does bear repeating: the pictures of the "Highway of Death" had not appeared on American television screens before Powell took the initiative with his recommendation that offensive action be curtailed. It was fear, not the reality, of adverse public reaction that guided Washington's decisions. Such a situation borders upon the bizarre. That the conduct of a war that was being waged in a distant theater at immense cost after months of preparation should be dependent upon the possibility of public revulsion may be commendable at a personal level, but it makes no sense for states. States cannot divorce their conduct of foreign policy and war from the nature of their domestic institutions, but the implications of the Information Revolution reference armchair warfare is clearly certain to have a major impact on the balance of the parts of the Clausewitzian trinity of the military, society, and the state by stressing the political dimensions of warfare at the expense of the others. At very best, Powell's insistence on ending the campaign because of fear of public reaction betrayed a remarkable, profound distrust of American society.[46]

In very large measure the shock brought about by the bunker bombing and fear of the impact on American domestic opinion of pictures of the bombing of Iraqi units fleeing from Kuwait was the result of their being contrary to claims of precision and detachment that had been stressed by the U.S. political and military leadership throughout the 1991 campaign. These claims, in turn, were the product of two elements in U.S. national security strategy: the insistence on divining the end-state of the campaign, and the desire to control events and to be seen to control events. Perhaps the best illustration of this imperative was the handling of the flanking attack, specifically the desire to leave nothing to chance during the approach to contact phase. As Svechin so accurately wrote more than half a century before these events, the battle of annihilation necessarily involves an element of risk, and while AirLand Battle does not have to exhibit Deep Battle characteristics to be AirLand Battle, the contrast between the conduct of the ground offensive in 1991 with such offensives as Bagration in 1944 or Oder–Vistula in 1945 is very striking— specifically these latter offensives' willingness to leave things to chance. It was the desire in the conduct of operations in 1991 to avoid the unknown and to control the battle, because it was tied to the certainties provided by advanced technology, that calls into question the nature of war on account of the basis of the doctrinal disputes that have followed in the wake of this campaign.

* * *

The basic doctrinal dispute is interservice and primarily revolves around the claims of the air lobby, specifically Warden's Five Circles concept and Deptula's idea of Inside-Out Warfare, which, simply stated, in combination claim that a state's command and control systems can be gutted by strategic air attack and an enemy thereby defeated without the necessity of "outside-in warfare," which is the manner in which warfare has been conducted throughout history. The basis of this view of war is a perceived vulnerability of a state to paralysis by a technologically superior enemy.

One of the ironies of twentieth-century military thought is that whereas Mahan had his counterpart in Corbett and land warfare came into the possession of many schools, Douhet only had disciples: the Five Circles and Inside-Out Warfare concepts form part of an unbroken, singular air culture that has existed for almost as long as the use of the aircraft in war. As such, these concepts labor under the legacy of persistent failure, since in various wars air power has never been able to deliver upon the promises of its advocates, and these present concepts, and even more obviously the concept of "Parallel Warfare," lay themselves open to the charge that they are merely failure recycled under a new name—the "one-more-effort-down-the-old-path-and-we-will-make-Douhet's-ideas-work" argument that independent air forces have employed during and since the Second World War.[47]

Given that the rationale for independent air forces lay and perhaps continues to lie in a strategic bombing role, perhaps this line of argument is inevitable, but in considering the 1991 campaign and the present doctrinal debate, one is left to wonder how much of these ideas represent rational argument and how much dogmatic assertion—articles of faith. But this question obscures the real ones, whether it really does offer the opportunity to makes Douhet's ideas work, whether new technology will alter the very nature of war. Concepts such as the Five Circles and Inside-Out Warfare, Parallel Warfare, Rapid Dominance, and, most recently and all but unbelievably, Shock and Awe have as their base the assumed effectiveness of modern weaponry of unprecedented accuracy and destructive power, and certainly this cannot be disputed. But what can be disputed is the assumption that new-found and future capability will produce results that have hitherto proved elusive. The basis of doubt on this particular score lies in the reality that whereas technology in the form of the destructiveness of weaponry is linear and predictable in terms of cause and effect, society most definitely is neither. The new concepts of warfare have as their premise a view of an enemy state and society unchanged and unchanging other than the damage inflicted upon both by one's own offensive action, and such a concept as "Shock and Awe" is explicit in its faith in technology, its successful application and an ability to control the process—witness:

The ability to impose massive shock and awe . . . to be able to "turn the lights on and off" of an adversary as we choose, will so overload the perception, understanding and knowledge of that adversary that there will be no choice except to cease and desist or risk complete and total destruction.[48]

And presumably, being rational, mend its ways, as, of course, did the Japanese when faced with such a choice in 1941. Resisting the temptation to question the circumstances that might lead a superpower to threaten a lesser society with "complete and total destruction" and the various limitations that the possession of the means to "turn the lights on and off" would inevitably entail, any consideration of warfare, and specifically of warfare in the twentieth century, suggests that societies possess enormous capacity for adaptation and endurance and that the main impact of bombing campaigns has been to strengthen the will to resist. The simplicity of this statement conceals a profound point of change that such concepts as Inside-Out Warfare and Shock and Awe present. It is not so much that Inside-Out Warfare claims to be able to affect an enemy capacity that will result in air power being able to achieve what has hitherto been elusive, whereas critics of this claim would hold to the belief that the concept of strategic bombing will never be brought to fruition because the basic idea is inherently flawed. It is, rather, that the air lobby argument has blurred the distinction between the nature of war and the conduct of war and that its basic premise, technological effectiveness, runs counter to the fundamental characteristic of war. War is a human activity, not a laboratory exercise in applied technology, and doctrine is the servant, not the determinant, of war. Herein lies the gravest problem presented by the current obsession with doctrine, which is even more serious than that represented by the absurdities of "Shock and Awe." The latter, at least in part, do start from a premise based upon the changing nature of society and technology as they might affect the conduct of war. Present doctrine, from the insularity endowed by assumed orthodoxy, would dictate a concept of operations that would, in turn, determine a vision of the nature of war. This is explicit in the concept of "Parallel Warfare," which comes complete with a basis of knowledge and correct anticipation of every aspect of an enemy's capabilities and intentions.[49] By inverting what is the natural order of a relationship that is not singular but embraces both the nature and the conduct of war and one in which the various parts are mutually dependent and related, present doctrine in its certainty and purpose represents nothing but "danger on the utmost edge of hazard."[50]

Any consideration of warfare over the last 200 years, and particularly in the twentieth century, points to a societal capacity to endure that is not to be underestimated. Human resilience, and the capacity of people bound together by common identity, language, culture, and institutions to adapt and to continue to offer resistance even in the most appalling of circumstances, has been demonstrated not just in the two world wars of the twentieth century but also, and perhaps even more significantly, in other conflicts since 1945. This, and the ability of non-Western societies to survive conditions that would deeply divide democracies, represents a clear indication of the critical importance of moral as opposed to material factors in the conduct of war. Any suggestion that the ability to destroy the capacity to resist on a scale and at a pace that are unprecedented will profoundly alter the will and ability to resist would seem to have little historical basis. At the same time the level of expectation and demand in terms of war being portrayed as clean, swift, minimal in its claims on life and, critically, carrying with it the certainty of victory may well present those who insist upon the efficacy of modern doctrine and weaponry with all but impossible problems of fulfilling wholly unrealistic public expectation.

The idea of Inside-Out Warfare may be proven by future events, but in its present context it would seem to be part of a much wider concept, which suggests, indeed insists, that war can be controlled. The insistence on the defined "end-state" of conflict by the U.S. military in the last decade has its origins in the Vietnam experience, yet it begs a number of questions even as it is based upon the need to soothe a potentially volatile electorate. If in 1941 Roosevelt had been subjected to such requirements, the United States would probably still be waiting to enter the Second World War; but the more pertinent point about this "end-state" demand is its being indicative of a desire to control the peace or at least set the agenda for peace, yet the conduct of peace necessarily presents greater problems than the conduct of war. The experience of twentieth-century warfare would suggest that the ability of any single nation or associated group of nations to control the terms of reference of war is illusory: as Clausewitz had taught us, in war everything is uncertain, and wars invariably assume courses and outcomes very different from those intended by their authors. The whole notion of being able to control warfare, whether it be definition of "end-state" or offensive operations of surgical precision, runs directly counter to the fundamental Clausewitzian element in war—chance. War is not the preserve of the intellect and is not intrinsically rational or scientific. Man made War in his own image, complete with all the elements of human failure, misjudgment, and incompetence therein, and, hopefully, thus it will remain. Current doctrine and predictions for the future of war that are now on the table would seem to assume otherwise—that somehow the certainties provided by technology will provide certainties in the conduct of war that will in themselves transform the nature of war. Doctrine cannot be divorced from the past, but if, as Svechin is credited as having written, doctrine is the daughter of history, then, on the basis of some of the more recent doctrinal papers I have had the misfortune to read, I am left to ponder the identity of the father, and still more the question of whether or not the parents were married. Current doctrine would seem to represent neither the daughter nor the product but the end of history, and the end of the primacy of Man in terms of the nature and conduct of War.

"Segui il tuo corso, e lascia dir le genti."[51]

NOTES

1. Lieutenant-General John J. Tolson, *Airmobility, 1961–1971* (Washington, DC: Department of the Army & GPO, 1973), pp. 97–101, 209–214.

2. To the experience of Vietnam I would add two other examples, though their relevance is somewhat problematical: The first, the American and Soviet air lifts to their Middle East associates in the course of the October 1973 war, was a demonstration of strategic capability, not a comment on air mobility per se. The second was the Soviet air lift of an armored division from the Addis Ababa area to a position behind the Somali formations attacking Harar in the course of the Ogaden war in January–February 1978. This little-known episode contributed to the rout of Somali forces at Harar and Dire Dawa and undoubtedly confirmed the potential of air mobility at the operational and tactical levels.

3. In the interest of accuracy it needs be noted that the idea of the air–land battle was probably first articulated in April 1975 by Major-General John H. Cushman in a briefing to TRADOC; the idea was acknowledged in FM100-5 1976, but it was too advanced for its time, and it was not until after Active Defense was authorized that this idea began to emerge as an alternative; see Colonel Harry G. Summers, Jr., *On Strategy II: A Critical Analysis of the Gulf War* (New York: Dell, 1992), pp. 147–148.

4. APD Operations, para. 0504. In fairness, it needs be noted that the British paper, *Design for Military Operations: The British Military Doctrine*, Army Code 71451, D/CGD/50/8, provides a summary of the Maneuver Warfare concepts in two of its sections—"Characteristics of Manoeuvre Warfare" and "Manoeuvrist Concepts"—see pp. 4.22–4.25. Under the former is listed joint effort, the concentration of strength (firepower) against weakness, emphasis upon the defeat and disruption of the enemy rather than the holding of ground, seizure of the initiative and surprise, momentum, and tempo as the means of inducing shock; this section also states the need for the mobile action to be complemented by positional defense.

5. As the Russians found to their very considerable cost in central Groznyy on 31 December 1994, when the 131st Motor Rifle Brigade is reported to have lost 20 of its 26 tanks, all but 18 of its 120 BMPs, and all six 2S6 Tunguska air defense vehicles, mostly to RPG-7; the 81st Motor Rifle Regiment, also inside Groznyy at the same time, suffered similar losses. For the comment that the Russian conduct of operations inside Groznyy made the Charge of the Light Brigade look like a stroke of genius, see *Red Thrust Star*, PB-30-96-3, July 1996. This action demonstrated the continuing effectiveness of general-purpose, low-technology weaponry in the close-quarter battle.

6. The latter had survived at least 33 attacks that had involved a minimum of 380 fighter-bombers between 3 April 1965 and 28 January 1968 in the course of

Rolling Thunder, and attained a certain notoriety on account of its powers of resistance. It was not until the raid of 13 May 1972, involving 14 fighter-bombers, that a span was knocked off its abutment and the superstructure so mangled that the bridge was closed to rail traffic for months. The figures are not complete with respect to raids between April and September 1967; see A. J. C. Lavelle, *The Tale of Two Bridges; The Battle for the Skies over North Vietnam* (Washington, DC: Office of Air Force History, 1981).

7. These are listed in Richard E. Simpkin, *Race to the Swift: Thoughts on Twenty-First Century Warfare* (Washington, DC: Brassey's Defense, 1982), p. 24. There Simpkin writes: "Thus, both in general military understanding and in its association with maneuver theory, 'operational' has taken on a third meaning divorced from organizational level. As I at least see it, for a concept, plan or warlike act to be considered as 'operational', it must meet five criteria. It must: have a *mission* lying at one remove, and one remove only, from an aim which can be stated in politico-economic terms (in other words from a strategic aim); by a *dynamic, closed-loop system*, characterized by speed and appropriateness of response; consist of *at least three components*, one of which reflects the opponent's will; by *synergistic*—that is the whole must have an effect greater than the sum of its parts; be *self-contained* within the scope of its mission. As we shall see, the blitzkrieg concept stemmed from thinking of this kind [italics in original]." Much of what Simpkin wrote would seem to be somewhat obscure, but the significance of *Race to the Swift* lay in its presenting the challenge of the future at this particular time.

8. The program *Defence of the Realm*, BBC1 Television, 5 September 1996.

9. In effect AirLand Battle could have gone to press in mid-1981, when Starry unveiled the new thinking in two open papers. Starry's departure from TRADOC and his replacement by a successor, Lieutenant-General Glenn K. Otis, who entertained certain reservations about the proposed new orthodoxy, delayed the process. Otis, much more than Starry, was responsible for setting the ideas of the simultaneous battle in depth in an operational context, specifically in terms of incorporating the concept of the operational level of war.

10. The Israeli withdrawal from the Sinai was not completed until April 1982, but the Camp David talks (September 1978) and the treaty of March 1979 in effect closed down this front, notwithstanding the assassination of President Sadat of Egypt in October 1981.

11. Inevitably, figures vary between sources. Richard P. Hallion in *Storm over Iraq: Air Power and the Gulf War* (Washington, DC: Smithsonian Institution Press, 1992), pp. 97–98, indicates that the Israeli air force accounted for 64 Syrian aircraft in the first two days of operations and states that the Israelis did not suffer the loss of a single aircraft. Anthony H. Cordesman and Abraham R. Wagner, *The Lessons of Modern War*. Vol. 1, *The Arab–Israeli Conflicts, 1973–1989* (Boulder, CO: Westview Press, 1990), p. 202, gives Syrian losses as 22 or 23, with another 7 damaged on 9 June, 25 on 10 June, and 18 on 11 June, "bringing its total to 79 to 82 Syrian fighters shot down." The total Syrian losses during Operation Peace for Galilee are given as 92 and Israeli losses as 3, including one A-4 Skyhawk and one F-4 Phantom.

12. *Force XXI Operations*, TRADOC Pamphlet 525–5, 1 August 1994, pp. 3–11.

13. Colin S. Gray, "A Case for a Theory of Victory," *International Security*, 4, No. 1 (Summer 1979), pp. 54–87, and Colin S. Gray and Keith Payne, "Victory is

Possible," *Foreign Policy*, No. 39 (Summer 1980): 14–27.

14. Somewhat surprisingly, it would appear that the requirement that Iraqi forces be subjected to a 50% attrition rate originated with the SAMS graduates—see Eliot A. Cohen et al., *Gulf War Air Power Survey*. Vol. II, Part 2, *Effects and Effectiveness* (Washington, DC: Government Printing Office, 1993), p. 170.

15. See footnote 28.

16. *Conduct of the Persian Gulf War: Final Report to Congress* (Washington DC, US Government Printing Office, 1992), p. 84.

17. There is a curious parallel between Schwarzkopf's definition of objectives as trapping Iraqi formations with their backs to the sea and Schlieffen's memorandum of December 1905 with respect to a campaign against the French army: "By attacks on their left flank we must try at all costs to drive the French eastward against their Moselle fortresses, against the Jura and Switzerland. The French army must be annihilated"; see Gerhard Ritter, *The Schlieffen Plan: Critique of a Myth* (New York, Praeger, 1958), p. 145.

18. Robert H. Scales, Jr., *Certain Victory: The U.S. Army in the Gulf War* (Ft. Leavenworth, KS: US Army Command and General Staff College Press, 1994), p. 146.

19. The Third Army was the military component of Central Command in its operational guise. For the purposes of this narrative—that is, the execution of the attack through the desert—it is sufficient to note that its main offensive formations were XVIII and VII Corps, the First Cavalry Division being constituted as theater reserve.

20. Scales, *Certain Victory*, pp. 241–243; Richard M. Swain, *"Lucky War": Third Army in Desert Storm* (Ft. Leavenworth, KS: US Army Command and General Staff College Press, 1994), pp. 245–247.

21. See, for example, Scales, *Certain Victory*, p. 254, and *Final Report to Congress*, p. 287.

22. Scales, *Certain Victory*, pp. 247–251.

23. Norman Dixon, *On the Psychology of Military Incompetence* (New York: Basic Books, 1976).

24. And, according to at least one U.S. Army officer, one corps commander was "supervising" the operations of battalions (private communication).

25. Lieutenant-Colonel H. T. Hayden (ed.), *Warfighting: Maneuver Warfare in the U.S. Marine Corps* (London: Greenhill Books, 1995), p. 30; my suspicion is that the observation is perhaps a little overharsh but nevertheless well founded.

26. H. Norman Schwarzkopf, *The Autobiography: It Doesn't Take a Hero* (New York, Bantam Books, 1992), p. 382; *Final Report to Congress*, pp. 230, 245, 262; *Field Manual 100-5, Operations*, 14 June 1993, pp. 6–16.

27. Scales, *Certain Victory*, pp. 128–131.

28. Schwarzkopf, *It Doesn't Take a Hero*, p. 380. Note, however, that on the following page Schwarzkopf writes that at the very same meeting: "At last I turned to the plan for the ground offensive—a fully realized version of the envelopment I'd proposed to Powell three weeks before." It is somewhat difficult to reconcile these two statements with those of others pertaining to these and related developments at this time.

29. Thomas A. Keaney and Eliot A. Cohen, *Gulf War Air Power Survey, Summary Report* (Washington, DC: Government Printing Office, 1993), p. 22; see also Eliot

A. Cohen et al., *Gulf War Air Power Survey*. Vol. I, Part 1: *Planning* (Washington, DC: Government Printing Office, 1993), pp. 149, 161. According to the second source, p. 149, based upon Schwarzkopf's order, the air campaign was to "cut key bridges, roads and rail lines to block withdrawal of RGFC forces, cut bridges, roads and rail lines to block reinforcement and/or resupply of Iraqi forces from the west and isolate Iraqi forces in the KTO, and to provide air support (CAS) throughout all phases." Leaving aside the point that, arguably, it was not in the Coalition's interest to block the movement of reinforcements into theater, the second source, p. 161, notes that Schwarzkopf "Fearing an early withdrawal . . . directed that bridges be struck early in the air campaign (in Phase I) not simply to stop the flow of supplies into the theater but to interrupt the retreat of the Guard (from) the theatre." It needs be noted, however, that while the wording of this interpretation of events—to interrupt the retreat—is elusive, this is not what the order itself stated, as the footnote quoting the directive makes clear: the phrase used was "to block (the) withdrawal."

30. *Final Report to Congress*, pp. 315–316.

31. This comment is made in full knowledge of the operations of 24th Mechanized Division and its drive down the Euphrates valley and on the flank of First Armored Division as the latter moved to the main battle. There would seem to be two possible conclusions to be drawn from these events: that an outflanking movement could have been achieved if either the 24th Mechanized Division had been tasked to advance on Basra via the Euphrates valley from the outset or the 24th Mechanized and First Armored Divisions had been "paired" for such a drive. As it was, arguably the 24th Mechanized Division was one day from Basra by the time operations were halted—my own estimate is that probably two days was more accurate—and that the responsibility for such a situation rests with the plan of campaign, not the 24th Mechanized Division's conduct of operations.

32. Perhaps it would be more accurate to state a day rather than a step behind requirement. Whatever word is used, however, the basic idea was in part provoked by a consideration of Swain, *"Lucky War,"* and by one somewhat odd fact: that this account provides maps drawn from Scales, *Certain Victory*, and that the latter appears to have taken all its maps from corps sources, not the Third Army.

33. Lieutenant-General John H. Cushman, USA, Letter on the article "Pushing Them Out the Back Door," U.S. Naval Institute *Proceedings*. Vol. 119/7/1,085 (July 1993), p. 14. Further to this point, it is perhaps worth noting the provisions of *P.U. 36 Soviet Field Regulations* concerning the conduct of the battle in depth and the battle of annihilation: "The enemy should be pinned down over the entire depth of his dispositions, encircled and destroyed. The task of long-range task groups is to penetrate to the depth of the main enemy defence, disrupt his reserves and headquarters, destroy his artillery groups, *and cut the line of withdrawal of his main force"*—see Richard Simpkin, *Deep Battle: The Brainchild of Marshal Tukhachevskii* (London: Brassey's Defence, 1987), p. 170; see also a comment written in 1929: "The art of the attacker is . . . to unleash the entire mass of forces quickly enough to break (into) the flank and rear area of the enemy forces, *to cut his withdrawal routes and to disrupt any new groupings of forces the enemy is preparing"*—V. K. Triandafillov, *The Nature of the Operations of Modern Armies*, transl. William A. Burhans (London: Frank Cass, 1994), p. 153, italics added.

34. Taken from the title of the book produced by *U.S. News and World Report* Staff and published by Times Book, Toronto, 1993.

35. It is interesting to note two sets of comments, both made about the 1991 campaign, that illustrate the depth of the division that air power seems to generate. On the one side, this campaign attracted the comment that it pointed to the future in which there would be no front lines or flanks—see "Viewpoint: What the Russians learned from the Gulf War," *Aviation Week and Space Technology*, 5 October 1992, p. 78; and "Soviet Lessons Learned: Operation Desert Storm," *Marine Corps Gazette*, February 1992, p. 39; and that it was the first space war—see "The Soviet Military and the New Air War in the Persian Gulf," *Air Power Journal*, Winter 1991, pp. 64–77; and "Space: A New Strategic Frontier," *Air Power Journal*, Spring 1992, pp. 14–23. On the other side, this campaign was also described as "the mother of all anomalies, not a model for the future"—see "Lessons of the Gulf War," *Newsweek*, June 1994, pp. 24–25.

36. *Final Report to Congress*, p. 159.

37. Swain, *"Lucky War,"* p. 83.

38. Keaney, *Gulf War Survey*, pp. 101–102.

39. Reference to the Al Firdos bunker incident is illustrative of the extent of Iraqi communications resources and the problems that U.S. planners faced in seeking to close down the Iraqi command system. This bunker was one of 4 main command centers and 17 subcenters available to the Iraqi high command, which, with a maximum overhead of 37' of reinforced concrete, were so heavily protected that the Americans lacked enough bombs to first penetrate their thickness and then put bombs through the penetration to be able to destroy them. The planners solved the problems thus presented with the realization that the bunkers did not have to be destroyed to be rendered nonoperational, the calculation being that single smart bombs delivered against ventilation systems would send shock waves and dust throughout the interior and render the posts uninhabitable and unusable for a period. In addition to economizing on resources, this form of attack allowed the Americans to inflict progressive damage and impose rising costs upon the Iraqis while still allowing intelligence to continue to monitor communications traffic. No more than four bombs were used against any single target. After the air offensive began, the Americans began building a heavy bomb—the 4,700-lb GBU-28—capable of penetrating Iraqi bunkers; two were used successfully in the last hours of the campaign.

40. There is reference in Keaney, *Gulf War Survey*, p. 109, to a comment made by an Iraqi, presumably about this battle, in which he states that one brigade lost more in 30 minutes of air attack in 1991 than it lost in eight years of the Iran–Iraq War. Michael R. Gordon and General Bernard E. Trainor, *The Generals' War: The Inside Story of the Conflict in the Gulf* (New York: Little Brown & Co., 1985), p. 286, give the same reference, but citing a 15-minute span. The point about this episode is, however, that air power was critical in ensuring that Iraqi second-echelon formations were not able to get into Khafji after it had been taken. Air power ensured the defeat of the Iraqi effort and the piecemeal destruction of the formations committed to this offensive; the greater part of the three Iraqi divisions committed to this offensive were destroyed without being able to get into the battle—see Gordon and Trainor, *The Generals' War*, pp. 266–288.

41. Scales, *Certain Victory*, pp. 261–262. It also needs to be noted that the B-52 strikes had very little effect in the destruction of Iraqi material; indeed, it has been alleged, apparently with some cause, that these strikes were singularly inaccurate. But interrogation of Iraqi prisoners in 1991 indicated that the air offensive undoubtedly had one critical effect in terms of breaking what little Iraqi resolve existed in ordinary line formations at the outset of hostilities. An unanticipated side-effect of Western television coverage during Desert Shield was to convince ordinary Iraqi soldiers of the hopelessness of their position. They had been led to expect victory and found themselves faced with the prospect of a war that they realized would begin when American preparations were complete.

42. The original B-2 program was to have resulted in the building of 132 bombers, but in the early 1990s this number was reduced to 20 and their principal role changed from that of a strategic bomber with nuclear capability to a conventional bomber with precision-guided munitions. The cost of the B-2 is dependent upon what figures are used. The $1,300,000,000 price tag, the official figure used by the U.S. Air Force, seems to be based upon procurement costs. The 1994 Defense Authorization Act limited funding to a ceiling of $28,968,000,000 (at 1981 prices) for 20 aircraft. But with only 15 operational aircraft, the bill was $44,389,000,000 of which $24,808,000,000 was development and $19,581,000,000 was procurement costs. Thus the overall cost per aircraft was $2,959,000,000, and, as the 1995 General Audit Office report stated, "After fourteen years of development and evolving mission requirements, including six years of flight testing, the air force has yet to demonstrate that the B-2 design will meet mission requirements." Should more B-2s be ordered, each will cost about $500,000,000 (source: GAO/NSIAD-95-164). The B-1, scrapped by Carter and resurrected by Reagan at a cost that was so embarrassing that seemingly it was never announced, was beset by massive problems, could not meet operational requirements, and did not see service in the 1991 campaign. While some of the 100 that were built continue in service or are being converted to the conventional role, admittedly with very great difficulty and at a cost of some $2,700,000,000, after which they will still not be able to meet all their mission requirements, others have been reduced to service with the Air National Guard and yet others appear to have been scrapped or, to use a dreadful pun, to have gone to the bone yard (source: GAO/AIMD-96-28).

43. Hallion, *Storm over Iraq*, pp. 251, 362.

44. The number of satellite communications terminals in theater rose from three on 2 August 1990 to 7,200 by the end of the campaign, while the number of automatic voice network systems in European NATO stood at 40 compared to the 265 in service in Saudi Arabia in March 1991—see Keaney, *Gulf War Survey*, pp. 193, 214–215.

45. As a side issue, contrary to Iraqi claims, the bunker was not a civilian air raid shelter but a fully operational communications post in which were sheltered families of the secret police, gathered there for their own safety in the knowledge of what awaited them at the hands of the population should the regime be destroyed. The bunker was never used as an air raid shelter in terms of being opened to the general public.

46. In reality the manner of the ending of the ground campaign begs a question that has not been addressed properly since 1991. By the time the cease-fire was

unilaterally imposed at Washington's insistence, such was the confusion and traffic congestion at the rear of VII Corps that its lead units and formations—that is, those best placed to attempt the encirclement and annihilation of fleeing Iraqi forces—had been reduced to less than 10 hours' fuel. At best, therefore, it is very doubtful if VII Corps could have pressed its advantage had the campaign been prolonged by another day. In such circumstances one is left to wonder not only whether Washington's actions were not in part designed to forestall the possibility of VII Corps being seen to grind to a halt and unable to trap fleeing Iraqi formations, but also whether this is the reason that Schwarzkopf initially attempted to resist Powell's insistence on a halt to proceedings but then complied. The assumption that VII Corps could have continued operations had it not been for the cease-fire would seem to be, at best, very dubious, and not simply because of logistical difficulties: after four days of intense operations, either in battle or in the advance to contact, the men of the lead units were about as exhausted as their fuel supplies. This certainly applied to the British First Armoured Division, which was earmarked to lead the assault against Basra, the U.S. formations being tasked to get behind the city and into the Tigris and Euphrates valleys.

47. And not just the U.S. Air Force. The recurring theme in U.S. military thinking has been a certainty provided by technology and disproved by events, firepower as in Vietnam being an obvious example. Most certainly the belief in the efficacy of firepower in securing victory survived Vietnam—witness the observation that the United States "should capitalize on American technological prowess and not think that we can win by sending out small counterinsurgent teams to beat the guerrillas at the type of war they know best"—see Samuel P. Huntington, "American Military Strategy," *Policy Papers in International Affairs,* No. 28, pp. 3–17. This, and certain of Huntington's other assertions, would seem to embrace some highly dubious assumptions, not least that the military could impose its own mark on guerrilla wars by offensive action and that "the offensive aimed at the center of enemy power was the core of American strategy. It has, unfortunately, been lost during the last thirty years." Since Huntington marked 1951 as the watershed in U.S. thinking with reference to offensive and defensive, it would seem that he is implying that both the Korean and Vietnam wars could have been won by offensive action. No further comment seems necessary.

48. Harlan Ullman, "A New Defence Construct: Rapid Dominance," *Royal United Services Institute Journal,* October 1996.

49. See Colonel David A. Deptula, *Firing for Effect: Change in the Nature of Warfare* (Arlington, VA, Aerospace Education Foundation: 1995).

50. John Milton, *Paradise Regained,* Book 1, lines 94–95.

51. "Follow your own course, and let people talk" Dante, quoted in Marx's preface to his *Das Kapital.*

Index

Northwest Europe, 26, 76–78, 80–84, 86–89, 93–95, 100–101, 105–106, 121, 124, 128
Norway, 62–64, 93, 107, 121

Offensives: 1917, French spring, 38; 1918, German spring, 25, 39, 42; 1940 campaign, 113, 117, 220, 234, 237; Lvov–Sandomiercz, 45, 127; Vistula–Oder, 45, 101, 127, 249
Ogarkov, Nikolai, 48, 207, 224
Oil/oil prices, 18, 93, 179–180, 183, 189, 192
OMG concept, 203
OODA Loop, 206
Operational art/level, 48, 109, 112–113, 116–117, 126, 189
Operations: Bagration, 125, 127, 249; Barbarossa, 84, 118; Deliberate Force, 9; Desert Shield, 229, 247; Downfall, 100, 102; Husky, 86–87; Instant Thunder, 238–239; Jupiter, 93; Liberty Canyon, 198; Market Garden, 102; Neptune/Overlord, 1, 73, 81, 86–87, 101–103; Roundup/Sledgehammer, 80–83, 87–88, 101; Shingle, 87; Torch, 79–80, 91, 93
Osgood, Robert, 162
Osirak, 9
Ostpolitik, 186
Outbreak of war (1914), 33, 52, 55

Pacific, 3, 7, 9, 62, 82, 101–102, 104, 128, 160, 216
Pacification, 167
Pakistan, 163
Palestine/Palestinians, 36, 172, 175–176, 189, 193, 213–216
Parallel Warfare, 250–251
Paris, 18, 20, 60, 149, 156, 174, 178, 216
Passchendaele, 38
Patriot HIMAD system, 199
Patton, George S., 89, 127
Pearl Harbor, 129, 159
Peking, 144, 160
Persian empire, 23–24
Persian Gulf, 212, 225

Peru, 173
Pétain, Henri-Philippe, 147
Peter the Great, 113, 115
PGM, 208, 246
Philippines, 143, 160
Phoenix missile, 197, 200
Poland, 5, 37, 64, 101, 107, 114, 130
Portugal, 7, 20, 78, 150–152, 156
Powell, Colin, 230–231, 237, 245, 248
Prague Spring (1968), 17
Prokhorovka, 120
Protracted operations, 36, 43, 46, 57, 104–105, 108, 113, 217, 219, 242–243
Protracted war (Maoist), 156, 168–169, 173
Prussia, 54, 57

Quebec separatism, 175, 178

Race/racism, 50, 54–55
Radio, 40, 216
Railways, 40, 51, 61, 83, 103, 208
Rationalism, 58, 68
Reagan, Ronald W., 211–212, 220, 222–227
Red Army Faction, 175, 178
Reprimitivization of war, 184–185
Republican Party, 20, 156, 226
Revolution in military affairs, 14, 135
Revolutionary war, 141–143
Right, the, 15–17, 19–20, 66, 180
Rights of Man/liberalism, 54, 58
Romania, 37, 59, 64
Romanian military, 119
Rome/Roman Empire, 75, 79, 141
Rommel, Erwin, 75
Rhine, the, 102–103
Roosevelt, Franklin D., 80, 99, 135, 223, 252
Ruhr, the, 8, 103
Rural-based insurgency, 143, 151, 153–154, 156, 158, 169, 172–173, 227
Russia, 35–38, 48–50, 56–57, 59, 64–65, 113–115, 216; *see also* Soviet Union
Russian military, 36, 43, 115
Russian revolutions, 38, 117; civil war/intervention, 117

About the Author

H. P. WILLMOTT is a Lecturer with the Greenwich Maritime Institute at the University of Greenwich. He has written extensively on modern military and naval subjects, including the critically acclaimed, *The Great Crusade: A New Complete History of the Second World War.*